In 1989 engineer and scientist Maurice Cotterell found a way of calculating the duration of long-term magnetic reversals on the sun. Using this knowledge, he was able to break the codes of ancient sun-worshipping civilisations – first the Mayas of central America, then those of Tutankhamun of Egypt and those of Viracocha in South America.

His own unique decoding process reveals amazing pictures from archaeological treasures that explain the spiritual mysteries of life; why we are born, why we die and why this has to be.

His work, best described as 'adventure fact', brings together modern science, spirituality and ancient wisdom to unlock the secrets of the past, present and future.

In 1992 Cotterell was awarded the Voluntario Cultural medal for his contribution to Mexican culture.

What they said about his previous books:

'An incredible discovery' *Daily Express*

'One of the most amazing books I have ever read in my life'
Colin Wilson, bestselling author

'Cotterell puts up enough evidence to make even the most sceptical take note'
Daily Mail

D1244992

Also by Maurice Cotterell

Astrogenetics
The Amazing Lid of Palenque Vol. 1
The Amazing Lid of Palenque Vol. 2
The Mayan Prophecies
The Mural of Bonampak
The Mosaic Mask of Palenque
The Supergods
The Tutankhamun Prophecies
The Lost Tomb of Viracocha

The Terracotta Warriors

The Secret Codes of the Emperor's Army

Maurice Cotterell

headline

First published in 2003
by HEADLINE BOOK PUBLISHING

First published in paperback in 2004
by HEADLINE BOOK PUBLISHING

10 9 8 7 6 5 4 3 2

ISBN 0 7472 6444 9

Typeset in Palatino by Avon DataSet Ltd, Bidford-on-Avon, Warks
www.avondataset.co.uk
Printed and bound in Great Britain by
Clays Ltd, St Ives plc

Papers and cover board used by Headline are natural, recyclable products
made from wood grown in sustainable forests. The manufacturing processes
conform to the environmental regulations of the country of origin.

HEADLINE BOOK PUBLISHING
A division of Hodder Headline PLC
338 Euston Road
London NW1 3BH

www.headline.co.uk
www.hodderheadline.com

Contents

Credits

Sources of Illustrations and Quotations

All illustrations, drawings, artwork and photographs by M. Cotterell and A. Perry (graphics, K. Burns) except those specified below:

Text figures: 7, 9, 10, 12, 14, from *The World's Religions*, Ward Lock & Co., London (1890); 16, after *Compendium of Works and Days*, O-Erh-T'ai (1742); 17a, Corel 15073, 17b Corel 5074; 26, 46 (part), 47a, 48a (part), A50 (part), A51 (part) the sarcophagus Lid of Palenque, after Augustin Villagra (1952); 27b, tau cross, Greek ivory staff, Tarascon, eighteenth century, Victoria & Albert Museum, London; 27b, tau cross, walrus-ivory, English, mid-twelfth century, Victoria & Albert Museum, London; 29, woodcut engraving, after Wu Cheng'en (eighteenth century); 30 and 60b, paper-cut monkey, after the Chinese Tourist Organisation; 65a, after Guamán Poma de Ayala (sixteenth-century woodcut engraving); A33d, A71 (insert) mask, after Vautier de Nanxe; A34 mosaic skull, British Museum; A57, after James Churchward (1931); A61a, Corel 90045.

Colour plates: plate 2, jade dragon, fourteenth century, Ashmolean Museum, Oxford; plate 15; jade burial suit of Prince Liu Sheng, William MacQuitty Collection; plate 16a, jade burial suit of Princess Tou Wan, Robert Hardy Picture Library, London.

Quotations: *Chinese Classics*, Vols. I–V, James Legge, University of Hong Kong Press (1960); *Sacred Books of the East*, Vol. X, Max Muller (trans.), Oxford (1881); *The Popol Vuh*, University of Oklahoma Press (1947); Ssu-ma Ch'ien, *Records of the Historian (Sima Quin)*, W. Burton, New York (1958); Bible quotations, (Special Command) Eyre & Spottiswode (1897); *The Geeta*, Shri Purohit Swami, Faber & Faber (1935); *Collection of the Most Important Military Techniques* by Tseng Kung-Liang (1044).

Acknowledgements

With sincere thanks, as always, to G, and VH; to my wife Ann for her continuing support; to Kevin Burns for help with the graphics and artwork; to editor Hugh Morgan; to the team at Hodder Headline; to my literary agent Robert Kirby and all at Peters Fraser & Dunlop.

CHAPTER ONE

The Secret Army of the First Emperor

The Potter's Field

That cold crisp day, in the spring of 1974, is one the people of Lintong province will never forget. For a brief split second the vaporised breath of three young farmers was all that remained of the men who, moments earlier, had toiled together.

It seemed that the field, three kilometres (two miles) from Xiyang, had swallowed them up, together with the drill, the tripod and several wooden buckets that were to provide – once they had recovered from the shock of the fall – a means of escape.

They had tumbled into an ancient passageway, which collapsed around them, sending clouds of dust billowing high into the sky above. As it cleared, they found themselves surrounded by an army of warriors in full battledress; a life-size army of terracotta soldiers that gazed, expressionless, at the unexpected intruders.

Within hours, archaeologists from the nearby town of Yanzhai arrived to seal the site from prying eyes.

Test digs confirmed that more than 8,000 life-size terracotta soldiers, buried more than 2,000 years ago, in around 220 BC, filled four concealed underground chambers.

Archaeologists were surprised to find that the shapes of the faces (taken together with the shape of the head and the hairstyle) of the

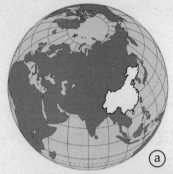

Modern-Day China

Figure 1. (a) and (b)
Political boundary of
modern-day China
(white).

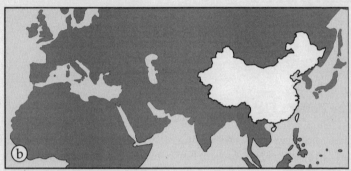

China During the Ch'in Period

(c) China during
the Ch'in period,
221–206 BC
(hatched), against
a backdrop of
modern-day
China (white).

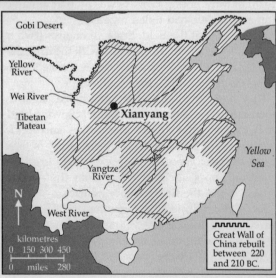

Gobi Desert

Yellow River

Wei River

Tibetan Plateau

● Xianyang

Yellow Sea

Yangtze River

N

West River

kilometres
0 150 300 450

0   miles   280

Great Wall of
China rebuilt
between 220
and 210 BC.

The Last Refuge of the Dragon King

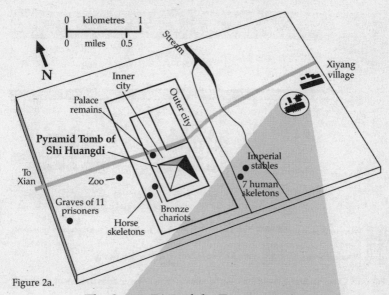

Figure 2a.

The Secret Pits of the Terracotta Army

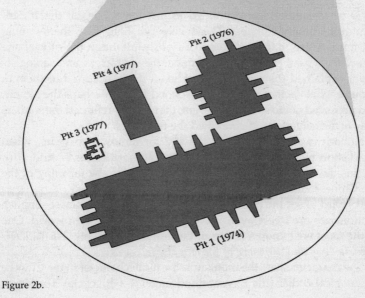

Figure 2b.

The Covered Tunnels

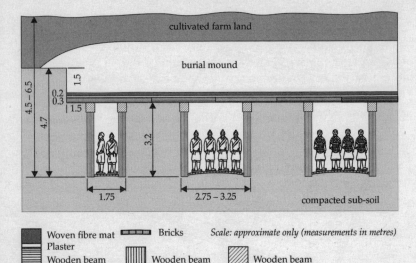

Figure 3. Cross-section view of three of the tunnels (also referred to as *trenches* or *corridors*).

8,000 or so soldiers corresponded to just ten shapes of the 10,516-character Chinese alphabet. These were: ryh, jiah, your, shen, yuung, jih, muh, fehng, tiarn and guor. Curiously, although the official site record from Xian provides the names of the characters, archaeologists never explained their *meaning*. Perhaps it never occurred to them to enquire what each of the characters stood for. Or perhaps they knew, and preferred not to say. In any event, they hastily reburied the soldiers they had excavated and concealed the test holes.

Nobody was allowed near the site for almost two years, when excavation recommenced, although the authorities never said why. To this day the official site guide refuses to give the meaning of the ten Chinese characters.

It's hard to see the reason for the secrecy. After all, Chinese–English dictionaries are freely available throughout the Western world. One of the most well known is that of the author Lin Yutang: *Lin Yutang's Chinese–English Dictionary of Modern Usage*.

The character shen, the monkey, is the ninth character in the Chinese astrological zodiac (the 12-year duodecimal [2 + 10] cycle). *The Mayan*

Prophecies, *The Supergods*, *The Tutankhamun Prophecies* and *The Lost Tomb of Viracocha* each explained that 9 is the highest number that can be reached before becoming one (10) with God. Because of this, ancient sun-worshipping civilisations used the number to represent God, and the number 999 to represent a Supergod, a spiritual teacher (the opposite of 666, the number of the beast in Revelation, in the Bible).

The Ten Face Shapes, according to Lin Yutang's Dictionary

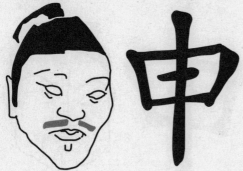

shen

N. (1) A letter in the duodecimal cycle:

The Duodecimal Cycle

Chinese Animal	Western Animal	Chinese Zodiac	Hours
Tzyy	Rat	Aries	11 – 01 a.m.
Choou	Ox	Taurus	01 – 03
Yirn	Tiger	Gemini	03 – 05
Maau	Rabbit	Cancer	05 – 07
Chern	Dragon	Leo	07 – 09
Syh	Snake	Virgo	09 – 11
Wuu	Horse	Libra	11 – 01 p.m.
Weih	Sheep	Scorpio	01 – 03
Shen	**Monkey**	Sagittarius	03 – 05
Yoou	Cock	Capricorn	05 – 07
Shyu	Dog	Aquarius	07 – 09
Haih	Pig	Pisces	09 – 11

Figure 4a.

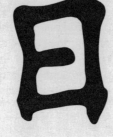

ryh

N. (1) The sun.

jiah

N. (1) <u>The first</u> of the ten characters in the decimal cycle. (Note: The 60-year Chinese astrological cycle is described using permutations of either the duodecimal or the decimal cycles; five of the Duodecimal cycles (5 x 12) or six of the decimal cycles (6 x 10). This is the Jiahtzyy system, also known as Ganjy.)

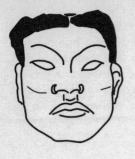

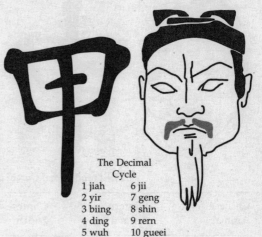

The Decimal Cycle

1 jiah	6 jii
2 yir	7 geng
3 biing	8 shin
4 ding	9 rern
5 wuh	10 gueei

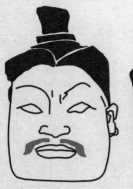

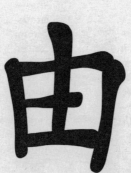

your

N. Reason: <u>story</u> or <u>course of events</u>; reason, how something happened; basic cause.

Figure 4b.

yuung

N. (1) A drumstick. (2) A dry measure. *Yuungdauh,* n., (1) <u>A tunnel</u>. (2) <u>Covered corridor or passageway</u>.

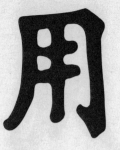

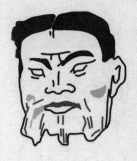

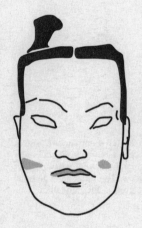

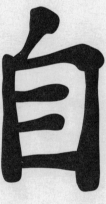

jih

Prep. <u>Up to</u> (a point or period of time): until recent times; <u>until now</u>.

muh

N. (1) The eye: with angry <u>look</u>; meets the eye; (distress, wounded soldiers) meet the eye everywhere; <u>focus eye or attention (on person, thing)</u>.

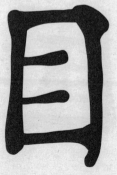

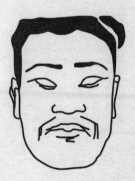

Figure 4c.

fehng

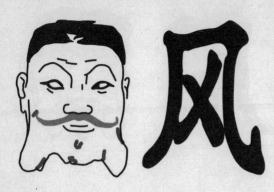

V.i. & t. (1) <u>Incant, read with intonation</u>. (2) Satirise, ridicule, persuade or make a person <u>see a point by clever analogy</u>. *Fehngjiahn*, v.t. & n., remonstrate (or remonstration) with (ruler) by clever analogy. *Fehnsuhng*, v.t., <u>read</u> (poem, etc.) aloud <u>with intonation</u>; read your letter <u>as if to memorise</u>.

tiarn

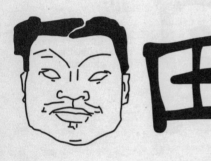

N. (1) A surname. (2) Farm: good farm; paddy field; dry land, farm for wheat, cotton, etc. <u>The mind considered as ground for cultivation</u>.

guor

N. & adj. A country, nation, national: inside the country; supported by the central government; national product; national treasures such as ancient objects of art, imperial seals, etc.

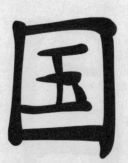

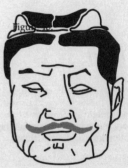

Figure 4d.

Chinese mythology tells the story of the monkey; how he had to complete 81 tasks (9 x 9) before he could get to heaven. From this we can infer that the character shen, the monkey, number 9, refers to God.

The Secret Message of the Ten Face Shapes

Bringing the dictionary definitions of the ten characters, as given by the ten face shapes, we thus have:

Focus the eye on the soldiers in the covered tunnels. Read the meaning of the national (Chinese) characters differently; use the mind to conjure (understand) the story which spans from the beginning of time until now; a story about the sun and God.

Or, put another way:

Look at the soldiers in the tunnels carefully and decode the secret story of the sun and God, from the beginning of time until now.

The Sun and God

In *The Mayan Prophecies*, *The Supergods*, *The Tutankhamun Prophecies* and *The Lost Tomb of Viracocha*, I explained how the leaders of the Maya, the Egyptians and the Peruvians possessed a scientific understanding of a very high order, one that modern man is only now beginning to grasp. They taught their people that the sun controls fertility on earth, that it controls personality determination (sun-sign astrology), and that solar magnetic reversals bring periodic catastrophic destruction to earth, erasing each civilisation in turn from the annals of history. These Supergods taught that the soul is imperishable, everlasting and – for the pure – destined for the stars, and that rebirth on earth awaits the rest. So they encoded their secrets into their treasures, giving those that failed this time a better chance of redemption the next time around.

The message conveyed by the face shapes of the terracotta warriors suggests that close examination of the soldiers will, in some way, lead to discoveries about the sun and to revelations regarding the spiritual side of life.

Before we attempt to decode the secrets of the warriors we need firstly to familiarise ourselves with how the sun affects life on earth, and Appendix 3, towards the back of this book, provides a brief and simple guide.

An understanding of how other civilisations encoded their secrets into their treasures would also be invaluable, and Appendix 4 reveals how the Egyptians, the Maya and the Peruvians concealed theirs.

Appendices 3 and 4 therefore, equip us with the investigative know-how to enable us to begin a journey that might explain why Emperor Shi Huangdi manufactured and buried more than 8,000 life-size soldiers, each weighing half a tonne, beneath a field near Xian. Was it really, as archaeologists would have us believe, to provide protection for his nearby pyramid and mausoleum? We can understand why any rational enquirer might view such a scenario with scepticism. After all, the soldiers can't move – they *are* made of clay. Or are we to believe that it was simply wishful thinking on the emperor's part, that perhaps he thought the presence of the soldiers might scare away tomb-robbers? But if that were the case, why bury and conceal the warriors so effectively that they might not be found for at least 2,000 years? The fact that his mausoleum has never been robbed (as far as we know) suggests that the presence of the army, and the ostensible protection it may have provided, was never an essential requirement. So why engage more than 700,000 labourers for more than ten years to manufacture and bury an army that served no purpose?

Clearly, if we are to find the answers to these questions we need to dig deeper; not just into the soil around Xian, but also into the hearts, minds and history of ancient China.

CHAPTER TWO

A Brief History of China

Texts, Silk, Jade and Immortality

Written accounts of Chinese history take us back to around 2697 BC, beyond which we rely on archaeological evidence and mythological belief.

This is primarily because character-writing did not exist during the early periods and also because materials on which to write either did not exist or have since perished. The first piece of paper known to contain writing (20 characters of the Chinese script) was found in 1942 in the ruins of an ancient watchtower in Tsakhortei, near Chuyen, which was abandoned by Chinese soldiers in AD 110 as they came under attack from the Hsiung-nu (pronounced 'shee-on-yu') tribe of barbarians from the north, dating the paper to the same time.

The oldest known surviving piece of *paper* in the world was also discovered in China, in a tomb near Shensi province in 1957, and dates back to between 140 and 87 BC. The tiny, ten-centimetre (four-inch) piece of disintegrated hemp fibres can, for the first time, be truly referred to as *paper*, given the sedimentary nature of the layered fibres – as against papyrus (from which the name derives), which is the husk, or pith, of the papyrus plant used by the Egyptians since at least 3000 BC.

Other materials were used in China prior to AD 110 to convey written historical records. One of the earliest of these used characters impressed, or scratched, into tablets of wet clay that were

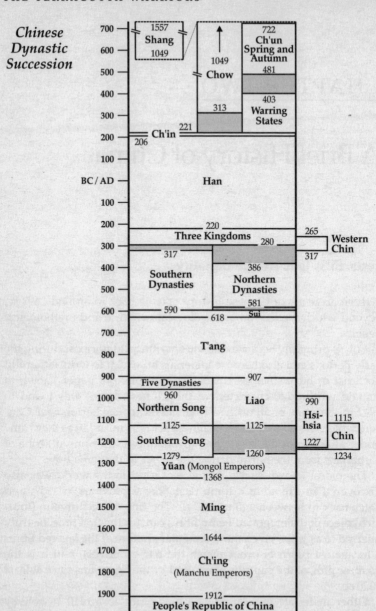

Chinese Dynastic Succession

Figure 5. Table of Dynastic Succession, c. 1557 BC – AD 2000 (see also Appendices 1 and 2).

subsequently baked hard in the sun (similar to the tablets of the Sumerians that contained their cuneiform writing, from around 3500 BC). Many of the Chinese texts from the time of the philosopher Confucius (551–479 BC) were made in a similar way. The Bamboo Books (discussed shortly) also provide valuable historical accounts going back to the beginning of Chinese civilisation, as do ancient bark books. Silk wall hangings began to appear with the domestication of the silkworm in China at around the same time. Beyond these periods, neither the material to convey the script nor any script at all existed. If we wish to probe ever deeper into antiquity, then we are left only with rock carvings, pictures scratched on to cave walls, megalithic monuments and stone circles that often perplex as much as they inform.

In China, complex picture-writing – using ideograms and pictograms – was used as early as the middle of the second millennium BC for divination and record-keeping purposes. Many examples, carved into tortoiseshell or cattle bones during the Shang period (1557–1049 BC; see figure 6), have been excavated from the fields around Hsio T'un. The inscriptions, which Chinese archaeologists now call *jia gu shu* (the study of bone writing), recount history from the Shang period, the peoples of whom lived in the region of Anyang (some scholars prefer older dates for the dynasties and take the Shang period back a further 1,000 years. It is also worth mentioning here that names of dynasties are often spelled differently in different texts).

So where do we begin our historical enquiries? And who were the scholars who laboured long and hard to lift the shroud of mystery that cloaked China's history for so long?

The Bamboo Books (from which figure A2, the Table of Chinese Emperors, is taken, in Appendix 2) take up the story from around 2697 BC with the appearance of the Yellow Emperor, Huang-ti, the legendary first emperor (not to be confused with Shi Huangdi, who became the first emperor of a *unified* China in 221 BC). Legends say that before Huang-ti was born, a bright star was seen in the sky. They say that he was born through an immaculate conception and became a superhuman hero figure who brought many benefits, including the introduction of writing, an advanced knowledge of astronomy and mathematics, agricultural irrigation, domestication of the silkworm and the consequential production of silk. Even more remarkably, legends insist that he performed miracles and never died – that he

China, from the Earliest of Times to 771 BC
(part Shang and part Chow periods)

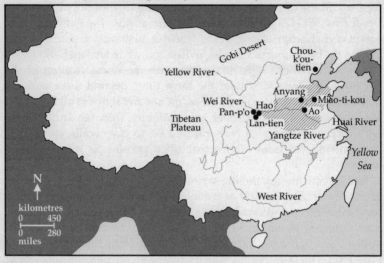

Figure 6. Map showing the prehistoric settlements of China up to 771 BC. The hatched area shows the boundary during the Shang period (1557–1049 BC).

simply flew to the sky as a dragon that became the sun and lived for ever. They called him the Son of Heaven.

The Chinese classics – the Five Ching (*books*) and the Four Shu (*writings*) – compiled around the time of Confucius and the philosopher Mencius (372–289 BC), provide the most comprehensive surviving accounts of Chinese history.

When the sages of China compiled the Five Ching, containing the truth on the highest subjects, it was decreed they should be accepted as law by all future generations. The Five Ching are primarily credited to the philosopher Confucius (figure 7):

Book	Compiler
The Book of Changes (Yi)	Confucius
The Book of History (Shu)	Confucius
The Book of Poetry	Confucius
The Record of Rites	Various
The Spring and Autumn Period (the Ch'un	Confucius

Ch'iu, a chronicle of events from 722 to 481 BC)

The Four Shu (also known as the *Shu Ching*, *Shu King*, *Shoo King* and *Book of Historical Documents*) are ascribed to:

Book	Compiler
Digested Conversations	Confucius
(The Confucian Analects)	
Doctrine of the Mean	K'ung Chi, grandson of Confucius
The Great Learning	Tsang Shan, a disciple of Confucius
The Works of Mencius	Mencius

This arrangement, though, must be flawed given that the *Doctrine of the Mean* actually appears as book number 28 in *The Record of Rites* and *The Great Learning* as book number 39 in the same treatise.

Other collections of the Ching have been proposed; the addition of *The Book of Music* to *The Record of Rites* once made the Five Ching actually Six Ching, and during the T'ang dynasty (AD 618–649) a compilation promulgated under the orders of Emperor Taizong identified 13 Ching, some of which have since been relegated to 'Smaller Classics'.

In the *Memoirs of the Former Han Dynasty* (206 BC–AD 23) a chapter referred to as The History of Literature attempts to set down the classics to their place in history (spellings and dates may differ from those in contemporary usage):

After the death of Confucius there was an end of his exquisite words; and when his seventy disciples had passed away, violence began to be done to their meaning. It came about that there were five different editions of the Chun Chiu, four of the Shu and several of the Yi. Amid the disorder and collisions of the Warring States [481–220 BC] truth and falsehood were still in a state of warfare, and a sad confusion marked the words of the various scholars. Then came the calamity inflicted under the Ch'in dynasty [221–207 BC], when the literary monuments were destroyed by fire, in order to keep the people in ignorance. But, by and by, there arose the Han dynasty, which set itself to remedy the evil wrought by the Ch'in. Great efforts were made to collect slips and tablets and the way was thrown wide open for the bringing in of books. In the time of the Emperor Hsio-wu [Wudi; 140–85 BC], portions of books being wanting and tablets lost, so that ceremonies and music were suffering great damage, he was moved to sorrow and said: 'I am very sad for this.' He therefore formed the plan of repositories, in which the books might be stored, and appointed officers to transcribe books on an extensive scale, embracing the works of the various scholars, that they might all be placed in the repositories. The Emperor Chang [Chengdi; 32–5 BC], finding that a portion of the books still continued dispersed or missing, commissioned Chan-nang, the Superintendent of Guests, to search for undiscovered books throughout the empire, and by special edict ordered the Chief of the Banqueting House, Liu Hsiang, to examine the Classical Works, along with the commentaries on them, the writings of the scholars and all poetical productions; the Master-Controller of Infantry, Zan Hwang, to examine the books on the art of war; the Grand Historiographer, Yin Hsien, to examine the books treating of the art of numbers; and the Imperial Physician, Li Chu-Kwo, to examine the books on medicine. Whenever any book was done with, Hsiang forthwith arranged it, indexed it, and made a digest of it, which was presented to the emperor. While this work was in progress Hsiang died and the Emperor Ai [Aidi; 6 BC–AD 1] appointed his son, Hsin, a Master of the Imperial Carriages, to complete his father's work. On this Hsin collected all the books and presented a report of them under seven divisions.

The collections later suffered damage in the troubles during the Han dynasty, which lasted from around AD 8 to 25. Mencius mentions how princes made off, in antiquity, with many thousands of records from which their own wrongdoings may have been condemned.

The Confucian Analects (also referred to as the *Book of Digested Conversations*, or *Discourses and Dialogues*), compiled by his disciples, was the term by which the collected sayings of Confucius were known. Only one copy escaped the Burning of the Books episode during the Ch'in dynasty and another was later discovered hidden in the walls of Confucius's house.

The accounts of Mencius, borrowing from the grandson of Confucius, K'ung Chi, fill a large part of the gap between the times of Confucius and those of the Ch'in.

Confucius

In the sixth century BC, China was ruled as a feudal kingdom by the Chow dynasty comprising primarily the areas that form today's Honan and Shensi provinces. Agricultural methods were primitive and food scarce. Polygamy was widespread and women abused. There was no religion and the misruled masses lived in chronic misery. Writing 250 years later, Mencius observed:

> The world had fallen into decay and right principles had disappeared. Perverse discourses and oppressive deeds were waxen rife. Ministers murdered their rulers and sons their fathers. Confucius was frightened by what he saw and he undertook the work of reformation (*The Works of Mencius*, Mencius, 310 BC).

It was in this climate that the great Confucius (K'ung Fu Tzu, the Master K'ung) was born. His family moved to Lu (modern Shantung) to escape the feudal wars that raged around them.

His father, Shu-leang Heih, an army officer, produced nine daughters and a crippled son by his first marriage. A second, at the age of 70, produced Confucius, who married at 19 to father two daughters and a son (Le).

At 20 he secured employment as Keeper of the Grainstore, progressed to Superintendent of Parks and, at 22, started teaching privately.

His popularity grew rapidly, so much so that by the age of 30 his reputation attracted the patronage of the Duke of Lu. This position of privilege allowed him access to the royal library and temple. When a civil war broke out he fled to exile with the duke to the neighbouring state of Tsou. When the troubles ended, Confucius returned to Lu, where, at the age of 50, he secured the position of Chief Magistrate in the city of Chung-too and impressed on the office his strict rules on conduct and administration that permeated every aspect of his life. He led by example, and his success gave way to the introduction of many reforms that fuelled his promotion through the ranks to the position of Minister for Crime.

On hearing of his position, the neighbouring Duke of Tsou sent for Confucius and offered him the city of Lin-kew together with its revenues, but Confucius declined the offer.

Confucius

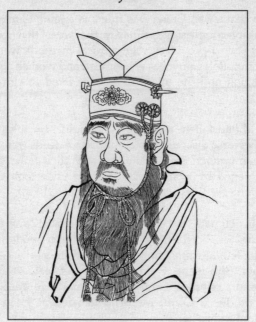

Figure 7.

As a result of good government, the state of Lu increased its population and popularity. Men became loyal and faithful, women chaste, and the people praised his ways. But it was not to last. The Duke of Tsou, fearing a takeover from the prospering Lu, arranged the downfall of the Duke of Lu by presenting him with a gift of 80 beautiful girls, a group of dancers, bands of musicians and 125 horses. The plan worked. Distracted from his duties, the ministries began to fail. Disillusioned, Confucius left and wandered from state to state seeking a post that would allow him to put into practice his ideas for relieving suffering among the poor.

He believed he could teach the rulers how to behave, what to encourage and what to forbid, in a climate where everyone knew their place:

If any ruler would submit to me as his director for twelve months,

The Warring States Period

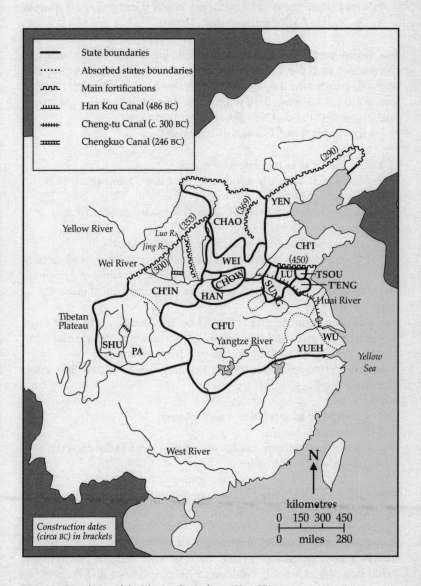

Figure 8. Boundaries of the Warring States from 403 to 221 BC.

I should accomplish something considerable and within three years I should attain the realisation of my hopes (Confucius, as reported in *The Works of Mencius*, Mencius, 310 BC).

But times were bad and the surrounding states began to align themselves with the state of the Chow, making Confucius unpopular with adversaries. At last, aged 70, he returned to Lu, where he devoted himself to teaching but died within two years. His funeral was lavish, and his grave outside Qufu became a pilgrimage.

As for his teaching, Confucius believed that:

1 The universe is regulated by order.
2 Mankind is basically good and capable of doing good works without motive *(Jen)*.
3 People do wrong through lack of knowledge and from lack of example.
4 Government must lead by high moral standards.
5 Development is both inward and outward; inward development required behaving in private as one would in public and outward development promoted self-sufficiency and ethical etiquette.

His teachings were at first collected by his disciples and later more systematically and methodically by Mencius. Later, the scholar Chu-His (AD 1130–1200) took up the mantle from Mencius.

Mencius's interpretation of the teachings resolved the five tenets into three qualities:

1 *I*, integrity: to act without self-interest.
2 *Li*: decent behaviour.
3 *Chih*: the development of a sound intellect to allow sound judgement.

Later scholars augmented these with *Hsin*, fidelity – keeping one's promise. The *Jen*, *I*, *Li*, *Chih* and *Hsin* became known as the Five Virtues of Confucius.

A disciple once asked Confucius if there was one golden rule to which a man should subscribe, to which he replied: 'Reciprocity. What you do not want to be done to yourself do not do to others.' In this way his teachings, like those of Jesus, were perceived as more akin to religion than philosophy. His journey along the path of virtue required attentive diligence in business and sincerity when dealing with others. When asked if he believed that injury should be repaid with kindness, he replied: 'With what, then, will you recompense kindness? Recompense injury with justice, and kindness with kindness.'

It was during visits to the library in Chow that he discovered the records of the four dynasties – Yu, Hea, Shang and Chow – which enabled him to compile the Four Shu, containing a hundred historical chapters, or Books, that he prefaced with a commentary from himself.

The nineteenth-century scholar James Legge translated the name shoo (Shu) as 'the pencil speaking' and hence was used as a reference to the early written characters of the language. Legge's translation was derived from the preface to the *Shwo Wan*, the oldest surviving Chinese dictionary, which points out that the original Chinese written characters resembled the objects they described and were at first called *wan* ('delineations'). As they developed to represent sounds, they were called *tsze* ('begetters'), and later, when set down on to stone tablets, bamboo or silk, they were called *shoo* ('writings'). The word *shoo* hence evolved to describe books.

In compiling the Four Shu (Shoo), Confucius assembled the best account of Chinese history to date, but as Legge points out:

> The book, even though as it is said to have come from the hand of Confucius, never professed to contain a [complete] history of China, and much less are we to look in it for the annals of history. Its several portions furnish materials to the historian but he must grope his way through hundreds of years without any assistance from Shoo. It is simply a collection of historical memorials extending over a space of about 1,700 years, but on no connected method, and with great gaps between them (*Chinese Classics*, Vol. III, James Legge, University of Hong Kong Press, 1960).

The copy of the Shoo found hidden in the walls of Confucius's house was studied by one of his disciples, K'ung Gan Kwo, in around 90 BC, who added his own commentary:

> He [Confucius] examined and arranged the grand monuments and records, deciding to commence with Yaou and Shun and to come

down to the times of Chow. Where there was perplexity and confusion he mowed them. Expressions frothy and unallowable he cut away. What embraced great principles he retained and developed. What were minute and yet of importance he carefully selected. Of those deserving to be handed down to other ages and to supply permanent lessons, he made in all one hundred books consisting of Canons, Counsels, Instructions, Announcements, Speeches and Charges (*Chinese Classics*, Vol. III, James Legge, University of Hong Kong Press, 1960).

Lao Tzu

The works of Lao Tzu (the Venerable Philosopher; figure 9) were conveyed by the historian Ssu-ma Ch'ien in around 100 BC and by the school of Confucius in around AD 250.

He was born in the state of Ch'u in today's Honan province in around 604 BC. Legend says that his mother carried him in her womb for seventy-two years, so that when he was at length delivered his hair was already white – hence the name: Lao Tzu, 'Old Boy'.

In real life he secured the position of Recorder for the Duke of Lu, at the capital city of Lo, where he looked after the royal library and later met Confucius.

The older Lao Tzu, already established as a great thinker of the times, was not impressed with the aims of Confucius that called for greater state control through centralised government nor with the rigid bureaucratic systems it beseeched and sustained. He preferred instead the simple life of a rural economy that flourished during the golden age of Emperor Shuhn (c. 2042 BC), when the earth was pure and unadulterated by the activities of men preoccupied with business and war.

Followers of Lao Tzu set down the basic tenets of his philosophy, Taoism ('the Way'), in the *Tao Te Ching*, a book of around only 5,000 characters that appeared around 250 years after his death. His philosophy emphasised the need for an individual to live in harmony with the environment, here and now, rather than the need to perform good deeds that would later yield returns either for the individual or the state. He believed that there exists a hidden principle of the universe that demands equilibrium in all things, not too much and

Lao Tzu

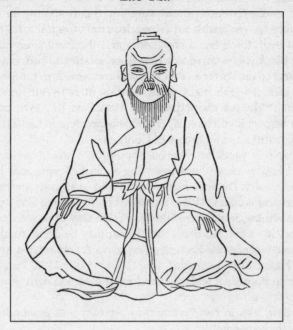

Figure 9.

not too little – the middle way. The middle way therefore would lead to harmonious existence while dis-equilibrium led to dissonance and unhappiness as things out of balance are brought back into line by natural forces.

In explaining this, he developed a model not too dissimilar from that used by modern physicists where the universe is divided equally between positive and negative energies. These he called Yin and Yang, which operate in dynamic tension between themselves. Yin is female and watery – the force in the moon and the rain which reaches a peak in winter. Yang is masculine and solid – the force in the sun and earth which reaches a peak in summer. The peaceful way is the middle way, the Tao. Tao embraces *everything*, and the inference is, therefore, that Tao is God, either in a physical form, as in the physical universe, or in spiritual form. All cause and effect is due to deviation from the middle way.

Through his philosophising he sought to fathom the mysteries of creation and existence, attempting for the first time to express conceptions he was unable to define adequately. Central to his teaching was that everything has a correlative and therefore everything was relative; black was relative to white, good relative to bad, hot relative to cold and so on. As far as Lao Tzu was concerned, to profess a thing was to lack it – the main point of dissent between himself and Confucius: 'Why talk about discipline if you have it?', 'Why talk of the need for respect if you have it?' There was no room in Lao Tzu's mind for the fanciful airs and graces of Confucius.

The aspiring sage, he believed, should act without presuming an outcome and work without assuming rank, believing that humility precludes rivalry. The wise man would avoid, at all costs, the pursuit of adoration and acclaim: 'When a work of merit is done and reputation [fame] is coming, to get out of the way is the way of heaven.'

Section 10 of the Tao deals with 'what may be done' (without the whiplash effect of cause and effect) and says: '. . . to act and expect not – this is called sublime virtue.'

Other sections deal with the conduct of the good man:

Take hard jobs in hand while they are easy and great affairs, too, while they are small.
The troubles of the world cannot be solved except before they grow too hard.
The business of the world cannot be done except while relatively small.
The wise man, then, throughout his life, does nothing great and yet achieves a greatness of his own.
Choosing hardship, then, the wise man never meets with hardship all his life (*The Way of Life*, Lao Tzu, trans. R. B. Blakney, New American Library, New York, 1955).

Other proverbs from Lao Tzu include:

- He that grasps loses.
- While one goes ahead, another lags behind.
- While one blows hot, another blows cold.
- The wise man simply puts away all excess and gaiety and grandeur.

- He who conquers others is strong; he who conquers himself is mighty.
- He who knows when he has enough is rich.
- He who dies, but perishes not, enjoys longevity.
- The sage thinks of all people as his children.
- He takes care of his own part of the contract and exacts nothing of others.
- He who knows his true life will fear no wild beast nor need he armour.
- The saint hoards not.
- The more he does for others, the more he has of his own.
- The more he gives to others, the more he is increased.
- This is the way of heaven, which benefits and does not injure.

This is the way of the sage, who acts but does not strive (*The World's Religions*, Bettany, Ward, Lock & Co., 1890). Thus ends the Tao.

After the Burning of the Books during the Ch'in dynasty, in around 208 BC, a more magical and shamanistic form of Taoism (that had little to do with the teachings of Lao Tzu) emerged. With encouragement from Emperor Wudi (during the rule of the Western Chin dynasty, AD 265–289), Taoists pursued the quest for magical recipes to find the elixir of life and the secrets of immortality.

The *I Ching* (the sacred *Book of Changes*) first appeared during the Chow dynasty (1049–313 BC) and is also referred to as the *Chou I, The Book of Changes,* of the Chow dynasty. Confucius added commentaries, as did later philosophers. Its short passages are regarded as the medium through which heaven can make its will known, a kind of oracle. It consists of sixty-four sections, each headed by a diagram of six lines, which may be solid or broken. Each diagram, which carries a name giving a clue to its interpretation, is selected through a random process of tossing yarrow stalks, or coins, into the air. The enquirer formulates a question before throwing and the book gives interpretations of the meaning of the hexagrams. It seems the broken/unbroken possibilities of the hexagram lines linked it to the bipolar nature of Yin and Yang of Lao Tzu and hence Taoism, but the two schools have little else in common.

Mencius

Mencius (figure 10) is the Latinised form of the name Meng-tsze, or Meng the philosopher (372–289 BC). The follower and admirer of Confucius wrote the fourth of the Four Shu, *The Works of Mencius*, in the tradition of orthodox Confucianism. His conception of morality was based on the belief that human nature was innately good, although he recognised that this goodness required cultivation.

During his lifetime the feudal nation was broken up into twelve monarchies at war: hence the name the Warring States period (figure 8).

Mencius naively imagined he could travel to each of the Warring States peddling a Confucian model of political correctness that would alleviate the prevailing disaffections. Having sold it to one leader, it would surely be adopted by the others, thus restoring order and a return to the feudal system. But this might only happen if each and all of the states were equally balanced, which was not the case. The mighty Ch'in were gaining ground and saw no advantage in such a scheme. Moreover, without participation from the Ch'in there was no incentive for other states to join in. In 310 BC, after searching for twenty years without success for a ruler willing to accept his philosophies, he settled down to finish the record of his teachings.

As well as subscribing to the Confucian ideals, he further proposed that man has a good heart (a conscience) and that 'he who has fathomed his own heart knows his own nature, and if one knows his own nature he also knows heaven'. Accordingly, he believed that every heart has the germ of perfection and only falls short of it by not taking advantage of opportunities, or missing them:

> The great man is he who does not lose his child-heart. He does not think *beforehand* that his words shall be sincere, nor that his acts shall be resolute. He simply abides in the right (*The Works of Mencius*, Mencius, 310 BC).

Like Confucius, he preferred the euphemistic synonym of 'heaven' in preference to the word 'God':

> When heaven is about to impose an important office upon a man it first embitters his heart in its purposes; it causes him to exert his bones and sinews; it lets his body suffer hunger; it inflicts upon

Mencius

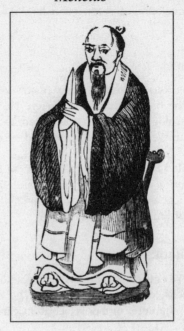

Figure 10.

him want and poverty and confounds his undertakings. In this way it stimulates his heart, steels his nature and supplies that of which the man would else be incapable (*The Works of Mencius*, Mencius, 310 BC).

By the third century AD, worship of the gods had begun to appear. From the fourth century, rivalry between Taoists and Mahayana Buddhists waxed and waned in line with the whims of the ruling court; in AD 550, Emperor Jian Wendi, in an attempt to establish religious order, forced Taoists to adopt Buddhism, while the Tang Emperor Gaozu (AD 618–626) suppressed all religion during the first five years of his office. Later, Xuanzong (AD 712–756) resurrected the Lao Tzu form of Taoism and bestowed the title of *Tao Te Ching* (*The Canon of the way of Virtue*) on the works of Lao Tzu, the name by which it is still referred today. He added a commentary and decreed that the book should replace the *Confucian Analects* as the standard text for guidance and development. A few years later it was usurped by the *I Ching*.

Ssu-ma Ch'ien

Much of what we know about the early history of China is due to the scholarship of the historian Ssu-ma Ch'ien. He was the son of the recorder and astrologer Ssu-ma Tan, who worked for Emperor Wudi (141–87 BC) of the Western Han dynasty and succeeded his father in office.

Ch'ien compiled his own account of Chinese history, the *Shih Chi* (*The Book of Historical Records*), between 103 and 97 BC, which included scientific, historical and biographical accounts of the preceding ages from the times of Emperor Yaur (2145 BC).

The Bamboo Books

The chronology of emperors set down in Appendix 2 is derived from the Bamboo Books, discovered in AD 279. The documents, divided into around 70 chapters, or books, contain rare accounts of early Chinese history.

News of the important discovery first appeared in *The History of Emperor Wudi* (AD 265–289):

> In the fifth year of his reign some lawless parties in the department of Keih dug open the grave of King Seang of Wei [died AD 279] and found a number of Bamboo Tablets written over in the small seal characters with more than 100,000 words; which were deposited in the Imperial Library (*Chinese Classics*,Vol. III, James Legge, University of Hong Kong Press, 1960).

Within two years the tablets were transcribed into modern characters and arranged chronologically into fifteen different categories, many of which deal with mythological stories. Two books, the *Yih King* and the *Book of Annals*, contain de facto historical accounts comparable to those in the Shu, spanning from the reign of the Yellow Emperor, Huang-ti, in around 2697 BC to the end of the Chow period (313 BC).

James Legge's *Chinese Classics*

Many regard the greatest English-speaking scholar of Chinese history to be the Christian missionary James Legge (1815–97), who wrote this of the publication of his great work, *Chinese Classics*:

> This work, the result of more than five and twenty years of toilsome study, was necessary in order that the rest of the world should really know this great Empire and so that our missionary labours among the people could be conducted with sufficient intelligence so as to secure permanent results. I consider that it will greatly facilitate the labours of future missionaries that the entire books of Confucius should be published with a translation and notes (James Legge, April 1886, Hong Kong).

In 1837 Legge joined the Nonconformist Church in England and studied divinity. On completion of the course he agreed to a posting in the Far East and in 1838, accompanied by his wife, sailed to Malacca to take over from his predecessor, Dr Robert Morrison, principal of the Anglo-Chinese College. Morrison had started the college with the aim of diffusing Christianity across China through the compilation and publication of a Cantonese–English dictionary and textbooks to teach English. He also intended to translate the Bible into Chinese, as well as set up a printing press in China if and when the opportunity arose.

In 1841 Legge capitalised on the taking of Hong Kong by the British (two years earlier) and seized the chance to establish a missionary school for Chinese children.

Legge's life in Hong Kong gave him the opportunity to study many aspects of Chinese scholarship, learn the language and to travel to Canton, on the mainland. He quickly realised that before he could instil Christianity into the hearts and minds of the Chinese he would firstly need to familiarise himself with their history and traditions through a thorough investigation of Chinese historical documents.

By 1858 he had accumulated sufficient translations to seek publication of his works, and a local businessman, Joseph Jardine, came to his aid with $16,000 to cover the cost of self-publication, using the printing facilities at the missionary press.

In 1861 *Chinese Classics*, Volume I – which covered *The Confucian*

Analects, The Great Learning and the *Doctrine of the Mean* – was published in Hong Kong. This was soon followed by Volume II – *The Works of Mencius* – and Volume III – the *Shoo King*, or *Book of Historical Documents*.

In 1867 Legge returned to London and within two years finished the last two volumes: Volume IV – *The She King*, or *The Book of Poetry* and Volume V – *The Ch'un Ts'ew* (*Chun Chui*) with the *Tso Chuen*, which he eventually published in 1871 (Volume IV) and 1872 (Volume V).

In 1873 he returned to Scotland and three years later accepted the appointment of a newly created Chair in Chinese at Oxford University. He died at his desk, in 1897, while working on other translations.

Dr Joseph Edkins of Shanghai, in a sermon following Legge's death, said this of his scholarship:

Even now when James Legge is no longer among us, these volumes, the outcome of his long continued toil, contain a rich store of facts by which the foreign observer in Europe and America can judge of China so correctly, because here are the maxims which are popular, here are the ideas that rule in the minds of the scholars and all the people. Here are the principles that sway every native coterie, through all the provinces. What the Bible is to the Christian; what Shakespeare is to the student of English or poetry; what the Koran is to the Mohammedan, these books are to the universal Chinese mind. To place these books in the hands of all who look with despair on a page of *Mencius* or *The Book of History* is a service of the most solid kind and the achievement of a most useful character. While he was engaged in this work he made it a point, from which he would not deviate, to regard direct missionary labours as demanding and receiving his chief attention (Dr Joseph Edkins, from *The Sinologue* (by Lindsay Ride) to *Chinese Classics*, Vol. I, James Legge, University of Hong Kong Press, 1960).

Joseph Needham

Another notable contributor to our understanding of the genius of early China was Joseph Needham, who from 1918 studied bio-chemistry and embryology at Cambridge University.

There, he met and befriended several Chinese colleagues who shared similar interests in history and science. Needham questioned why, on the one hand, the ancient Chinese were far more advanced than the rest of the world and yet on the other, why modern China, given its head start, was not centuries ahead of the rest of the world today. In an attempt to explain the paradox he decided to document the scientific and technological history of China.

In 1942 he travelled to China, as an envoy of the Royal Society, and was offered the post of Scientific Counsellor at the British Embassy in Chongqing, which gave him the perfect opportunity to travel the country. There he met doctors, scientists, engineers, librarians, historians and farmers, each of whom had a story to tell. This mine of information gave Needham the database, the empathy, the understanding and the knowledge to compile his *Science and Civilisation in China* (published by Cambridge University Press). The first volume appeared in 1954 and fourteen more volumes were published during the thirty years that followed.

Needham was astonished to find that almost everything across the wide fields of science, medicine, agriculture and engineering had been either invented or discovered first in China.

He never successfully resolved the paradox he set out to explain, although he notes that the Protestant Reformation, the rise of capitalism and the entrepreneurial bourgeoisie in Europe might all be factors of influence. But his research provides us with a wonderful insight into the ingenuity of the Chinese from 1400 BC onwards.

Silk

Some observers believe that trade in silk and the establishment of markets along the Silk Road, the transasian trading route, had a more far-reaching effect on the development of China than any other single influencing factor, punctuating as it did the deserts and mountains that had isolated that country from the rest of the world for so long.

Silk production (sericulture) was first celebrated by the Chinese more than 4,000 years ago.

Although silk was treasured for clothing, it also played a major part as a writing medium in chronicling the history of the nation – set down in silk books and silk scrolls – long before the appearance of paper, and as a valuable trading commodity it was exchanged for other goods. So silk not only recorded the history of China but played a major part in its development.

Researcher Yue Jue Shu, referring to a quotation from *Selections of Chinese Relics and Archaeology* (Foreign Languages Press, Beijing, 1995), credits the Yellow Emperor Huang-ti (c. 2697 BC) as the progenitor of domestic silkworm production and hence the production of silk.

Its production remained a closely guarded secret for more than 3,000 years until a group of Persian monks smuggled silkworm eggs out of the country in the sixth century AD.

Several moth larvae of the *Bombycidae* and *Saturniidae* families spin silk-thread cocoons within which they pupate, and the Chinese silk-moth variety is the most prolific producer, spinning around 275 metres (900 feet) around itself during a typical incubation. During the larval stage the caterpillar pupates – larval tissue is broken down and adult tissues and structures are formed.

After hatching, the flightless male moth sets off on foot in pursuit of sexually stimulating female moth pheromones. After several hours of mating, the female lays around 500 white pinhead- size disc-shaped eggs, which are kept cool during the first weeks of development. Increasing temperature triggers hatching between six and fifty-two weeks later. The newly hatched caterpillar feeds on the white leaves of the mulberry tree, increasing its body weight 10,000 times during its 28-day life.

Every six days the caterpillar sleeps for a day, before wriggling free to cast off its outgrown skin. After the twenty-eighth day it ejects a single silken thread to anchor itself down and, tossing its head in a figure-eight motion, wraps its body in seracin, a mucous-like liquid ejected from a spinneret (the opening of a tube that leads to the two silk glands that run the length of the body). This flows out at the rate of about 30 centimetres (12 inches) a minute. The seracin hardens on contact with the air to become the cocoon. Fourteen days later, the moth metamorphoses. It dies two to three days after mating. Thus the cycle continues.

Emergence of the moth, under normal conditions, would destroy the cocoon for silk-retrieval purposes, so for domestic silk production the pupa is killed before metamorphosis using hot air. The cocoon is then soaked and carefully unwrapped. Several cocoon threads are combined to form one single commercial thread used in the manufacture of silk fabrics. Around 110 cocoons are needed to make a silk tie and 630 to make a blouse. A heavy silk kimono takes around 3,000 worms that consume 61 kilogrammes (135 pounds) of mulberry leaves.

Wealthy members of the aristocracy, high-ranking officials and scholars wore fine silks, while peasant farmers made do with garments made from hemp, a coarsely woven grass. Supply of silk was controlled to prevent unauthorised persons acquiring the fabric. Even merchants trading in the material were forbidden from wearing it themselves.

It was valued more than clay tablets, tree bark and bamboo poles as a writing medium because it was lighter and hence easier to transport.

The Great Silk Road

In around 138 BC the Western Han leader Emperor Wudi, under attack from the troublesome Hsiung-nu nomads to the north (figure 18) dispatched the imperial envoy Chang Ch'ien to travel to the western regions in an attempt to secure the alliance and support of the Ta Yueh Chi, adversaries of Hsiung-nu. But the envoy was captured and interned for ten years. On his release, he continued his mission west, eventually locating the Ta Yueh Chi settled in Ta Hsia (modern Turkestan and Afghanistan), at the formerly Greek-controlled city of Bactria (figure 11), where he discovered a civilised and settled population.

Returning to Ch'ang-an in 126 BC, he told the court of his travels, of the strong horses in the west that would be useful in combat to the emperor's troops, of the Bactrian camel (plate 1d) that could travel over rough terrain for days without water and suggested the establishment of a trading route across Asia to Bactria and, later, onwards to the eastern Mediterranean and Red Sea ports.

Wudi accepted the envoy's advice and dispatched expeditions that established embassies along the proposed route linking the oasis cities of Central Asia as far as Bactria 3,000 kilometres (1,864 miles) to the west. The route established itself slowly over the centuries, but caravans came under increasing attack from raiders.

In AD 97 General Pan Ch'ao reasserted Han influence across Asia with an expedition of over 70,000 troops who made safe the trade routes as far west as the Caspian Sea.

Safety was further improved during Mogul rule (1279–1368), which secured the entire length of the route, which had by that time extended across the Gobi Desert, Samarkand and Antioch to Mediterranean ports in Greece, Italy, the Middle East and Egypt. It was during this period that the Italian merchant-explorer Marco Polo first reached China from the West to become a long-serving official of Emperor Kublai Khan. Returning to Italy twenty years later, he chronicled his journey in a book called *Travels* which gave Westerners an insight into the mysterious country in the East.

Trade flowed both ways. Spices, teas, ceramics, bronzeware, ironware, jadeware and lacquerware from the East were exchanged for gold, silver, cotton, camels and horses from the West.

Buddhism Travels to China

Religious and philosophical belief in China was divided between Confucianism and Taoism until the arrival of the third way, Buddhism, along the Silk Road.

Sri Lankan texts say that Prince Gautama Siddhartha, the Buddha (c. 563–483 BC), was born at Kapilavastu, between the Himalayas of Nepal and the river Rapti in the north-east of Oudh. There, the Sakyas ('the powerful') grew rice and traded with their neighbours, the Kosala, to the south-west.

The Sri Lankan records, written in Pali, the sacred language of Buddhism (an early modification of Sanskrit), refer to the founder as 'the enlightened one', a great teacher who preached salvation and deliverance to the people. He married and fathered one son, Rahula, who became one of his disciples.

At the age of twenty-nine Buddha left home to become a wandering ascetic. As a deep-feeling philanthropic philosopher, he contemplated the states of old age, weakness, decay and the horrors of sickness and death, and measured these afflictions of an imperfect world against the notion of a perfect creator. The resulting paradox would in time be overcome by the teaching of his own enlightened understanding.

Records provide an account of his departure:

The ascetic Gautama has gone from home into the wilderness, whilst still young in years, in the bloom of youthful strength, in the first freshness of life. The ascetic Gautama, although his parents did not wish it, although they shed tears and wept, has had his hair and beard shaved off and has put on yellow garments (*Sacred Books of the East*, Vol. X, trans. Max Muller, Oxford, Clarendon Press, 1881).

The Silk Road

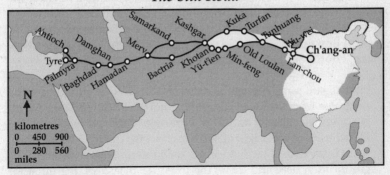

Figure 11. Boundary of China *(white)* during the Han period. The Silk Road extended from Ch'ang-an in the east, across Asia (eventually) to Antioch and Tyre in the Mediterranean.

Thus, seeking spiritual enlightenment he travelled for seven years, placing himself in succession under two notable teachers. Leaving them, unfulfilled, he travelled through the kingdom of Maghada and arrived at the town of Uruvela. There, in the beautiful forests he spent many years in self-discipline repressing desires and aspirations, awaiting spiritual enlightenment. Fasting, suppression of breath and other mortifications were all tried without success, and around this time five friends with whom he had travelled abandoned him.

Finally, sitting beneath a bo tree (tree of knowledge) near Buddh Gaya in Bihar, he meditated for five weeks, during which time he was shaken by a storm. During the storm he was visited by the serpent Maculinda, who provided protection by coiling himself around Buddha and fanning the canopy of his head above him.

After five weeks he passed through several stages of abstraction until he became enlightened about the transmigration of souls and the four sacred truths:

1 Suffering envelops the world.
2 Its cause is desire and attachment.
3 It can be overcome with nirvana (the extinction of desire, of suffering, of ignorance), the eternal state.
4 The way to nirvana is through Buddhism.

Realising that asceticism, like overindulgence, was futile, he chose the middle way between mortification and self-indulgence that would inevitably lead to peace, knowledge and enlightenment and ultimately nirvana through the eight-fold path: right faith, resolve, speech, action, living, effort, thought and concentration.

> Birth is suffering; old age is suffering; sickness is suffering; to be separated from the loved is suffering; not to obtain what one desires is suffering; clinging to life is suffering. This, Oh monks, is the sacred truth of the origin of suffering; it is the thirst for being which leads from birth to birth, together with lust and desire, which finds gratification here and there; the thirst for pleasures, the thirst for being, the thirst for power . . . this, Oh monks, is the sacred truth of extinction of suffering, the extinction of this thirst by complete annihilation of desire, letting go, expelling it, separating oneself from it, giving it no room . . . (Sermon to the Monks at Benares; *Sacred Books of the East*, Vol. X, trans. Max Muller, Oxford, Clarendon Press, 1881).

From this moment forth there would be no new births for him. He who walked in purity would end all suffering.

The teachings of Buddhism are deliberately vague with regard to the existence of the soul as a separately existing energy. On the one hand Buddhism believes in the endless cycle of birth and rebirth for less developed souls, and yet on the other hand it does not identify with the reincarnation of the same soul energy. This deliberate vagueness is overcome by a positive approach to spirituality rather than a negative one. It is not that the inner darkness is converted to light; it is rather that the being preoccupied with inner illumination crowds out the darkness. In this way the peaceful soul that reaches nirvana through the teachings of Buddha will not come back to earth.

Returning to Uruvela, Buddha converted a group of ascetics and their leader Kasapa after, according to the records, performing numerous miracles. The whole group moved on to Magadha and converted the king.

Strangers came from distant lands to listen to Buddha's teaching as he wandered the streets accompanied by his begging-bowl mendicants, a brethren of religious men – the Sangha – with shaven heads

Buddha

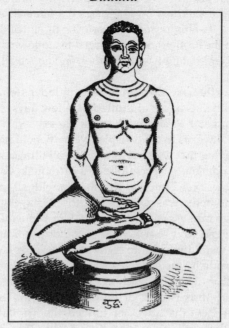

Figure 12.

and yellow robes who through choice had given up property, family ties and vanity and chosen instead a life of chastity.

> From time to time an unsurpassed teacher is born into the world as a guide to erring mortals, a fully enlightened one, a blessed Buddha who thoroughly understands the universe, the gods and men and makes his knowledge known to others. The truth doth he proclaim both in its letter and in its spirit, lovely in its origin, lovely in its progress, lovely in its consummation; the higher life doth he make known, in all its purity and perfectness . . . (Sermon to the Monks at Benares; *Sacred Books of the East*, Vol. X, trans. Max Muller, Oxford, Clarendon Press, 1881).

At the age of eighty Buddha embarked on a final journey from Rajagah, the capital of Magadha, to Pataliputta, the future capital whose greatness he prophesied. On the journey he was attacked by a great illness, which he subdued hoping to give a farewell address to the order. He knew that his journey was nearing its end and that he could no longer lead the brotherhood and urged his followers to be a refuge to themselves and not look for any other, and above all to be anxious to learn.

A mighty earthquake then arose with thunder from the heavens. He broke out into his hymn of exultation. A few days later he arrived at Kusinagara, Uttar Pradesh, where he passed away without complaint. His final words to his disciples were: 'Behold now, brethren. I exhort you, saying that decay is inherent in all things. Work out your salvation with diligence.' Then followed earthquakes and thunder.

His funeral was celebrated in Kusinagara with all the honour due to a king. His body was wrapped with 500 layers of bandages, enclosed in two iron vessels and cremated on a funeral pyre made of perfumes. Legend says that neither soot nor ash was left, just the bones, which were divided into eight portions, over each of which a mound was made by the groups who had claimed them.

After Buddha's death his teachings were sung by disciples in three divisions: the Sutras (words of Buddha), Vinaya (disciplines) and Dharma (doctrines) that together formed the Tripitakas, the three collections of the works of Buddha. King Asoka (262–239 BC), the king of Magadha, grandson of Chandragupta – who became a kind of second founder of Buddhism – established monasteries all over northeast India and inculcated its principles by having them carved into hillside rock along the main migratory routes into and out of the country. He adopted the philosophy as the state religion and in so doing helped spread the teachings.

First evidence of the diffusion of Buddhism across China appeared with the arrival of the first missionaries in around AD 150, when sections of the Dharma were carried on tree bark, and later silk, by travelling monks, who spread the philosophy northwards through the Himalayas into Central Asia and along the Silk Route to Tibet and China.

Confucianism and Taoism, so omnipresent and influential during the Warring States period, as we will see, changed the course of political, sociological and philosophical development in China and in turn changed the course of the wars themselves, facilitating the emergence of the Ch'in and their leader Shi Huangdi. But, today, both philosophies are less popular than Buddhism in modern-day China. The main form of Buddhism changed variously as it diffused and disseminated; in south-east Asia the Theravada School of Buddhism (the school of the elders) was favoured, believing that the meditative life was the way to break the chain of samsara, the endless cycle of birth, death and rebirth. Its three main goals strive to attain a true insight into the nature of things, to become a fully enlightened one who lives alone and does not teach and to become a fully awakened Buddha.

In China, Korea, Japan and Tibet the Mahayana (the great vehicle) form of Buddhism, developed from around AD 150, encouraged individuals who have reached the state of nirvana to become a trainee Buddha (a bodhisattva) and so save others.

At first traditionalists in China, content with Confucianism and Taoism, were not impressed by the new Buddhist teachings. But, during the Tartar Partition period (AD 317–589; figure 19) Mahayana Buddhism gained new ground with the teachings of Bodhidharma, the Indian Buddhist teacher who arrived there in around AD 520 and founded the Ch'an school of Buddhism (which developed into the Zen form of Buddhism in Japan in around the twelfth century). This emphasised silent meditation with sudden interruptions from a master that encouraged the awakening of the mind.

Esoteric Buddhism (Tantrism), yet another variant popular in Tibet and Japan, teaches that enlightenment is already within the true sage, from a previous incarnation, and that with proper guidance it can be developed.

Buddhism declined rapidly in India by the thirteenth century as it came under pressure from Islam and Hinduism.

Jade

Another highly prized trading commodity was jade.

The semiprecious stone was more precious than gold to the ancient Chinese, who believed that, because it lasted for ever, it could confer immortality. Alchemical Taoists ground the stone into powder, which they then consumed in the belief that it would create a bridge within them that would lead to heaven and immortality. The emperor and nobles were buried in jade suits, like the ones of Prince Liu Sheng (plate 15) and Princess Tou Wan (plate 16a) discussed later.

Jade Deposits

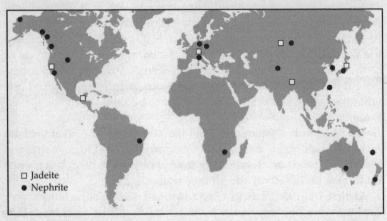

Figure 13. Jadeite comes from Guatemala, California, Switzerland, Siberia, Japan and Burma. The slightly softer, less precious nephrite is found in North America, Brazil, Zimbabwe, Italy, East Germany, Poland, Siberia, western China, Japan, Burma, Australia, New Zealand and New Caledonia.

China's early supplies of jade came from the Yurunkax, the White Jade River that separates the Takla Makan desert from the Kunlun mountains (the jade mountains) in north-west China's Xinjiang province. Other supplies began to arrive from the seventeenth century from Burma in the south-east, Korea in the north-east and Taiwan in the south. It was worked by craftsmen into tools, jewellery and objets d'art and bartered in exchange for imports.

Differing combinations of heat and pressure determine the global formation of jade (figure 13) which falls into two categories: jadeite, a silicate of sodium and aluminium, and nephrite, a silicate of calcium and magnesium. The amount of iron in the stone determines the colour, which can range from white (mutton-fat jade) through green, to red and black.

Jade is harder than steel, comparable to quartz in hardness, and can only be worked by stones harder than itself, like diamond-tipped grindstones or wheels. The Chinese drilled holes in the stone using hollow bamboo tubes charged with sand containing crushed quartz. Today, true jade can be distinguished from inferior types using spectrometers to measure the signature of reflected light.

The Silk Road enabled silk, jade and other commodities to be traded until around the sixteenth century, when it fell into decline with competition from the safer sea routes.

China through the Ages

The Yellow Emperor, of around 2697 BC, was the legendary first emperor of China who tamed the Yellow River with dykes and canals. Hence the name Huang (yellow) and Ti (son of heaven). The Bamboo Books say that he was followed by the Emperors Che, Cheuen-Heuh, Kuh and then by Yaur and Shuhn (see the Table of Emperors in Appendix 2, figure A2a, which shows the succession of emperors after Yaur – the foremost emperor whose existence can be substantiated from archaeological record).

Legge says that, of the founding fathers, Emperor Yu, the next in line, should rightly be regarded as the founder of the Chinese empire because the historical accounts of the others, 'having much of legend about them', raise suspicion.

He believes that early settlers, descendants of Noah and his fabled ark, began to move eastwards between the Black and Caspian Seas in around 2,000 BC and journeyed between the Altaic mountains in the north and the Tauric mountains in the south until they came across the fertile Yellow River valley, where they settled. Thus the modern Shensi province was the cradle of Chinese civilisation. There, the early settlers consolidated their strength under the rule of chieftains. Gradually, they migrated in all directions, overcoming geographical obstacles as they went.

The 'black-haired people', as they became known, brought with them the ideas of settled labour, the cultivation of grain for food, flax for clothing and the mulberry tree to feed the silkworms. They were acquainted with astronomy and practised intercalation to anchor down the calendar to the agricultural seasons. They also used the written Chinese characters handed down from earlier times.

According to Ssu-ma Ch'ien's account, Yu was the great engineer who takes the credit for containing the Yellow River flood waters through hydraulic conservation works:

'The inundating waters seem to assail the heavens,' Yu said, 'and in their extent embraced the hills and overtopped the great mounds so that people were bewildered and overwhelmed ... I opened passages for the streams throughout the nine provinces and conducted them to the seas. I deepened the channels and conducted them to the streams.' Thirteen years Yu spent mastering the waters without once returning home to see his wife and children. By his extensive water works he brought water benefits to all the people. The flood ceased and fields were irrigated. To his own family came the privilege of founding the Hsia Dynasty. The descendants of Yu reigned down to 1588 [BC] when the dynasty was overthrown by the Shang.

God (Heaven) was designated the Ruler and the Supreme Ruler, and it was through God's ordination that kings reigned and princes dispatched justice. On the common people he conferred a moral duty. All powers that exist in the world were from him. Wrongdoings would be punished with calamities while continued persistence resulted in the loss of dominion over others and loss of title.

The Duke of Chow in his *Establishment of Government* provides a simplistic account of the history from Yu to himself:

Yu [c. 1989 BC] the great, founder of the Hea [Hsia] Dynasty, sought for able men to honour God. But the way of Kee [Kwei, c. 1588 BC], the last of his line, was different. He employed cruel men and he had no successors. The empire was given to T'ang [c. 1557 BC] the Successful, who greatly administered the bright ordinance of God. By and by T'ang's throne came to . . . the house of Chow [c. 1049 BC], whose chiefs followed their fitness for the charge by finding out men who would reverently serve God (*Chinese Classics*, James Legge, University of Hong Kong Press, 1960).

Although the ancient texts give accounts of the early civilisations, the best archaeological evidence before 1935 set the start date of Chinese dynastic history at around the beginning of the Chow period (1049 BC). In 1935, oracular inscriptions found on bones excavated from the Shang capital at Anyang (figure 6) supported Ssu-ma Ch'ien's accounts of the times between Yu (1989 BC) and the Chow dynasty (1049 BC).

Emperor T'ang brought the first centralised government to the various tribal groups which led to advances in art and technology. Bronze casting techniques were perfected, leading to the introduction

Emperor Ch'in (Qin) Shi Huangdi

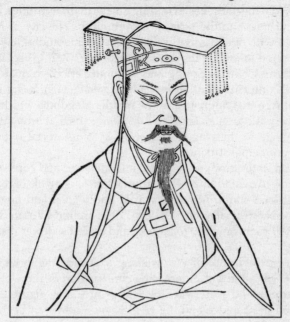

Figure 14.

of quality bronzeware and weapons, like the halberd dagger. The simultaneous invention of the chariot and the bow was to ensure the Shang dynasty's military supremacy and their concomitant hold on power for the next 500 years. Despotic rule by the last Shang ruler, Te-sin, led to revolt, allowing the nearby Chow, descendants of the Ch'i who had settled in the fertile Wei valley, to rise to power. Te-sin (of the Shang dynasty) was succeeded by Woo (of the Chow dynasty) who overturned the oppressive rule of Te-sin to take control around 1049 BC.

During the reigns that followed, the Chow dynasty brought significant developments in agriculture within which a feudal system developed and flourished. Fiefdoms, ruled by nobles, were established. These were often brothers of the emperor and were called on to support campaigns with revenues obtained from peasant farmer surpluses. But population growth forced migration of the people to new settlements in all directions, and these soon organised themselves

43

into states with their own programmes. At the same time the Hsiung-nu tribe from the north began raiding the northern territories, bringing terror and havoc to the peasant communities. The city of Hao was destroyed with one massive assault from the marauding invaders.

The period following the destruction of Hao (722–481 BC) is known as the Ch'un Ch'iu, or Spring and Autumn Period (from an account given by Confucius in his *Spring and Autumn* annals). It was the great Classical Age that flourished in the middle kingdoms which saw the rise of the philosophers Lao Tzu and Confucius that brought about a great change in thinking, bureaucratic systems, social organisation and governmental structure.

Various states grouped together into alliances and confederations in an effort to defend themselves from incursions by the barbarians in the north and south. Alliances waxed and waned and larger states began to absorb smaller ones. Before 770 BC around 1,700 fiefs existed. Within 100 years only 200 remained, and by 500 BC fewer than 20 had survived.

In 486 BC the Prince of Wu, wishing to invade the more northern states of Sung and Lu, ordered the construction of the world's first man-made inland waterway, the Han Kou Canal (figure 8), which connected the Yangtze and the Huai Rivers (now part of the longer Grand Canal that extends north to connect Hangchow with Beijing). The canal not only transported goods and troops but provided much-needed irrigation and flood control. At around the same time, discoveries and developments in iron casting saw the advent of the iron ploughshare, which increased agricultural productivity. The consequential shedding of farm labour swelled the ranks of state armies that raced to equip themselves with the latest weapons of war – iron swords and arrowheads. Clearly, there were many other factors that led to the confrontationary unease that swept the land, but once armed they began to fight, and from 403 to 221 BC the states of Ch'i, Yen, Chao, Han, Wei and Ch'u and Ch'in were at war (figure 8) in an internecine struggle for supremacy.

The elevation of Zheng, the son of an earlier Chow warlord, to the throne of Ch'in in 246 BC was dramatically to change the course of the war. One of the factors that led to his success over neighbouring Han was the construction of the Chengkuo Canal that connected the Jing River and the Luo River (figure 15), tributaries of the Wei, in around 246 BC. Ssu-ma Ch'ien explains what happened:

The Chengkuo Canal

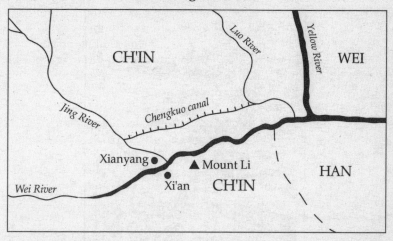

Figure 15. The Chengkuo Canal, connecting the Jing and Luo Rivers, was opened in 246 BC. Thousands of acres of poor land were thus irrigated, raising productivity of the previously infertile plain, a major factor that enabled the Ch'in to prosper and conquer the surrounding feudal states.

... how the king of Han wished to prevent the eastern expansion of Ch'in by exhausting it with projects. He therefore sent the water engineer Cheng Kuo to the king of Ch'in to convince him that a canal should be built between the Jing and Luo Rivers. The proposed canal would be 300 li [a measure of land equating to 400 metres/1,313 feet] long and used for irrigation. The project was half finished when the plot was discovered. The Ch'in ruler was stopped from killing Cheng Kuo by the engineer's own argument. 'Although this scheme was intended to injure you,' he said [referring to the fact that the scheme was originally proposed as a hair-brained project intended to deplete the coffers of the Ch'in] 'if the canal is completed it will bring great benefit to your state.' The work was then ordered to be continued. When finished, it irrigated 40,000 ching [green pastures] of [previously] poor land with water laden with rich silt. The productivity of the fields rose to one chung [full capacity] for each mu [a measure of land; 6.6 mu equals 1 acre]. Thus the interior became a fertile plain without bad years. Ch'in then grew rich and strong and finally conquered

45

The Seed Drill

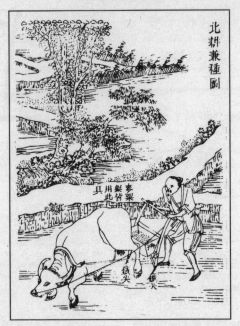

Figure 16. An engraving from the *Compendium of Works and Days* compiled by O-Erh-T'ai (1742), showing an early ox-drawn (iron) seed drill known to have been used at least by the second century BC in China (wooden versions precursed these during the third century BC).

all other feudal states. The canal was called after Cheng Kuo who built it.

At around the same period, the multi-tube seed drill appeared (figure 16), greatly facilitating the sowing of wheat. Chao Kuo, a government official from around 85 BC comments:

The [seed drill] ploughshares were all drawn by one ox, with one man leading it dropping the seed and holding the drill simultaneously. Thus 100 mu could be sown every day.

The combined effect of irrigation, mechanical sowing and the consequential increases in yield from the extra 227,000 acres in the Wei valley sustained a growing army while the waterway itself improved deployment of troops and supplies.

Now just two states remained: Ch'in and Ch'u. Zheng's massive and well-equipped army quickly subsumed the Ch'u. For the first time ever the nation was united under one leader who, in 226 BC, changed his name to Ch'in (leader of the Qin), Shi – the first – Huang – yellow – Ti (Di in modern usage; hence the name Shi Huangdi throughout this text) – Son of Heaven – the first emperor of a *unified* China, sent by God to rule the greatest nation on earth.

He could now, at last, turn his attention back to the Hsiung-nu who, during the warring years, had sacked the unprotected northern territories at will. But the border was 6,435 kilometres (4,000 miles) long. His answer to the problem was to build a defensive wall that connected sections of walls (shown and dated in figure 8) built by previous administrations. The finished wall would be the biggest and longest the world had ever seen, to keep out the marauding barbarians. It would cross deserts, marshes and mountain peaks, rising to 2,438 metres (8,000 feet) in altitude. Its length would be 4,828 kilometres (3,000 miles), from Mount Jeyshi in North Korea to Linshao in western China. It would be built in local materials along its length, from dry stone in some places to beaten-earth walls in others. It would be 6 metres (20 feet) high and as much as 4.8 metres (16 feet) wide with 7.9 metre-high (26-foot-high) beacon towers that carried platforms, each communicating with the next using smoke signals by day and torch beacons at night – the world's first data communications highway sending messages across the country, from the western borders to the centre of the capital, in hours.

For every one of the 700,000 conscripts, soldiers and peasants engaged in building the wall, five others supplied the materials and the food, tools, horses, camels and carts required to sustain progress. In all, three and a half million workers toiled for ten years on the greatest project the world has ever known. One million died during the construction of the wall, which increased in length by 482 kilometres (300 miles) a year, almost 1.6 kilometres (1 mile) a day.

The astonishing achievements of the first emperor were many. Rural communities, protected by the wall, flourished in the north. Canal systems connecting the northern and southern states accelerated growth. But the public works projects of walls, canals, roads, as well as the construction of the emperor's own mausoleum, which occupied

The Great Wall of China

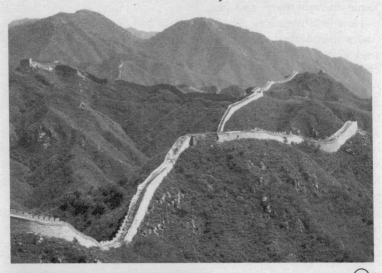

(a)

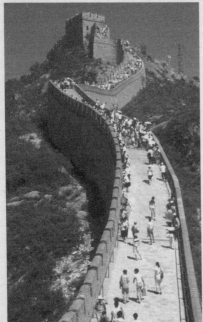

(b)

Figure 17. The Great Wall of China, built during the reign of the first emperor to deter Turkish and Mongol invaders, stretches inland from Mount Jeyshi, in North Korea, to Linshao in the west, a distance of 4,828 kilometres (3,000 miles). It was extended westwards, and rebuilt, during the Han, T'ang and Ming Dynasties.

700,000 workers, sapped the will of the people, who became unsettled. Three attempts were made on Shi Huangdi's life. During his brief reign he retreated into isolation. Following requests from advisers (more on this later) he ordered the burning of many of the treasured books, and 460 dissenting scholars, who forced a rebellion, were executed.

Preoccupied more and more with the quest for everlasting life, the Son of Heaven embarked on tours of the kingdom in search of the elixirs of immortality. During a tour along the eastern shores of Shandong he sickened and died. The heir to the throne, Meng T'ien, committed suicide, and the younger, weaker, son, Er Shi, took the throne in 210 BC. Within three years the peasants revolted. Er Shi was killed. The mighty Ch'in dynasty that had brought China together had torn itself apart in less than 15 years.

In 206 BC a rebel army attacked the Ch'in capital of Xianyang and burned what books remained, consigning, for a while, the history of China to the shadows of oblivion.

Our account of Chinese history could end here, leaving readers to speculate on how dynastic China became the Communist republic of today. But continued historical enquiry suggests that Shi Huangdi was not the last in the line of the so-called Sons of Heaven to rule in China. It would therefore be premature, for the sake of a brief synopsis of dynastic succession, to terminate our enquiries here.

Following the collapse of the Ch'in, soldiers deserted the Ch'in army and defected to the rebel Nung. A power struggle ensued between several rebel leaders who wished to return to the feudal system, but attempts to re-establish the old order failed. In an effort to suppress the re-emergence of feudal institutions, the Han emperor Gaodi (206–195 BC) sought a compromise with rebel leaders. He distracted the maladjusted feudal princes with gifts of land and granted fiefdoms – but only to his own supporters (who would willingly relinquish them when asked to later). He made sure that the new settlements were contained within the preferred framework of provinces controlled by governors and magistrates whose loyalties lay with the emperor. He thus slowly eliminated rivalries, allowing successors to inherit a prosperous and united empire (figure 18).

Uprisings proliferated with widespread unease until the appearance of Emperor Wudi (141–87 BC), who completed the dismantling of the feudal system. The administrative system of the Ch'in was retained and Confucian ideals prospered. The imperial system was consolidated with the establishment of a civil service. The neglected and crumbling Great Wall was restored and reinforced, once again fortifying the northern borders against Hsiung-nu incursions. Garrisons and embassies were established along the Silk Road, which prospered, with trade boosted by the output of manufactured goods from state-controlled factories.

By the end of the later Han period merchants and landowners had become wealthy at the expense of the rest of society, which gave them the leverage to exert economic pressure over the ruling classes. The civil service was taken over by the landowners, and funding for military campaigns began to dry up. The Great Wall again began to crumble, allowing the barbarians free access to the northern farmlands. Unable to fight off the intruders, the Han formed an alliance with the Hsiung-nu barbarians of the south, against those of the north, in exchange for goods. The shifting of the capital from Ch'ang-an, in the Wei River valley, to Loyang, in the Yellow River valley, shifted the hub of economic activity eastwards, introducing fierce competition from the Huai River settlements which had prospered since the arrival of the Han Kou Canal. These factors led to the fragmentation of the empire into the Three Kingdoms (AD 221–280) of Wei, Wu and Shu (figure 19).

These three struggled for supremacy until Wei, under control of the Western Chin dynasty, asserted its control over the others to briefly reunify the country. But the situation was not to last; alliances with barbarians had allowed immigration and settlement of tribal members inside the boundary of the Great Wall. Civil strife rallied the support of different groups with, at one time, the Hsiung-nu supporting one prince and the Tartars, another group of barbarians from the north, another.

The northern provinces became the battleground for warring barbarian kings. In AD 383 500,000 Tartar soldiers and 270,000 Tartar cavalry charged the Chin at the battle of Fei Shui. But the lines of the Chin held, and the Tartar withdrew to a line in the sand further to the north (figure 19). China was partitioned, with the Tartars controlling the north and Chinese dynasties to the south.

In AD 581 troops of Yang Chien, the half-Chinese and half-barbarian general, invaded the south from the north and defeated Ch'en, the last of the six dynasties that ruled during the period of disunion.

The Han Period

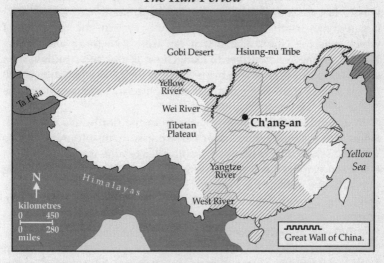

Figure 18. Boundary of China *(hatched)* during the Han period, 206 BC–AD 220.

The Three Kingdoms Period, AD 221–280, and The Tartar Partition Period, AD 317–589

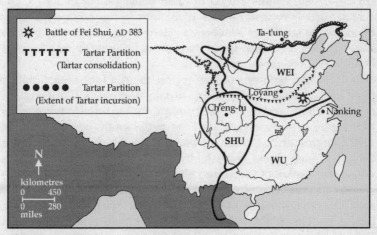

Figure 19. Boundaries of the Three Kingdoms from AD 221 to 280 and the division of China during the Tartar Partition *(see legend)* between AD 317 and 589 (as detailed by the Southern Dynasties and Northern Dynasties in Appendix 1).

51

China was reunified, but only briefly, under the Sui dynasty which was to last for less than 40 years. Emperor Sui Yangdi (AD 604-617) began construction of a nationwide canal system, the backbone of which was the Grand Canal that ran from Che (near present-day Beijing) on the Yellow River to Hangchow. It took three million men six years to build, enabling boats to navigate 1,800 kilometres (1,120 miles) inland from Beijing, a feat of engineering comparable to the building of the Great Wall itself.

In around AD 618 military attacks from the north, this time from Korea, put the Sui regime under fierce pressure for resources. Troops were conscripted from the land, leading to a famine-inspired rebellion that gave way to the T'ang dynasty (figure 20). Some see the T'ang period as the golden age during which China expanded to become a great world power. Art and trade flourished until once again, in AD 907, northern invaders caused a break-up that allowed the emergence of five different dynasties controlling ten different kingdoms (figure 21). It was reunited 50 years later under the Song (AD 960–1279) – apart from the north-west state of Hsia, which was under control of the part-Tibetan Tunguts, and Liao which was occupied by the Kitan barbarians in the north-east.

The period that followed the wars between the Hsia and Song (1032–44) saw another period of rapid development in Song China despite further incursions from barbarians in the north who forced the capital to shift from K'ai Feng to Hangchow further south (figure 22). A cultural revolution swept the country, bringing better education, literacy, art and commerce.

In 1126, after ten years of war in Liao, the Kin (one-time vassals of their Liao masters) swept south to take control of K'ai Feng and northern China, and in 1141 the country was partitioned between the Kin empire in the north and the Song in the south (figure 23). But by 1279 Genghis Khan, a Mongol leader from the north, reached K'ai Feng, occupied China and established his own dynasty, the Yuans, who controlled all of China by 1279.

After less than 90 years the Mongols were pushed out by the last of the *Chinese* dynasties, the Ming, who set up their new capital in Beijing, rebuilt the Great Wall – bigger and better than ever before – and extended its length to around 7,242 kilometres (4,500 miles). They improved and extended the Grand Canal, and foreign expeditions increased trade and prestige. The empire was finally lost to the foreign

The T'ang Period

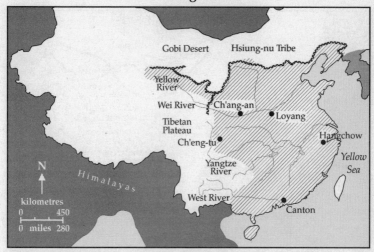

Figure 20. China *(hatched)* during the T'ang period, AD 618–907.

Period of the Five Dynasties and Ten Kingdoms

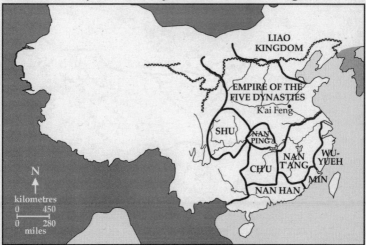

Figure 21. Between AD 907 and 960 China was divided between the Five Dynasties, to the north, and into Ten Kingdoms (only nine kingdoms are shown above; the tenth, the Sung, rose from the ashes of the surrendering states).

The Early (Northern) Song Period

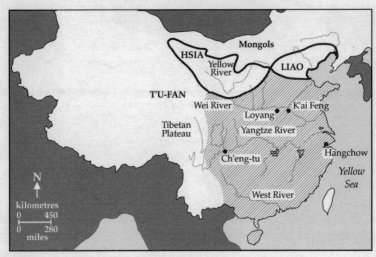

Figure 22. Song China *(hatched)* up to AD 1125.

The Later (Southern) Song Period

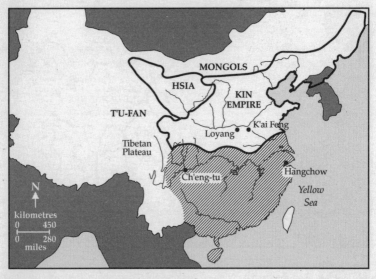

Figure 23. Song China *(hatched)*, AD 1126–1279.

Modern-Day China

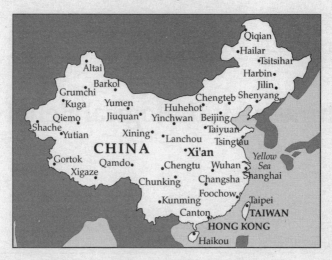

Figure 24. Political map of modern-day China showing principal cities.

Manchu dynasty of the Ch'ing (1644–1911) who, forever in fear of a Chinese revolt, spent more time looking over their shoulders than looking forwards. The country fell into rapid decline, and Chinese technology for the first time began to fall behind the rest of the world. In 1911 the Chinese eventually overthrew the weakened Ch'ing government and formed a republic.

CHAPTER THREE

Chinese Mythological Belief

Numerical, Pictorial and Mythological Encoding of Information

Appendix 3 details the areas of knowledge the ancients wished to encode together with their reasons for doing so. But this does not explain *how* they encoded it.

To understand how the first emperor might have encoded his secrets into the terracotta warriors we need to examine how the Maya, Peruvians and Egyptians encoded theirs and the methods they chose to encode them.

An essential requirement of any encoding system is that it announces, to the initiated, the existence of concealed information – without revealing the information itself. Appendix 4 shows how artefacts were labelled to facilitate future recognition and identification. It also shows how the ancients favoured the use of numbers, pictures and mythological stories to protect, compress and preserve their knowledge, because numbers and pictures transcend future language barriers.

Mythological stories called for a cast – as well as a plot – which gave rise to a pantheon of gods that could, in the distant future, be brought to life after ages of incarceration in carvings, paintings, jewellery and architecture. This mind-blowing finale would exemplify their brilliance and their intellectual superiority to modern man.

The Chinese, too, had their mythological beliefs which, curiously and remarkably, shared much in common with other ancient civilisations. Most of all, they worshipped the feathered snake as the highest of gods, they were keen astrologers and astronomers, and they revered the monkey.

The Dragon

The dragon in Chinese mythology was part bird, part snake and part stag (plate 2). Lord Pacal, the priest-king of the Maya in around AD 750 in Mexico, was known to his people as Quetzalcoatl, the plumed serpent, and as a stag; decoded pictures from the Mosaic Mask of Palenque and the Mural of Bonampak (Appendix 4 and plate 3) show Lord Pacal in both forms. In the simplest sense, the feathers referred to the soaring spirit in the sky, while the snake referred to the body on earth that shed its skin (reincarnated).

Mythologically, the expression referred to the perfect being, the most venerated of the gods. Tutankhamun of Egypt was likewise known as the feathered snake. He carried the mark of the bird and the snake on his forehead (figure A58).

In both the esoteric and scientific senses, the term 'feathered snake' refers to the sun itself (figure A57). Viracocha, the legendary white god of the Mochicas who walked the land of Peru performing miracles more than 1,500 years ago, was also known by the same eponym (figure A59). He scratched pictures into the deserts around Nazca in Peru, to convey the same message (figure A60). The drawings show the feathered snake clearly, together with the baby bird that symbolised spiritual rebirth. Close inspection of the one shown in figure A60a shows the bird with five claws on one foot and only four on the other. In China, ordinary dragons had legs with only four claws on each foot, distinguishing them from the more grandiose imperial dragon that had five-clawed feet, one to control each corner of the heavens while the other controlled his chambers in the centre of the universe. Close inspection of the Chinese dragon in plate 2 shows one leg with five claws and the other leg with only four; one claw is missing – associating that dragon (that feathered snake) with the feathered snake of Peru.

The bas-relief representation of Viracocha, from the Gateway of the Sun at Tiahuanaco, Bolivia, also shows Viracocha with one finger missing (figure A59).

As Appendix 4 explains, priest-king feathered snakes shared much in common. They were all conceived through an immaculate conception; when they were born a bright star was seen in the sky; during their lives they all performed miracles, and when they died they journeyed to the heavens to become the brightest of the night-time heavenly bodies, the planet Venus, the purest source of light in the heavens. Venus, known since ancient times as the twin star (figure A23), is the brightest source of light in the night sky and so resembles a star. Sometimes the planet appears in the morning sky, to the east (as the morning star) before the sun rises, and at other times (292 days later) in the evening sky in the west (as the evening star). Generally speaking, whenever the expression *twins* is mentioned (or illustrated) in ancient texts we can be sure that the reference is to Venus.

In Chapter 2 we became acquainted with the Yellow Emperor of around 2697 BC, the legendary first emperor who tamed the Yellow River with dykes and canals. This is how the Bamboo Books describe his life:

His mother was called Foo-Paou. She witnessed a great flash of lightning which surrounded the star ch'oo of the Great Bear with a brightness that lighted the whole country about her and thereupon became pregnant. After twenty-five months she gave birth to the emperor in Show-K'ew. When born, he could speak. His countenance was dragon-like, his virtue that of a sage. He could oblige the hosts of spirits to come to his court and receive his orders ... By means of the heavenly lady Pa, he stopped the extraordinary rains caused by the enemy. When the empire was settled, his sage virtue was brightly extended and all sorts of auspicious indications appeared.

In his first year, when he came to the throne, he dwelt in Yew-Heung. He invented the cap with pendants and the robes to match. In his twentieth year brilliant clouds appeared; and he arranged his officers by names taken from the colours of the clouds (from the Bamboo Books, Part I, as quoted by James Legge, *Chinese Classics*, Vol. III – *The Shoo King* – Hong Kong University Press, 1960).

Many accounts say that Huang-ti did not die but went up to heaven on a dragon. Hang Ch'in-fung gives the following passage, quoted by some writers as from the Bamboo Books:

> Hwang-ti went away as one of the Immortals. One of his ministers, Tso-ch'e, cut an image of him in wood and led the princes to pay court and reverence to it (quoted by James Legge, *Chinese Classics*, Vol. III – *The Shoo King* – Hong Kong University Press, 1960).

The Bamboo Books provide the lineage of the early Chinese emperors. Huang-ti was succeeded by Emperor Che. His mother was Neu-tsee, who witnessed a star-like rainbow floating down a stream to the islet of Hwa. Thereafter she dreamed she had received the star and bore Shaou-haou (Che). When he ascended the throne, there was the auspicious omen of phoenixes (when a kingdom is tranquil and its ruler fond of peace then the phoenixes come and dwell in it; when a kingdom is disordered and its ruler fond of war then the phoenixes leave). Some say that the emperor's name was T'sing and that he did not occupy the throne but led an army of birds and dwelled in the west, where he arranged his officers by names taken from birds.

Che was succeeded by Emperor Chuen-heuh. His mother was Neu-ch'oo. She witnessed the Yaou-Kwang star (Benetnasch) go through the moon like a rainbow which impregnated her in the Palace of Yew-fang, after which she bore Chuen-heuh near the Jo-water. When he was thirteen he documented calendric calculations and the delineations of heavenly bodies. At twenty he acceded the throne and died aged seventy-eight.

Chuen-heuh was succeeded by Kuh, Kuh by Yaur and then by the emperors listed in Appendix 2.

As we know, on succession to the throne Emperor Zheng, leader of the Ch'in in around 220 BC, changed his name to Qin (leader of the Ch'in), Shi (the most excelled and admired), Huang (yellow), di (= ti) (the Son of Heaven).

The insignia of the dragon was chosen by every Chinese emperor. Figure 25 shows a terracotta model of Qin Shi Huangdi, the first emperor of a *unified* China, wearing the ceremonial robes of office decorated with two dragons, each of which carries a pearl, the symbol of wisdom that had the power to illuminate the heavens. Two pearls hence associated the emperor with Venus.

The carved picture on the Amazing Lid of Palenque, the tomb lid

Qin Shi Huangdi as the Twin-Star Venus

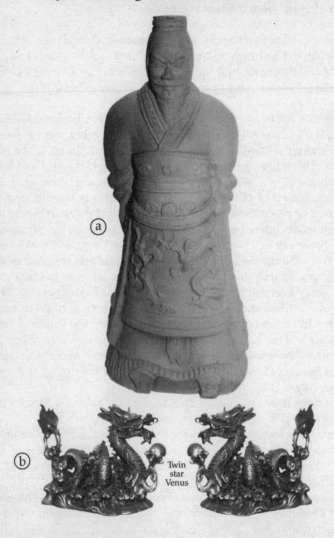

Figure 25. (a) Terracotta replica of the first emperor shown wearing a silk robe decorated with his insignia of two dragons (two feathered snakes), each a metaphor for the sun. Each dragon carries a sphere representing a pearl, symbol of wisdom and Venus, the white planet. The design on the robe therefore identifies the emperor with two white planets – the twin-star Venus, symbol of the Supergods (see figures A69–A72).

The Amazing Lid of Palenque
Story: Cosmogonic Destruction

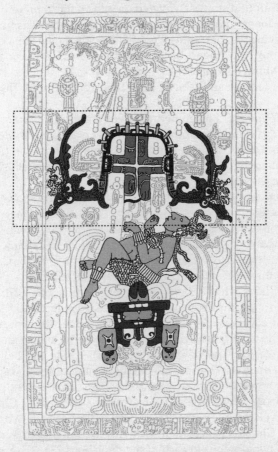

Figure 26. The story of 'cosmogonic destruction', one of many detailed on the Amazing Lid of Palenque, the tomb lid of Lord Pacal of the Maya. The area box-framed represents a tau cross (see figure 27). The central cross adorned with loops and marker pegs represents the four quadrants of the sun's magnetic fields covered in magnetic loops and sunspot marker pegs. Beneath this a female reclines following the birth of two 'solar babies' *(shown upside down with the solar symbol on their stomachs)*. Their sad mouths and downwards direction suggest they are stillborn. Tonatiuh, the sun-god *(upside down in between the babies)* licks the female in an attempt to increase fertility. The story suggests that the sun's radiation failed the reproductive needs of the people. The female is shown opening her legs to the sun to improve fertility levels. The first emperor of China was associated with two dragons and the sun, like Lord Pacal of the Maya.

that covered the sarcophagus of Lord Pacal (decoded in Appendix 4), also features two dragons (figure 26) with conjoined bodies that snake over and around a cross covered in schematic representations of magnetic loops and sunspot markers. The central character, Lord Pacal (playing the role in this scene of an open-legged female) reclines between the two dragon heads beneath the cross. Decoded stories from the Mural of Bonampak (Appendix 4) associate Lord Pacal with the god of fertility and rebirth, Xipe Totec (pronounced 'shy-pee-toe-tec').

In *The Supergods* I examined the lives and times of other spiritual leaders who shared common traits with Lord Pacal of Mexico and showed that many of the decoded stories from his treasures (Appendix 4) overwhelmingly suggest that he and Jesus of Nazareth shared the same antecedents.

The section of the lid, box-framed in figure 26 (and shown in figure 27a), represents a tau cross. The classical Greeks named the nineteenth letter of the Greek alphabet, 't' (tau), after 'Taw' (or Tawret-Thoeuris, the hippopotamus goddess of the Old Kingdom Egyptians, who was the patron of women in childbirth). It seems that, after the Crucifixion of Christ, the cross of the Crucifixion was referred to as a 't' or 'tau' – which explains why these tau cross talismans (figures 27b and 27c) evolved to show the death of Christ on the cross; figure 27b shows the handle of a Greek ivory staff from the eighteenth century, which features the Crucifixion within a cantonned envelope, a known solar symbol (see *The Tutankhamun Prophecies*), inside the belly of two conjoined dragons. Figure 27c, a twelfth-century English walrus-ivory carving, shows the circular sun at the centre that carries peripheral sunspot loops. Inside the sun the Madonna suckles the Christ child. Angels on either side of the sun turn away the heads of two conjoined dragons. Christ is hence identified with the sun, the cross of the sun and with two dragons in each of the depictions 27a, 27b and 27c.

The specific areas highlighted on the lid in figure 27a hence tell the story of how the sun's radiation (the cross of the sun covered in magnetic loops) failed the reproductive needs of females (the central reclining character), resulting in the stillborn birth of babies (the two upside-down babies with sad, downward-shaped mouths beneath the female). In between the babies, the sun-god (upside down) licks the female to stimulate fertility – clearly without success. Hence, this story, one of many contained in the design of the lid, tells the story of

The Tau Cross

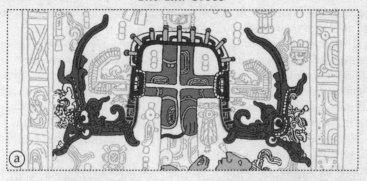

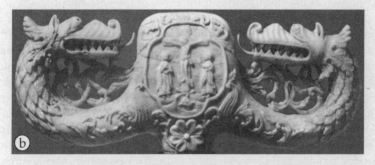

Figure 27. (a) Tau cross from the Amazing Lid of Palenque, c. AD 750, showing a cross covered in sunspot loops inside the belly of two conjoined dragons. (b) Tau cross showing a scene of the Crucifixion with Christ on the cross together with Mary and St John inside a cantonned envelope in the conjoined belly of two dragons *(from a Greek ivory staff, Tarascon, eighteenth century)*. (c) Tau cross showing Mary with the Christ child inside the sun, which carries magnetic loops around the perimeter, inside the belly of two conjoined dragons *(walrus ivory, English, mid-twelfth century)*.

cosmogonic destruction, the story of how the sun's radiation failed the reproductive needs of the population (figure A8), leading to a decline of the Maya in around AD 750.

It is likely that the dragons in figures 27b and 27c depict the ancient custom of Silene in Libya, which required the first born of every family to be sacrificed to the dragon that lived in a swamp (a similar belief was held in Palestine – a practice known as Moloch). The ultimate sacrifice of the first born for Christians was that of the Christ child, who was crucified on the cross and reborn three days later.

Dragons are therefore associated with the sun, fertility, sacrifice, Christ, the Crucifixion of Christ, and rebirth. The dragons on the Amazing Lid of Palenque thus associate Lord Pacal with the same concepts, as do the dragons on the robes of the first emperor.

The Venusian symbolism of the two pearls carried by the emperor's insignia similarly associates the first emperor with Jesus (figure A70), who was also associated with Venus. In the Book of Revelation Jesus unambiguously declares: '. . . I Jesus am the root of David and the bright and morning star' (Revelation xxii, 16). It also associates him with Lord Pacal's decoded picture from the Amazing Lid of Palenque (figure A71), which shows the rebirth of Lord Pacal as the twins (Venus); and with Tutankhamun – a large mural in his tomb at the Valley of the Kings in Egypt shows Tutankhamun embracing Nut, goddess of the night sky and the stars; in the next scene Tutankhamun turns into twins and embraces Osiris, god of resurrection and everlasting life, in the sky (figure A72) – and with Viracocha Pachacamac, god of the world for the Mochica, whose appearance preceded that of Viracocha at Tiahuanaco, where a group of statues suggest that he was reborn as the twins, the children of Viracocha Pachacamac (figure A73).

The dragon was thought to regurgitate pearls, which are thus associated with rebirth.

Astrology and Astronomy

Astrology was taken seriously by the emperors of China. Ssu-ma Ch'ien comments:

> Since man's earliest existence, through succeeding generations, was there ever a time when the rulers failed to observe the sun, moon

and planets, record their motions and expound their meanings? Raise the head and contemplate the vastness of the heavens; look around and marvel at their manifestations on earth. There is the primeval force, and such was related by the sages long ago (*The Books of Ssu-ma Ch'ien*, AD 200).

Another account reports a discourse that took place at the palace of Emperor Yuandi:

The Emperor Yuandi, wishing to choose an auspicious day for his enthronement, summoned the sage T'ai Yang and the Grand Astrologer Ch'en Cho to choose the day which they deemed the most appropriate. T'ai Yang selected the twenty-fourth day of the third month, that being the day of the Third Stem [see below] and the Seventh Branch [the seventh period (animal) of the duodecimal table]. Ch'en Cho chose the First Stem and the Fifth Branch. Said Ch'en Cho: 'The King of Yueh, on the advice of the astrologer Fan Li, chose such a day to return to his own land.'

T'ai Yang declared: 'Quite so. But the King of Yueh had been a prisoner of Emperor Wu and was inwardly rebellious. Fan Li chose such a day because the virtuous influence was directed outwards, while destructive influence pointed at the centre, and so attacked the palace of the Emperor Wudi. Our own king has no such inner resentment, and his throne is lawfully endowed by Heaven.'

The king carefully listened to the arguments of the two philosophers and accepted the advice proffered by the sage T'ai Yang (from *The History of the Chin Dynasty* c. AD 300. Source: *Doctors, Diviners and Magicians of Ancient China* by Kenneth J. DeWoskin, Columbia University Press, 1983).

When it was time for Buddha to die, he summoned all the animals in the land to a farewell speech. But only twelve arrived. First came the rat, who was followed by the ox. Then came the tiger, the rabbit, dragon, snake, horse, sheep, monkey, cockerel, dog and finally the pig. The monkey was special because he arrived in position number nine (the number of a Supergod; see figure A69). Each of these had their corresponding sun-sign used by sun-sign astrologers in the West (figure 4a), and even pairs of hours within each 24-hour period were dedicated to the procession of animals.

65

The 'stems' in the system of Chinese astrology refer to the five types of alternating polarity elements: metal, water, wood, fire and earth. Elements assume either a regenerative sequential relationship or a destructive sequential relationship. In the productive sense, each element generates the next: wood burns and produces fire, fire burns and produces ash, which turns to earth; earth contains ore that produces hard metal, metals melt and are therefore associated with water – just as hard ice melts into water, and water produces plants and wood. In the destructive sequence, each element destroys the next but one element: wood destroys the earth by drawing away water; fire melts metal, earth pollutes water; metal chops down wood; and water puts out fire.

The Chinese astrological system is an allegorical way of referring to the complex way in which solar wind particles bombard the earth cyclically. The twelve-year cycle (figure A24), together with the positive and negative polarities of the five elements, results in a longer cycle of sixty years.

There is no doubt that the Chinese understood the super-scientific causal relationship between the 11.5-year sunspot cycle and the 12-year Chinese astrological cycle (explained in Appendix 3).

Attempts to construct a chronological history of the country began during the Han dynasty, when scholars linked particular dates to the 60-year cycle. It was assumed, by Ta-nou, an officer of the Yellow Emperor, that the cycle had been first used during the reign of Huang-ti but was not used for chronological purposes until the Han dynasty. In the *General Survey of History by Ssu-ma Kwang*, the author Lew Shoo says:

The years of the sovereigns before and after Fung-Sin, down to King Le, are, I apprehend, dark and hardly to be ascertained; and we borrow the names of the Kea-tsze cycle to chronicle them. When did the practice of borrowing the cycle names to chronicle the years commence? It commenced in the time of the usurper Wang Mang (AD 9–23). [Note: the ten bipolar stem characteristics (positive and negative combinations of the elements earth, wood, fire, water and metal) were named from kea to kwei and the twelve branch characters (the twelve animals, from tze to hae; the expression kea-tsze therefore refers to both the twelve-year cycle (the twelve animals) and to the sixty-year cycle.]

The Great Bear Celestial Clock

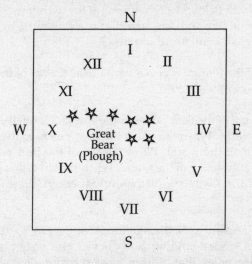

Figure 28. As the earth turns, the handle of the Plough (the tail of the Great Bear) makes one revolution per year. The sky, shown as a square, representing the four corners of the heavens, is divided into twelve equal parts. When the tail points east, it is spring, and when it points to the west, as shown here, it is autumn.

The *Book of the Shoo King* acknowledges that 'the first calendars of the Chinese were founded on observation of the rising and setting of celestial phenomena, such as the constellation of Orion, the star cluster Pleiades and the star Arcturus'.

Other (later) dates were calculated with reference to solar eclipses. Confucius's chronicle of the *Spring and Autumn* period commences in 721 BC. The first of thirty-six eclipses mentioned in the book took place three years later, on 14 February 719 BC.

Another ancient method, used for seasonal calculations, referred to the revolutionary cycle of the constellation of Ursa Major (the Great Bear), the seven stars of which make up the Plough. The Reverend John Chalmers (in the Appendix entitled *Astronomy of the Ancient Chinese* to the Prolegomena in James Legge's *Chinese Classics*, Vol. III) says that the Plough was also known in China as the 'Northern Bushel':

... under the name of the Northern Bushel it is sometimes confused with the North Pole and also with one of the twenty-eight mansions in Sagittarius [the zodiacal sign that is represented by a centaur, half horse, half man, firing an arrow].

The *handle* of the Plough is also referred to as the *tail* of the Bear. The scholar Hoh-kwantsze notes:

When the tail of the Bear points to the east (at nightfall), it is spring to all the world. When the tail of the Bear points to the south, it is summer to all the world. When the tail of the Bear points to the west, it is autumn to all the world. When the tail of the Bear points to the north, it is winter to all the world (Legge, *Chinese Classics*, Vol III).

Chalmers's appendix is disingenuous in regard to the level of astronomical understanding he believed the ancients in China possessed. He notes that '... the most common, and the earliest, division of the ecliptic is that of the twenty-eight mansions. These are of very unequal extent and consequently very inconvenient for any purpose other than astrology.'

He then, using only the very latest astronomical knowledge of the 1890s, attempts to reconcile unrelated scientific phenomena. Not surprisingly, he ties himself up in knots by comparing angular values of the mansions to the direction of the tail of the Great Bear and concludes, understandably confused: 'this discrepancy does not seem however to trouble their minds at all, and we may safely leave it unexplained.'

To be fair, Chalmers was unaware of the twenty-eight-day cycle of the solar wind (as measured on earth) and of its four unequal sectors, or quadrants, discovered in 1962 by *Mariner II* spacecraft (see Appendix 3). He was also unaware that the super-science of the sun had been well understood by the ancients millennia before his own arrival. And yet, incredulously, he concludes the piece by noting, somewhat puzzled:

This division of the ecliptic is, with some slight variations, common to the Arabians, the Hindoos and the Chinese; a fact which seems to point to the common origin of these races, or to their intercommunication at a period of which history gives us as yet no information (Revd John Chalmers, Appendix to the Prolegomena, *Chinese Classics*, Vol. III, Hong Kong University Press, 1960).

The first mention of one of the days of the sixty-year cycle appears in *The Book of the Shoo King*, (Pt. IV, Bk. IV, p. 1) when referring to the twelfth month of the first year of the Emperor T'ae-k'ang, 1957 BC. The first attempt to arrange the years in cycles of sixty is found in *Ssu-ma Ch'ien's Historical Records* in a table constructed for purposes of intercalation beginning in 103 BC for a period of seventy-five years.

The Chinese believe that Huang-Ti introduced both the twelve-year and sixty-year calendars in around 2697 BC.

The Monkey

The monkey, the ninth animal of the twelve-year cycle, features importantly in Chinese mythology. Legend has it that it took the creator god P'an Ku 18,000 years to chisel the universe. With every day that passed he grew six feet taller until he was finished. His body then became the physical universe, his head the mountains and his breath the wind. The sun and moon were made from his eyes and the stars from his beard. His limbs became the four quarters of the heavens and his blood the rivers, his skin the soil, his hairs the trees and plants, his teeth and bones the rocks and minerals and his sweat the rain. The lice on his body became the human race. P'an Ku is usually shown carrying the hammer and chisel from which he made the universe, surrounded by four creatures known as the four celestials: the tortoise, symbol of longevity and the north; the phoenix, symbol of the empress and the south; the dragon, associated with the emperor, power and the east; and the unicorn, the Ch'i-lin, the west. The burning of the Ch'i-lin's horn was said to produce a light that conferred the ability to see into the future by staring into a bowl of water. The four celestials hence conferred on P'an Ku long life (of the tortoise), beauty (of the bird), authority (of the dragon) and clairvoyance (of the unicorn).

Monkey, so the story goes, was born with magical powers from a stone egg deposited on the side of Mount Aolai in the Eastern Sea, following P'an Ku's creation of the world. He quickly rose among the family of monkeys to become the king and reigned for 300 years.

Monkey's Journey to the West

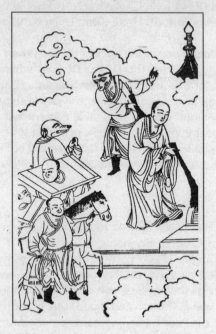

Figure 29. Eighteenth-century engraving by Wu Cheng'en showing the journey of the monkey *(top centre)* accompanying the monk Tripitaka *(right).*

The story of the monkey's journey is given in a document entitled *Xi you ji (The Journey to the West)*, written by Wu Cheng'en in the sixteenth century.

One day Monkey returned home to Mount Aolai to find a demon robbing his home. He fought the demon with bare hands and eventually won but, concerned that a similar incident might happen again in the future, decided to arm himself with a weapon. He called on the Dragon King of the Eastern Sea to supply a weapon, an iron bar. It turned out that the bar had magical properties; it was magnetic, allowing Monkey to travel to faraway places and find his way back home again.

In the seventh century the Buddhist monk Xuan Zhang (who became known by the name Tripitaka) wanted to journey to India in search of the sacred Buddhist texts (the Tripitakas) but feared he might get lost on the way. He called on Monkey, with his magic compass, to show him the way to India and back. On hearing of Buddhism and the promise of immortality, Monkey decided to join the world of men and accompany Tripitaka on his journey. As he travelled, Monkey acquired wisdom and was given the name the Sun, the enlightened one.

On their journey the travellers picked up a companion, Pigsy (another monkey), and after surviving fourteen years and eighty perils they came to the home of Buddha at the Mountain of the Soul. But Buddha decided they should have one more test before handing over the sacred texts. Before they could have everlasting life, they would have to complete one more task, a total of eighty-one tasks in all (9 x 9).

After an absence of sexteen years, Tripitaka returned home to translate the 520 books into Chinese.

On arriving back in China they took the books to the emperor in Chang'an, where they were received with ceremony.

Tripitaka, Monkey and Pigsy received the highest of accolades for their dedication; Tripitaka was again permitted to take up his place at Buddha's side, having suffered for his sins; Monkey was made the 'God of Victorious Battle' and Pigsy the 'Chief Heavenly Altar Cleaner'.

When the time arrived for Monkey to die, he was visited by two messengers from the underworld. He explained to the messengers that he had been given immortality, to no avail, and the messengers carried him away to the underworld. On arrival in the underworld, Monkey inspected the register of the dead and found his own name: 'Soul number 1,735, Sun, the enlightened one; 342 years and a fateful death.' Monkey scratched out the entry and was able to return home.

News of Monkey's sojourn in the underworld reached the great Jade Emperor, the Dragon King, and Yama, god of the underworld, who complained about Monkey's behaviour. As a result, it was decided that Monkey should be sent to heaven, where he could be supervised.

Thus it was that Monkey took up the post of 'Keeper of the Heavenly Horses' but, realising that his position was actually low down in the heavenly hierarchy, he demanded greater recognition. He was given the grander title of 'Great Sage Equal of Heaven' and progressed to the rank of the 'Guardian of the Garden of Heavenly Peaches' that belonged to the Queen Mother of the west, Xiwangmu who – every 6,000 years, when the fruit ripened – held a great feast for the immortals, who by eating the peaches renewed their immortality.

One day Monkey gorged himself on the peaches and drank from the gourds that contained the elixir of immortality belonging to the philosopher Lao Tzu. He was arrested and taken before the Jade Emperor, who wished to sentence him to death – not a realistic option given the great quantities of immortality-conferring substances he had consumed.

They tried to burn him, but even after forty-nine days he survived. The Jade Emperor called on Buddha to admonish Monkey. Buddha held Monkey in the palm of his hand and gave him an opportunity to escape, saying that if he could jump off his hand he would rule over all heaven. If not, he would have to return to earth to work hard and achieve immortality that way.

Monkey leaped from Buddha's palm and found himself at the foot of a hill. He plucked a hair from his arm and wrote his name on a nearby rock to prove the distance he had managed to travel away from Buddha. He then returned to claim the reward for his escape. But Buddha pointed to the name 'Monkey' written on the end of his finger, and Monkey realised that he had never left the hand of Buddha at all.

Mythological and Numerological Encoding of Knowledge during the Ming and Ch'ing Dynasties

The Forbidden City at Beijing, constructed from 1406 to 1420, was the imperial palace during the Ming and Ch'ing dynasties. Originally there were said to have been 9,999 rooms. The site is divided into two parts, an Inner Court and an Outer Court. The three main halls are arranged symmetrically around a central axis.

There are three main halls in the Outer Court – the Hall of Great Harmony, the Hall of Middle Harmony and the Hall of Preserving Harmony – where the great ceremonies were held; and three more in the Inner Court – the Palace of Heavenly Purity, the Hall of Harmonious Union and the Palace of Earthly Tranquillity. These were flanked on either side by the six Eastern Palaces and the six Western Palaces, the living quarters for imperial consorts. The layout of the city thus conformed to the number 666 (six buildings in the centre with six buildings on either side).

Plate 4 shows the massive doors from the Hall of Middle Harmony. Each of the doors contains nine rows of bronze (solar-style) studs (now painted black) and each row contains nine studs, referring to the story of Monkey, the ninth (9) animal in the zodiac who completed eighty-one tasks (9 x 9) to get to heaven and achieve immortality. His number was hence 999, the number of a Supergod.

Plate 4a shows the Hall of Great Harmony. The approach ramp of the nearby Hall of Preserving Harmony boasts the largest carving in Beijing, at 16.75 metres (54.95 feet) long, 3.07 metres (10 feet) wide and 1.07 metres (3.5 feet) thick. The 250-tonne slab of mutton-fat jade is ornately carved with clouds and nine dragons. Steps on either side of the ramp, are decorated with carvings of birds, snakes, stags and solar symbols (feathered snakes, stags and the sun).

The monkey, for the Maya and Peruvians, symbolised the written word. One of the line drawings of Nazca shows a monkey embracing a large pyramid shape (figure A67), one in a series of three believed to represent the statues of Viracocha and the children of Viracocha (the twins) at Tiahuanaco (figure A68). One of the fingers of the monkey is missing, associating the monkey with Viracocha (figures A59 and A60), who brought mankind knowledge, writing and wisdom.

Bringing the evidence together:

- The dragon is an amalgam of the feathered snake and the stag.
- The dragon was the chosen insignia of the first emperor.
- When the Yellow Emperor and his successors were born, a bright star was seen in the sky. When the Supergods were born, a bright star also shone in the sky.
- The Yellow Emperor and his successors were born through immaculate conceptions, as were the Supergods.
- The first emperor, with his terracotta army and the Great Wall of China, performed miracles, as did the Supergods.
- When the Yellow Emperor and his successors died, they became stars in the heavens, as did the Supergods.
- The feathered snake eponym was a feature shared by the Supergods, Lord Pacal of the Maya, Tutankhamun of Egypt and Viracocha and Viracocha Pachacamac of Peru.
- The stag eponym was shared by the Supergod Lord Pacal and the first emperor.
- The dragon, featured on the mutton-fat jade carving (plate 2), is

The Monkey

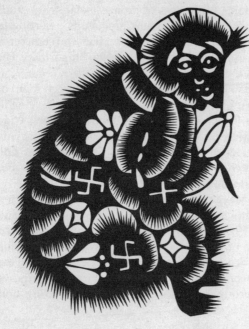

Figure 30. Paper-cut figure of a monkey eating a peach, the symbol of immortality (after a picture from the Chinese Tourist Organisation). Several types of solar symbol can be seen on the fur: the sun as a flower with petals; a swastika (representing the radiating solar wind, figure 58d); a cross (representing the cross-sectional schematic of the solar wind; figure A6a), and as a solar cross (figure A6a).

shown with one claw missing – which is the mark of the Super-gods, Viracocha and Viracocha Pachacamac of Peru.

- The ceremonial robes of the first emperor feature two dragons, as do the Lid of Palenque and other tau crosses, associating the first emperor with the decline in fertility, the sun, sacrifice, the Crucifixion of Christ and rebirth.
- Twin dragons carry twin pearls, which associate the first emperor with the twin-star Venus, a common association shared with all the Supergods.
- The face shapes of the terracotta warriors emphasise the importance of the story of Monkey, whose number is 9 and who completed 81 tasks (9 x 9) before reaching heaven. Monkey is thus associated with the number 999; the number 999 is the number of the Supergods, the highest number that can be reached before becoming one (1,000) with God.

The Chinese paper-cut figure of Monkey (figure 30) shows Monkey eating a peach, the symbol of immortality. His fur is decorated with solar symbols: the swastika – representing the radiating solar wind (figure 58d); as a cross – representing the cross-sectional schematic of the solar wind (figure A6a); as a solar cross (figure A6a); and as a flower with petals – representing the sun and sunshine, and we note that the Supergods were all associated with the sun (light).

The evidence suggests that the Yellow Emperor and his successors were indeed Supergods, truly the Sons of Heaven who understood the super-science of the sun and the higher orders of spirituality. As Supergods, they would have visited the earth to teach mankind the higher precepts. Appendix 3 explains how the sun affects life on earth, how we are spiritual beings by nature and how and why the ancients encoded this knowledge into their treasures. Appendix 4 explains the methods of encoding and how the Supergods used specific numbers to convey the same messages, the solar numbers 26 and 37 that refer to the rotational duration rates of the sun's magnetic fields (see Appendix 3); the number 1,366,560 that represents the duration of one solar neutral sheet magnetic shift on the surface of the sun; and the numbers 666 and 144,000 from the Book of Revelation in the Bible that tells of the revelation that appeared to St John. The meaning of the revelation is unknown and allegorical and has perplexed many through the ages. It tells of:

> . . . a beast which rises from the sea . . . which has seven heads and ten horns and . . . the dragon gave him his power and his seat and great authority . . . here is wisdom, let him that hath understanding count the number of the beast: for it is the number of a man; and his number is six hundred three score and six . . . (Revelation, xiii, 1–18).

Revelation continues:

> I saw four angels standing on the four corners of the earth [north, south, west and east] holding the four winds of the earth, that the wind should not blow on the earth, nor on the sea nor on any tree. And I saw another angel ascending from the east having the seal of the living God: And he cried with a loud voice to the four angels, to whom it was given to hurt the earth, and the sea, saying, 'Hurt not

the earth, neither the sea, nor the trees, till we have sealed the servants of our god in their foreheads.' And I heard the number of them which were sealed; and there were sealed an hundred and forty-four thousand [144,000] of all the tribes of the children of Israel (Revelation, vii, 1–4).

The Temple of Heaven in Beijing was built around the same time as the Forbidden City. It burned down in 1889 but has since been restored to its former glory. It was here, during the Ming and Ch'ing dynasties, that the emperor worshipped as the priestly Son of Heaven. The temple complex is laid out within a rectangular courtyard. The circular Great South Altar occupies one end of the courtyard on a platform made from three concentric circles of white marble, one inside the other, the largest measuring 64 metres (210 feet) and the inner one 27.43 metres (90 feet) in diameter. Twelve white marble stairways of one type and twelve stairways of another type traverse the three levels (12 x 12 = 144). The upper terrace is paved with marble slabs forming nine concentric circles, the inner circle of which is made of nine stones. The emperor kneels on the centre stone in the circle when worshipping heaven at the winter solstice. On the next level down tablets portray the spirits of the sun, moon and stars and the god of the year. The Temple of Heaven sits in the centre of these and carries three slated pagoda-style canopies each of which reduces in diameter as the roof rises to a conical peak topped with a bronze circle. The plan of the temple resembles a plan view of the sun with its magnetic fields and polar cap. Another enclosure, about three kilometres (two miles) in circumference, contains four altars, one to the god of heaven, one to the god of earth, one to the planet Jupiter and the other to Shin-nung, who is fabled to have invented agriculture. Four marble tablets containing the names of the gods of cloud, rain, wind and thunder rest on the Altar of the Heavens and five tablets bearing the names of mountains, lakes and seas of China.

Each long side of the rectangular courtyard is punctuated by a stairway that leads to a reception hall. The one close to the circular platform is larger than the other three. Inside the courtyard, three more temples set out to follow a square bracket do not quite envelop the circular terraces.

The dome of the temple inside is ornately decorated, and four large, equally spaced poles (beams) rise from the floor to provide support for the concave dome above. The top end of the beams are joined by eight other short beams around the dome producing an inner circle of twelve poles around the dome at ceiling level; twelve more poles form an outer circle of support (again, 12 x 12 = 144).

It is clear that the ancient practices and rites performed by the Son of Heaven continued from the earliest of times up to at least the Ming and Ch'ing periods because both the Forbidden City and the Temple of Heaven contain the esoteric numbers of 666, 999 and 144.

We need to keep these (and other numbers relating to astronomical constants involved with the super-science of the sun) in mind, when examining the terracotta soldiers of Shi Huangdi.

CHAPTER FOUR

The Secret Codes of the Terracotta Warriors

The Great Pyramid of China

The pyramid-shaped earthen mound of Shi Huangdi lies 35 kilometres (21.74 miles) east of Xian in Lintong province, on the slopes of Mount Li, just south of the Wei river and north of the Lishan mountains. It rises to 76 metres (249 feet), making it just lower than the height of the Giza pyramid of Khufu in Egypt (which rises to 147 metres/481 feet). But its circumference, at 1,250 metres (4,101 feet), makes it the largest pyramid in the world by land area. It was enclosed by two perimeter walls that delineated the inner city and outer city limits (figure 2a). Each had four gates. The pyramid was orientated to face the North Star – synonymous with the ruler who kept his place in the centre of the universe while others turned around it.

Construction of the mausoleum beneath the pyramid began a year after Shi Huangdi (259–210 BC) acceded the throne (as emperor) in around 221 BC and therefore must have taken the estimated workforce of around 700,000 conscripts less than eleven years to build.

In 1977 the remains of a palace were discovered north-west of the pyramid, and three years later two teams of bronze horses with chariots were found in a pit between the city walls, 20 metres (66 feet) to the west of the pyramid, close to a smaller pit containing horse remains. In 1979 thirty-one small pits were found about 150 metres (492 feet) to the west. Archaeologists named the pits 'the zoo' because of the skeletons of rare birds and animals they contained. The shallow graves of eleven prisoners (skeletons bound around the wrists and ankles) were found nearby. To the south-east, 'imperial stables' containing horse bones together with terracotta figures of grooms were found in ninety-one pits.

The mausoleum within the pyramid has yet to be explored. However, an account compiled from the original architect's plans by Ssu-ma Ch'ien in around 110 BC describes the tomb at around the time it was sealed. W. Burton (in *The Records of the Historian of Siam Qian*, New York, 1958) explains how the ceiling of the mausoleum was inlaid with pearls and precious gems to emulate star patterns in the sky and how the entire underground palace was built to resemble a miniature model of the empire, complete with mountains, valleys and rivers and lakes of mercury. Lamps, fed by tanks of whale oil, illuminated the twinkling stars above and flickered in the shimmering lakes of mercury below.

In the centre of the lake lay a series of sarcophagi that contained the body of the emperor, which (in keeping with practices adopted by other royal personages) may have been clothed in a suit of everlasting jade, like that of Prince Liu Sheng (plate 15) and Princess Tou Wan (plate 16a). Childless concubines, sacrificed to accompany the emperor into the afterlife, lay alongside.

The treasure-filled mausoleum was protected from unauthorised incursion by tripwired booby traps set to fire bronze-tipped bolts from arrays of strategically placed crossbows. Concealed pits and self-closing doors further deterred intruders. Workmen – leaving for the last time – were caught between sets of self-closing double doors that sealed the tomb, trapping the victims inside for the sake of secrecy.

The pits containing the army of life-size terracotta warriors lie approximately 1.5 kilometres (0.93 miles) to the east of the outer city wall. Four pits, numbered in the chronological sequence in which they were discovered, contain more than 8,000 troops and chariots.

The Pits and the Warriors

First, the footprint of the pit (the ground plan showing the extent and limits of the intended excavation from the green-field site) was marked out with pegs in the field. Then the tunnels were excavated (figure 3).

The ground in each tunnel was tamped firm using the sawn end of logs before baked quarry tiles were laid to the floor. Ends of trenches were framed with timber jambs and lintels.

The warriors, each weighing around half a tonne, were ostensibly carried by horse and cart from the kilns several kilometres distant. There they were manoeuvred down the steeply sloping trench-access ramps into formation arrangement. This account, though, suggests a formidable feat of engineering. When my own life-size terracotta warrior arrived from the museum shop in Xian, getting it to the house from the car proved a logistical headache. It took three men five hours to shift the single kneeling archer over the 100-metre (328-foot) journey. The exercise required the laying of two parallel sawn and planed timbers in front of the soldier. The planks were soaked with water to minimise friction. The figure was then rocked from side to side, corner to corner, along the lines of timber to its final resting place inside the house.

This at least illustrated the practical difficulties that must have faced those who stocked the tunnels, except that their task was at least 8,000 times more difficult and the distance between the kiln and the tunnels many kilometres over difficult terrain rather than my own short journey over grass. The rocking of my archer, from corner to corner, also proved perilous, with one of the corners of the base snapping off at the first attempt. This in itself was also revealing, because it drew attention, incredulously, to the rear corner of the base of the archer where one of the corners was deliberately missing. (*Incredulously* because ancient civilisations used the same method – omission of pieces – to draw attention to the fact that a particular artefact concealed secret information (see Appendix 3, xix).

The Xian museum workshop manufactures copies of warriors, like the one I bought, using the age-old techniques employed to produce the originals. The body of each soldier is firstly constructed using string-like loops of coiled clay that are squeezed together to create a torso-shaped shell. Arms and legs are made in the same way and attached to the body. Hands are moulded separately and fixed into the open-ended wrist sockets using slip (wet clay). This basic frame is then clothed in hand-made pieces of clay fashioned to resemble the different uniforms. The finished model, apart from the head, is then dried slowly in a warm clay kiln before coal is added to the fire to raise the temperature to the required 1,000°C (1,800°F) for five days. Heads are moulded separately and sculpted by craftsmen, who add the individual hairstyles and facial features using clay veneer. Heads are then fired before being loosely inserted into position in a respective body (plate 13a). Each head is thus removable.

Around ten per cent of firings fail due to impurities in the clay, water or kiln gases or as a result of non-linear kiln temperature. Good specimens sound with a clink when tapped, whereas defective ones, returning a thud, are scrapped.

Traces of brightly coloured paint made from pigment mixed with a binder have been found on a handful of the warriors, persuading archaeologists that all the soldiers at one time were brightly painted (plate 10d and e shows an ostensible reconstruction of such a scheme), although there is no evidence to suggest that this was the case. In the same way, a few of the hairstyles had been coated with black charcoal.

With the troop formations in position, the tunnels were covered with pine logs and a layer of plaster powder scattered on top. Woven hessian-type matting covered the plaster, which subsequently hardened with the ingress of moisture. The mats were then covered with around 1.5 metres (4.92 feet) of earth (figure 3).

Our analysis will shortly reveal that the formations of the troops, as well as the terracotta figures themselves, contain the same encoded information that was found in the tombs of Lord Pacal of Mexico, Tutankhamun of Egypt, Viracocha and Viracocha Pachacamac of Peru and the Book of Revelation in the Bible (explained in detail in Appendix 4): the secrets of the sun and God explained with numbers.

When archaeologists excavated Pits 1 and 2, they found extensive damage caused by fire. According to *The Records of the Historian*, a rebel named Xiang Yu (232–202 BC) led a peasants' revolt in around 206 BC, towards the end of the Ch'in dynasty. His forces sacked and burned Ch'in palaces and then turned, in a frenzy, to the tunnels of the terracotta warriors. There, they launched an attack on the silent army of Shi Huangdi, looting weapons, smashing warriors and torching the chambers, some of which raged with fire for days. Pit 3 was also found to have sustained considerable damage but this was put down to natural decay when rotting roof timbers collapsed, smashing soldiers in the north-west chamber below into pieces.

Pit Number 1

Partial excavation began in Pit 1 in May 1974 but little effort was committed to the project for two more years and hence little progress made during the intervening period. Figure 31 shows the footprint of the pit, which measures 210 metres (689 feet) by 60 metres (199 feet). The nine parallel inner corridors (figure 32) measure approximately 3 metres (10 feet) in width, accommodating up to four parallel lines of troops interspersed with chariots, while the narrower east–west perimeter corridor, at just under 2 metres (6.5 feet) wide, accommodates only two lines of troops. Figures 32 and 34, together with plate 6, facilitate analysis of the numbers and formations of soldiers in the pit.

The east-end perimeter corridor is occupied with three rows of crossbow-carrying unarmoured standing archers. This vanguard delivered the first long-range attack and were followed by formations comprising armoured archers, infantrymen and charioteers.

Analysis of the formation at the east end shows that three unarmoured infantrymen are missing from the formation in the top right-hand corner, and also from the formation in the bottom right-hand corner of Pit 1. This causes difficulty when attempting to quantify the numbers of troops arranged vertically in these three rows; should the count of troops include the missing infantrymen or should the vertical columns be counted to exclude those in the perimeter corridor?

Counting the troops in the rows from top to bottom, as they are found, then each row contains sixty-eight troops (68, 68, 68). If the top and bottom groups of three are included in the vertical-row count, then the number in each vertical row increases by two, to seventy (70, 70, 70). Setting out the figures vertically (figure 32), it becomes clear that the intermediary numbers 69, 69, 69 are missing from the sequence. The analysis produces the horizontal numbers 666 and 999. 666 represents the mark of the beast, from Revelation. 999 (as discussed in Appendix 4) represents the number of a Supergod, the opposite to 666. However, here we are mindful that these numbers do not actually appear as themselves but are in fact missing. This amounts to an instruction to find the three missing sixes and three missing nines in the troop formations.

Inspecting the formations around the perimeter corridors, there are

Pit Number 1. Trench Layout

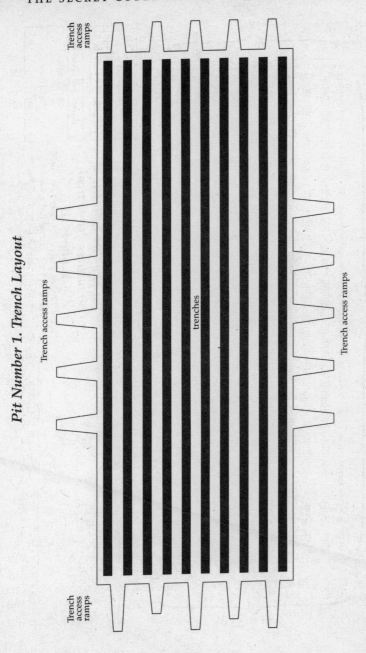

Figure 31. Footprint of Pit 1 showing trenches and trench access ramps (see plate 6 for battle formations).

THE TERRACOTTA WARRIORS

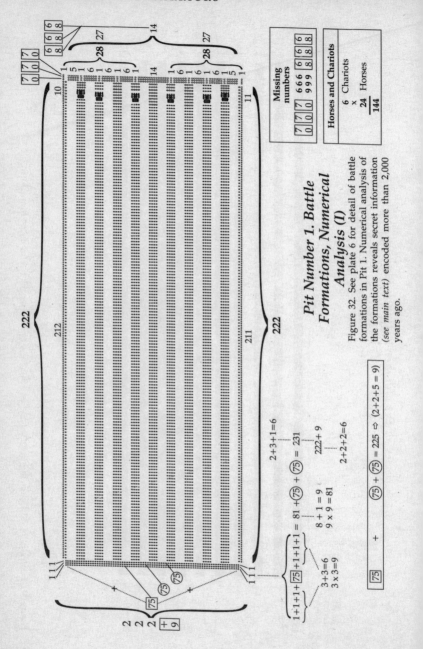

Pit Number 1. Battle Formations, Numerical Analysis (I)

Figure 32. See plate 6 for detail of battle formations in Pit 1. Numerical analysis of the formations reveals secret information (*see main text*) encoded more than 2,000 years ago.

84

222 troops along the top and 222 troops along the bottom. In the west facing corridor there are, however, a total of 231. This latter number should of course be 222, which would mean that the three rows together – 222, 222 and 222 – would amount to the esoteric 666. But 231 is 222 plus 9, which throws up the first of the three missing nines. On the western flank (plate 6), a horizontal row of three archers protects the inner troop formation that comprises three vertical rows of seventy-five (75 archers and two rows of 75 armoured infantrymen). Analysing these (figure 32), we see that $1 + 1 + 1 + 75 + 1 + 1 + 1 = 81 = 9 \times 9$, giving us the second and third of the missing nines. And more nines can be found easily; of the 81, $8 + 1 = 9$, and the $1 + 1 + 1$ (3) multiplied by the $1 + 1 + 1$ (3) = 9.

On the left, the cordon of archers facing west (plus the 3 facing north and the 3 facing south) protecting the two rows of 75 armoured infantrymen $(81 + 75 + 75) = 231$. $2 + 3 + 1 = 6$, which gives us one of the missing sixes. The $1 + 1 + 1$ archers to the north and the $1 + 1 + 1$ archers to the south provide the second group of missing sixes. The number of troops along the top and bottom perimeter corridors (222) amount to $6 (2 + 2 + 2)$, giving the last of the missing sixes. Other sixes, like the other nines, can be found when analysis of the numbers continues – and these are the only compound numbers that result from such an analysis.

This numerical analysis suggests that whoever placed the troops in the trench purposely wished to deliberately encode the figures 666 and 999.

The rows containing 68 troops facing east consist of a central block formation containing three vertical rows of 14 (the time it takes, in days, for one positive and one negative equatorial magnetic field of the sun to scan the earth). The lines above and below this contain 28 (the time it takes, in days, for four equatorial magnetic fields of the sun to scan the earth – one complete revolution of the sun's equatorial magnetic field in relation to the earth).

Horses and chariots were the principal measure of an army during the Warring States period (403–221 BC). The appearance of the chariot marked an evolutionary advance in warfare from the simple foot soldier involved in hand-to-hand combat. The wooden chariots in Pit 1 (plate 6) carried three charioteers and were drawn by a team of four life-size terracotta horses. The horses measure 1.5 metres (5 feet) high and 2 metres (6.5 feet) wide and are harnessed in a single row,

Chariot and Charioteers

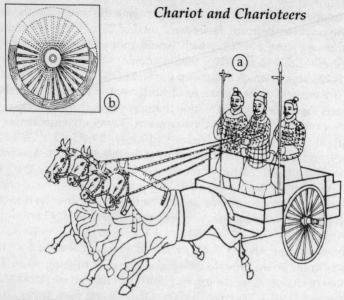

Figure 33. (a) Sketch of a horse-drawn chariot carrying three charioteers, from Pit 2. (b) Chariot wheel comprising six-piece rim with thirty spokes (6 x 30 = 180), one of a pair (2 x 180 = 360, the number of degrees in one circle). (c) Rear end of a team of chariot horses showing the tail shaped like the handle of the constellation of the Plough, often confused with one of the mansions of Sagittarius, home of the centaur, the half man, half horse that lived in the heavens.

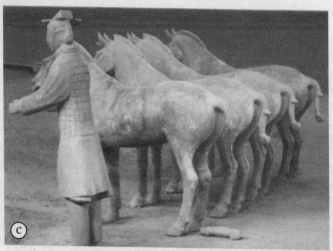

comprising two inner steeds connected together by a single shaft with a crossbar and two outer steeds.

Terracotta horse tails were fired separately, for later connection with a simple push-fit. Many became detached (figure 33), drawing attention to the unbalanced rear-end and the missing tail itself. Closer inspection reveals that the shape of the tails on the chariot horses corresponds to the shape of the star pattern that makes up the handle of the Plough (figure 28) which, as the Reverend John Chalmers observed (see Chapter 3), is also known as the Northern Bushel, confusing it with one of the mansions in Sagittarius of the same name. The shape of the tail therefore seems to connect the horse with the centaur of Sagittarius, which is half horse, half man, that lives in the heavens, implying that whoever designed the horses was not only aware of astronomy but that *'he was the archer that lived in the stars'*.

The chariots measure 150 centimetres (4.92 feet) wide and 120 centimetres (3.93 feet) long. Simple numerical manipulation of the numbers of chariots (6) and horses (24) in Pit 1 (6 x 24) produces, again, 144 (figure 32), the esoteric number mentioned in the Book of Revelation.

Each chariot wheel rim was made from six pieces of hardwood, as were the thirty radiating spokes of each wheel (6 x 30 = 180). Together, the chariot wheels contain the number (2 x 180) 360, the number of angular degrees in the radiating sun.

Cavalry horses (plate 8) stand 1.72 metres (5.64 feet) high and 2.03 metres (6.6 feet) long with plaited tails, in accordance with the specifications set down by the Chinese scholar Sun Bole (in his *Guide to Horse Selection (Xiang Ma Jing)* in around 621 BC, and his contemporary Jiu Fanggao, the founder of the school for horsemanship. These two set the standards of cavalry horses in terms of height, strength, speed and build.

The terracotta saddle is covered in rows of nails and decorated with tassels. The fact that the horses do not have stirrups gives an indication of the skill of the riders.

The total number of troops in Pit 1 amounts to 7,029 (figure 34) and the astronomical relevance of this is explained as follows. There are 781 time intervals of 87.454545 days that make up one sunspot cycle of 68,302 days (figure 35). Analysis of the waveform shows that 9 microcycles of magnetic activity, either side of interval 781, are free

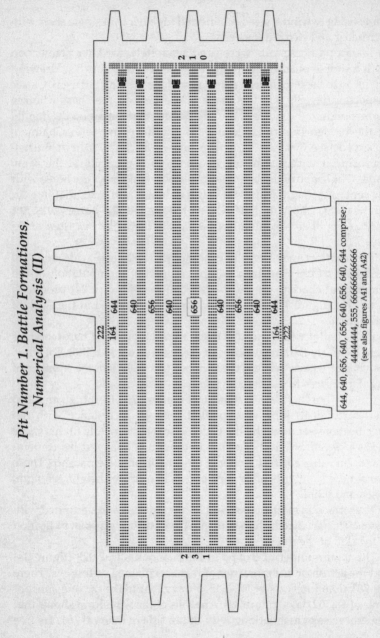

*Pit Number 1. Battle Formations,
Numerical Analysis (II)*

644, 640, 656, 640, 656, 640, 656, 640, 644 comprise; 4444444, 555, 66666666666 (see also figures A41 and A42)

Figure 34. There are 7,029 troops in Pit 1, which correspond to the number of time intervals in 9 sunspot cycles (9 x 781 = 7,029; see figure 35).

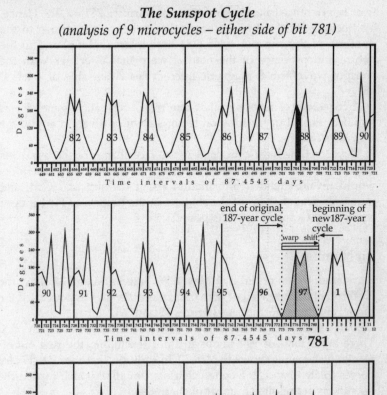

The Sunspot Cycle
(analysis of 9 microcycles – either side of bit 781)

Figure 35. Graph showing microcycles of magnetic activity that subsist on the sun's surface. To save space, only the last 16 microcycles (numbered 82–97) of one cycle and the first 10 microcycles (numbered 1–10) of the subsequent cycle are shown. Shift bits appear as solid vertical bars in microcycles numbered 88 and 10 (see also figures A15a–d). Shift bits shunt through the microcycle sequence (figure A20a) by 1 microcycle every 187 years (one long-sunspot cycle). Analysis of the sequence shows that 9 magnetic cycles, either side of bit 781 do not contain a vertical shift bit. 9 x 781 = 7,029, the number of troops in Pit 1. The total number of troops, therefore, in Pit 1 calls attention to the neutral warp of the sun, which contains the shift bits (see also Appendix 3).

from interference from the sun's neutral warp. 9 x 781 = 7,029. Hence, by stocking Pit 1 with 7,029 troops, our attention is drawn to the duration of the sunspot cycle (781 time intervals long) and to the nature and presence of the neutral warp that interferes with the sunspot waveform 9 magnetic microcycles either side of interval 781.

Archaeological texts say that one out-of-formation general was found in Pit 1, but his location is not shown or given in any of the drawings or texts.

The secret message contained in the face shapes of the terracotta warriors suggested that close analysis of the troops in the corridors would reveal encoded information about the sun and God, and numerological analysis of the soldiers in the tunnels of Pit 1 indeed conveys that knowledge, as expected.

Pit Number 2

Excavation began on Pit 2 in May 1976. Figures 36 and 37 show the footprint of the pit together with the exploratory digs that revealed the tunnel and troop formations (figures 38 and 39).

Plate 7 facilitates numerological analysis of the formations in Pit 2. There are a total of 999 troops in Pit 2 (excluding the two out-of-formation generals shown in plate 7). In addition, there are 116 cavalry horses (plate 8) and 89 wooden chariots, not all of which carried the maximum permissible number of charioteers.

The formation (in the top right-hand corner of plate 7) shows two blocks of 48 standing archers (2 x 48 = 96, the number of magnetic microcycles in one sunspot cycle; shown as microcycles numbered 1–96 in figure A15). These protect 4 blocks of 40 kneeeling archers (4 x 40 = 160) and 4 other blocks of 4 kneeling archers (4 x 4 =16), representing the 16 fundamental (hypothesised; figure A16) sunspot cycles that exist within each 187-year sunspot cycle.

At first, the numerological significance of the 89 chariots in Pit 2, in isolation, means little. However, the total number of chariots in Pit 1 (6), Pit 2 (89) and Pit 3 (1) again amounts to 96, the number of magnetic microcycles in one sunspot cycle.

Pit Number 2 (I)

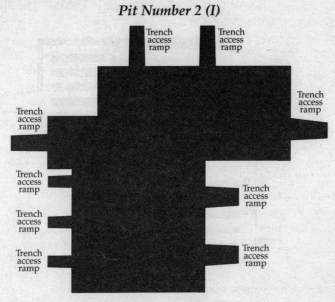

Figure 36. Footprint of Pit Number 2 showing trench access ramps.

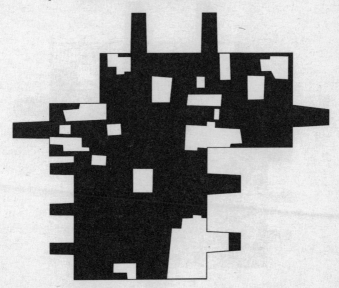

Figure 37. Exploratory digs (white) that revealed the buried army in Pit 2.

Pit Number 2 (II)

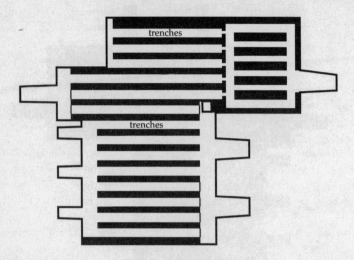

Figure 38. Trench layout established from test digs.

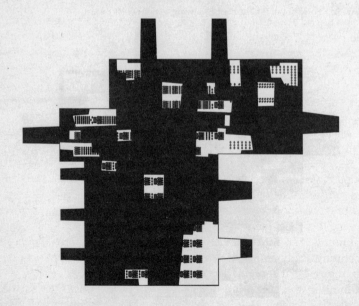

Figure 39. Buried army revealed by test digs in figure 37.

Pit Number 3

Pit 3 is unusual in that the relatively small size of the pit allows for the simultaneous analysis of the numbers of troops together with the deportment and orientation of troops (figure 40).

The first thing to notice with Pit 3 is that there are only 68 troops (not 666, not 999, and not 69). This suggests that a soldier is missing [archaeologists agree that one soldier appears to be missing], calling for a search for the missing soldier; this is to say that the presence of only 68 troops, and not the esoterically significant figure of 69, calls for a closer examination of the troops in the pit.

Closer examination reveals a glaring (ostensible) *defect* in the design of the pit and its contents. As it stands, it would be impossible for the chariot to exit the pit without a collision occurring between the right wheel of the chariot and the wall adjacent to the ramp.

To overcome this problem the chariot would have to turn to the left, anticlockwise, as it negotiated the ramp, to exit the pit safely. The requirement of such an essential manoeuvre implies that before the contents of Pit 3 can be decoded successfully, the notion of an *anticlockwise* rule needs to be embraced before decoding can begin.

The angle between the left-hand side wheel and the adjacent pit wall is greater than the angle between the right wheel and the right-hand side pit wall, to allow the chariot to perform the essential manoeuvre. With the chariot and charioteers successfully evacuated (figure 41), analysis of the formations can begin.

The deportment of troops in Pit 3 is unusual in that they appear to offer an embrace to each other (see also figure 42).

Counting the troops in Pit 3 (figure 42) *anticlockwise* (from the high-noon position), a row of two troops faces another row of two troops across the chamber. (The adjacent chamber contains a block of twelve troops that faces another block of twelve troops and therefore these groupings require separate analysis later.) Continuing anticlockwise, a row of three troops faces another row of three troops. Again, moving on, anticlockwise, four troops face another row of four troops. Again, continuing in an anticlockwise direction, the north-eastern chamber is anachronistically empty; it is the only chamber that does not contain any troops (i.e. it contains *zero* troops).

Counting the single-line formations in Pit 3 anticlockwise thus reveals the numbers 234 ZERO. Next to the empty chamber, two troops

Pit Number 3. Pit Layout and Troop Formations

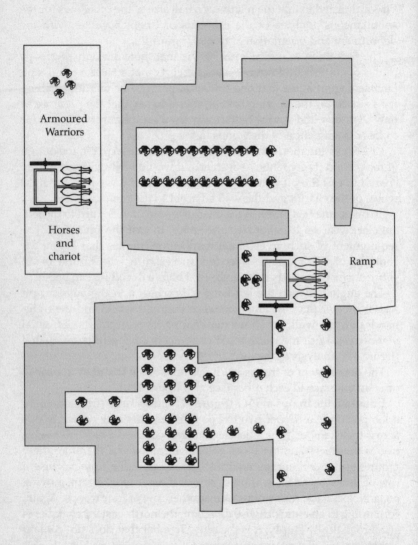

Armoured Warriors

Horses and chariot

Ramp

Figure 40. This is the only pit small enough to allow the simultaneous study of both the numbers and positions (deportment) of the soldiers with respect to each other. There are only sixty-eight soldiers in the pit; one soldier is missing (*see main text*). This calls for the observer to search for the missing piece, to study the pit and its contents more closely.

Pit Number 3. The Problem of the Ramp
(Analysis of the Ramp and Chariot)

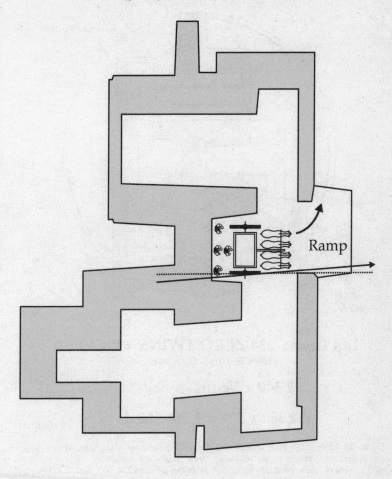

Figure 41. As it stands, the chariot could not leave the pit without a collision occurring between the right-hand side wheel and the pit wall. The only way to overcome this problem would be for the chariot (and the wheels) to move (spin around) to the left. When wheels move to the left they are said to move anticlockwise. The first clue, therefore, in decoding the meaning of the contents of Pit 3 involves a rule embracing the notion of anticlockwise (see figure 42). The angle and distance between the left wheel and the pit wall are greater that between the right wheel and the pit wall, thus allowing the chariot to perform the essential manoeuvre prior to exit.

Pit Number 3. Numerical Analysis (I)
The Birth of Venus (1,366,560)

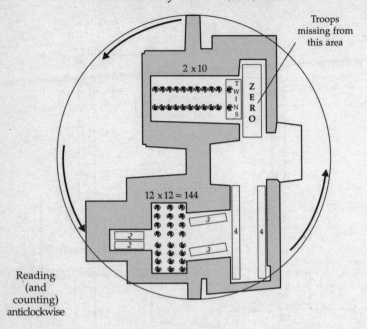

Top Layer: 234 ZERO TWINS = 2 x 10
(repeated on bottom layer)

= 2,340 x Venus interval (584 days) = 20 sunspot cycles

= 2,340 x 584 = 1,366,560 days

Figure 42. Once the horses, chariot and charioteers have left the pit, numerical analysis can begin. Deportment of the soldiers reveals single-line clusters of soldiers *facing each other*. These clusters are above identified as blocks labelled 2, 2, 3, 3, and 4, 4. The north-eastern chamber is curiously unoccupied. Following the earlier anticlockwise instruction, the single-line clusters read anticlockwise reveal the sequence 234. Then follows ZERO, the number of soldiers in the unoccupied chamber, then 2 soldiers (twins) in the north-west chamber (facing in a different direction from the other two lines of 10 soldiers in the same chamber). Together this message reads: 2,340 periods of the twins (Venus/584 days) amount to 20 (2 rows of 10). 2,340 x 584 = 1,366,560, the Mayan figure for the birth of Venus, the duration of 20 sunspot cycles (figure A36). Further analysis, again reading anticlockwise (omitting the previously counted blocks of numbers) throws up the expression 144 ZERO TEN TEN = 144,000.

Pit Number 3. Numerical Analysis (II)
666

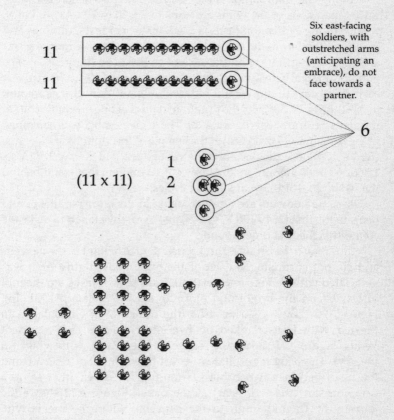

Figure 43. The reason for the embrace-like deportment of the soldiers now becomes apparent. Six soldiers with no partner to embrace (who do not love their neighbour) face east, the place where the sun is reborn on earth. The formation of charioteers, read anticlockwise, 1:2:1 (121), advises us that 11 is meant to be multiplied by 11 (11 x 11 = 121). Following this instruction, 6 (single soldiers) x 11 (soldiers in the north-west chamber) = 66 and, again, 6 x 11 (the second line of 11, in the north-west chamber) = 66, which, each taken together with the 6 single soldiers, throws up 666 and again 666, confirming that those who do not embrace (who do not love their neighbour) are reborn again (in the east) on earth, the place of 666.

stand alone facing eastwards without any partners to embrace. These are the only two troops in Pit 3 to share the same unique features, making them *twins*. Behind the twins stand two rows of ten troops facing partners (10, 10).

Reading the information anticlockwise, the instruction becomes: 2,340 revolutions of the twins amounts to 2 x 10 (= 20). As we know, whenever the expression *twins* is used, in ancient texts, carvings and paintings, it refers to the planet Venus, the twin-star (the morning star and the evening star) to all the ancient civilisations (figure A23). The periodic interval between successive appearances of Venus from planet earth is 584 days (figure A23). 2,340 revolutions of Venus hence amount to 2,340 x 584 = 1,366,560; the duration in days of one magnetic shift of the sun's neutral sheet (figure A20). The same number was contained in the treasures of Lord Pacal at the Temple of Inscriptions at Palenque (figure A36) once the decoding matrix had reached 9, 9, 9, 9, 9. Also, 1,366,560 days amount to 20 (2 rows of 10 soldiers that stand behind the twins; 2 x 10) 187-year sunspot cycles.

The same numbers are repeated again in the layer parallel to and beneath the first (234 ZERO TWINS) just in case we failed to make the connection the first time around.

Venus is also the brightest and purest source of light in the heavens and so, not surprisingly, each of the Supergods (figure A69) was associated with Venus. In Revelation, Jesus says: 'I Jesus am the root of David and the bright and morning star' (Revelation XXII, 16). Figure A70 shows a shrine, from the cathedral at Guadalajara in Mexico, with Jesus flanked by two silver spheres that represent Venus. Figure A71 shows the rebirth of Lord Pacal, with wings (in the sky). The baby regurgitates a pearl (the symbol of rebirth), and the pearl becomes two babies, twins (upside down) that share a common star (the twin star) at the navel. Figure A72 shows the journey of Tutankhamun to the heavens, where he meets Nut, goddess of the night sky, before becoming twins (Venus) to embrace Osiris (god of resurrection), who lived in the constellation of Orion in the heavens. At the Temple of Stone Heads, at Tiahuanaco in Bolivia (figure A73), Viracocha Pachacamac is accompanied by two baby twins in a formation that depicts the juxtaposition of the stars in Orion's belt.

Returning to the blocks of 12 troops that face each other: 12 x 12 = 144, the esoteric number from Revelation.

Returning to the complete complement of troops in Pit 3 (figure 43), the reason for the embrace-like deportment now becomes apparent; four (previously counted) charioteers face east (as do the twins) without partners to embrace. These stand in (anticlockwise) a 1, 2, 1 formation, which is 11 *multiplied* by 11, drawing our attention to the 2 rows of 11 troops (that include the twins) and also to the notion of *multiplication*. Multiplying the 6 east-facing troops by one row of 11 produces 66, and again multiplying the other row by 11 produces 66, i.e. 6, 66 and 6, 66. The final message of Pit 3 thus becomes clear: those with no neighbour to embrace (who do not love their neighbour) become one of the 666 to be reborn again in the east, on earth (the place where the sun is reborn on earth).

The appearance of the number 144 in the pits at Xian again connects the esoteric relevance of the terracotta formations with those of other ancient civilisations and the 144,000 destined for heaven in the Book of Revelation.

The decoded picture of Lord Pacal, from the Amazing Lid of Palenque (figure A52) shows him with the number 144,000 written on his forehead, and Tutankhamun carried 143 articles in the wrappings of his mummy; he was item number 144.

Pit Number 4

Pit 4 was empty.

Weaponry

More than 10,000 bronze weapons have been unearthed from the pits of the terracotta warriors; the eastern end of Pit 1 contained 279 arrows, 10,896 arrowheads and 22 bronze swords made from an amalgam of around 75 per cent copper and 25 per cent tin. The swords, knives, halberds (combined spear and battleaxe), daggers and bows were few in number compared with the arrows and arrowheads.

Many of the sword and dagger blades are engraved with a name which, according to archaeologists, refers to the name of the craftsman who made the weapon. A total of only 80 such names have been found, suggesting that the master craftsman (whose number was the heavenly 81; 9 x 9) was Shi Huangdi.

The accuracy and long-range effectiveness of the crossbow meant

Archers
(Reconstruction with Crossbows)

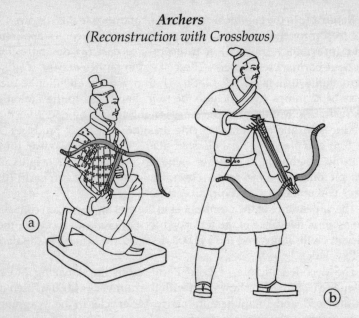

Figure 44. Sketches of (a) armoured kneeling archer and (b) unarmoured standing archer. In this reconstruction, by archaeologists, the type of weaponry carried by the soldiers has been inferred from their deportment; in this case, crossbows. However, the positions and shapes of the hands (see also plate 10e) conceal a secret numerical code (figure 63).

that the weapon was the one favoured by the military, and the archer (plate 10c and figure 44) was the rank most revered for strength and bravery.

An archery manual written by Feng Meng during the Han dynasty credits the invention of the crossbow to an archer named Ch'in who lived in Ch'u:

> Mr Ch'in considered, however, that the bow and arrow was no longer sufficient to keep the world in obedience, for in his time all the feudal lords were fighting against one another with weapons and could not be controlled by ordinary archery. He therefore added, at right angles to the bow, a stock and established a trigger mechanism within a box or housing, thus increasing its strength. In this way all the feudal lords could be subdued. Mr Ch'in transmitted the invention to the Three Lords of Ch'u ... and it was

from them that Ling Wang [539–527 BC] got it. As he himself said, before their time the men of Ch'u had for several generations guarded their frontiers with only bows of peachwood and arrows of thorns (Joseph Needham, *Science and Civilisation in China,* Vol. 1, Cambridge University Press, 1954).

In 1044 the author Tseng Kung-Liang provided an account of how the weapon was used in battle:

The crossbow is the strongest weapon of China and what the four kinds of barbarians most fear and obey... The crossbow is the most efficient weapon of any, even at distances as short as five feet. The crossbowmen are mustered in separate companies, and when they shoot nothing can stand in front of them, no enemy formation can keep its order. If attacked by cavalry, the crossbowmen will be solid as a mountain, shooting off such volleys that nothing can remain alive before them. Therefore the barbarians fear the crossbow. Truly for struggling around strategic points among mountains and rivers and defiles, overcoming men who do not lack bravery, the crossbow is indispensable.

And in regard to the method of using the crossbow:

... it is most beneficial when shot from high ground facing downwards. It only needs to be used so that the men within the formation are loading while the men in the front line of the formation are shooting. As they come forwards they use shields to protect their flanks. Thus, each in their turn, they draw their crossbows and come up; then as soon as they have shot their bolts they return again into the formation. Thus the sound of the crossbows is incessant and the enemy can hardly flee. Therefore we have the following drill: shooting rank, advancing rank, and loading rank (Collection of The Most Important Military Techniques by Tseng Kung-Liang, 1044, reported by Joseph Needham, *Science and Civilisation in China,* Vol. 1, Cambridge University Press, 1954).

The technologies employed in the manufacture of crossbows must be considered remarkable if not miraculous for the period during which they were developed. Stems of crossbow bolts (plate 10b) were made from cast iron doped with carbon – heralding the first appearance of steel known to man. Cast iron, smelted in Scandinavia from around AD 800, was unknown in the rest of Europe until around 1100.

Trigger mechanisms, cast in three pieces of bronze, were finely worked to enable friction-free, non-stick operation, despite the fact that all three pieces shared a common spindle inside a mortised chamber within the stock.

China's lead in metallurgical understanding arose from two main factors: the widespread availability of good-quality clays essential for lining the insides of the blast furnace, and an understanding of low-temperature smelting made possible through the ingenious discovery that the addition of iron phosphate during the smelting process lowered the melting point of iron substantially, from 1,130°C to around 950°C.

As we have already seen, the widespread use of iron throughout China led to other advances, from the cast-iron ploughshare in agriculture to the production of knives, woodworking tools, weapons and armour and to other advanced metallurgical techniques, like the production of corrosion-resistant chromium plate used to coat the bronze tips of the crossbow bolts, unknown in Europe until recent times.

The advanced metallurgical techniques used in the production of arrows was paralleled only by the specification and precision engineering involved in the manufacture. The sides of the triangular bolt tips feature the sectional concave curvature of a bullet, and the accuracy of each of the sides to each other remains perfect to a magnification factor of 20:1. Steel swords were ground with high precision comparable to those achieved by modern engineering techniques.

Body Armour

During the Warring States period iron-mail coat tunics (plate 10a) were worn as body armour. Only two examples have been found near the pits at Xian. Numerous horizontal rows of iron platelets over-lapped lower rows. Soft neck-scarves protected the wearer from abrasions from the tunic.

Examples of body armour displayed by the terracotta warriors vary according to rank, function and position in formation.

Terracotta Warrior Types (with Riveted Armour)

Figure 45. Sketches of some of the armoured warriors showing their deportment, when viewed from the rear.

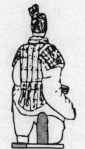

Kneeling archer

Junior officer (armoured at the front)

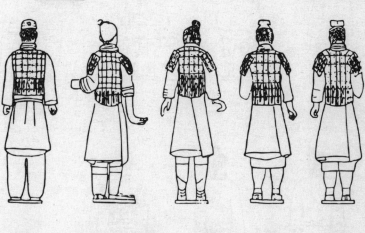

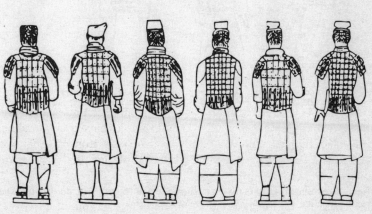

103

Terracotta Warrior Types
(without Riveted Armour)

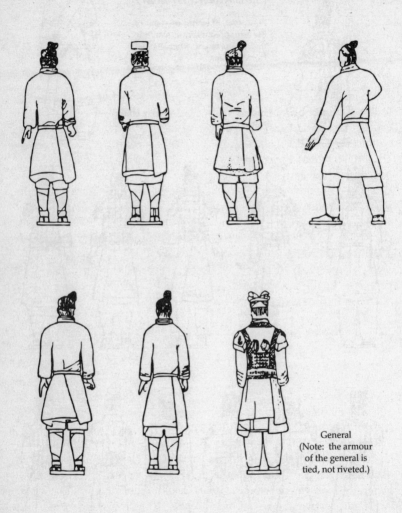

General
(Note: the armour
of the general is
tied, not riveted.)

Figure 46. Sketches of some of the unarmoured warriors showing their deportment, when viewed from the rear, together with an armoured general.

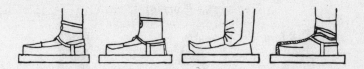

Figure 47. Sketches of various types of shoes worn by the soldiers. Others wore boots.

Sketches of the types of riveted armour are shown in figure 45. Other soldiers, primarily those protected by kneeling archers, wore only softer padded garments (figure 46) that provided little protection against the sword but allowed swiftness of movement, essential where advantage had already been gained and speed was of the essence to consolidate the gain.

There are many variations of uniform throughout the ranks. Some wear shin pads on bare legs; some wear shin guards beneath padded trousers covered by capes or long tunics. Others have no shin protection and some legs are simply bound with fabric. Some wear short trousers, others long trousers – some of which are padded.

Light footwear (figure 47), designed for mobility, was worn primarily by the unarmoured warriors and cavalrymen, while heavy leather boots were worn by the archers.

The Ranks

The General (figure 48). The number of generals found in the pits varies with the source of reference. As already mentioned, one general is said to have been found in Pit 1, but no location reference is given in any of the illustrations or texts. Two were found in Pit 2 in the positions shown in plate 7.

The general stands, ostensibly leaning on a sword with his hands crossed. One index finger points upwards. The term 'ostensibly' is used here because there is an alternative esoteric interpretation to the general's deportment which will be discussed later.

He wears two layers of robes beneath an armoured tunic that protects his chest, back and shoulders. The platelets of the armour are tied to the tunic rather than riveted, and the tunic is tied with bows, permitting removal off the shoulders rather than by lifting over the head. The rear of the tunic is considerably shorter at the back,

The General

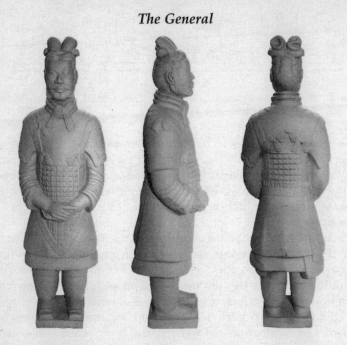

Figure 48. The hand gesture of the general (see figure 64) represents the number 9 (the highest number that can be reached before becoming one (10) with God), corresponding to the highest ranking officer. Only one general was found in Pit 1 and two in Pit 2.

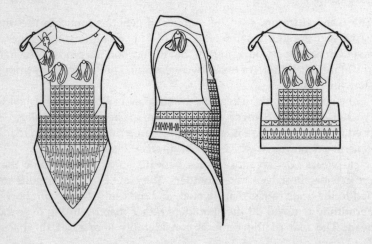

The Junior Officer

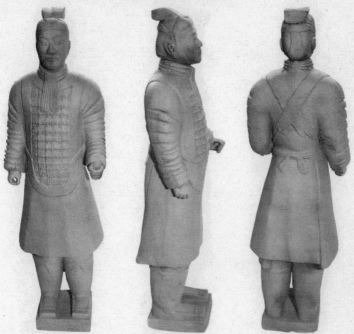

Figure 49. The junior officer wore the lightest armour of the armoured warriors.

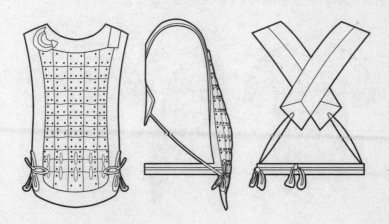

The Armoured Warrior

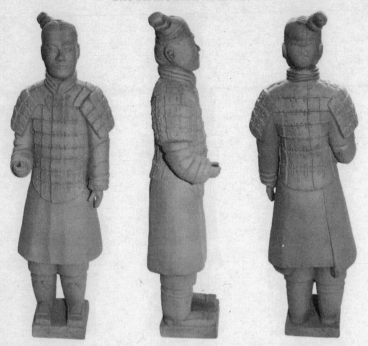

Figure 50. The heavily armoured warrior, like the archer, carried shoulder protection against falling enemy arrows and blows from clubs and axes.

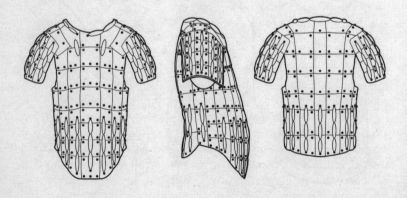

The Robed Infantryman

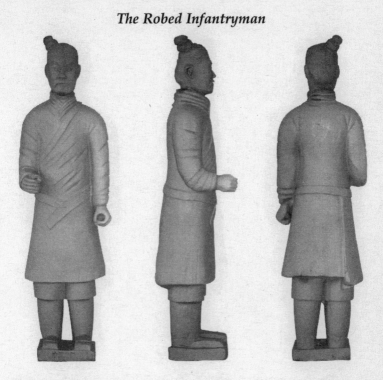

Figure 51. Robed infantryman.

confirming the general's leadership aim of forging forwards in advance and not in retreat to the rear, which would render him exposed to injury. The general thus displayed courage. His uniform sets him apart from all the other warriors. Shin guards and padded trousers protect his legs. His square-toed shoes are lightweight and curve upwards at the front, and shin pads protect the legs. He stands squarely on a square plinth.

The Junior Officer. Figure 49 shows a junior officer from Pit 2. An armoured cape covers his trousers, and a high-collared shirt and neck-scarf protect his neck. The platelets of his armoured tunic are, ostensibly, riveted, unlike the general's. The tunic ties with a crossed band at the back and like the general's, can be offloaded from the shoulders. He, too, wears square-toed shoes and stands on a square plinth.

The Cavalryman

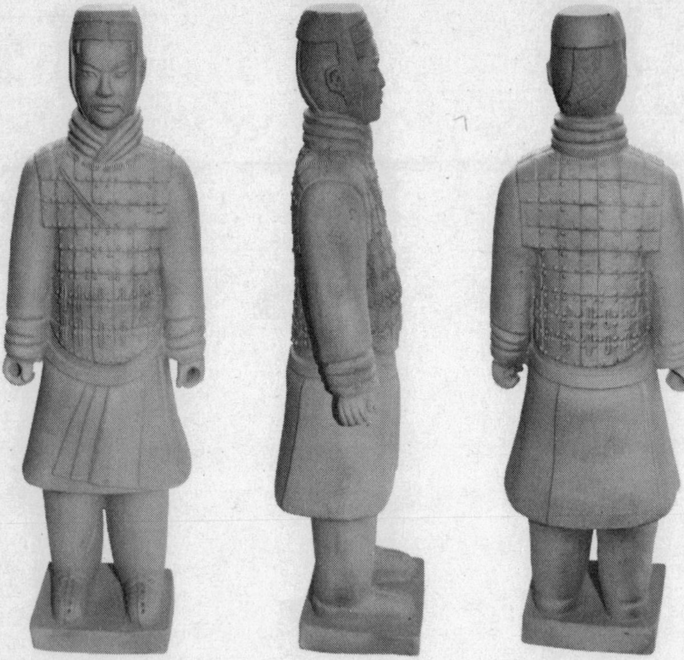

Figure 52. The cavalryman (see also plate 8) wore full body armour, slightly heavier than that of the officer. Unlike the officer, his arms were unprotected, not for reasons of rank, but to enable freedom of movement when controlling the reins of the horse.

The Armoured Warrior (figure 50). This one, from Pit 3, wears robes covered by a turtleneck, heavily armoured cape designed to protect the chest, back and shoulders during hand-to-hand combat. The lower platelets of the tunic are tied together by thong and rivet. The tunic can only be offloaded by lifting over the head, thus making the lower-ranking officer bow, in deference to generals and officers. He stands in square-toed shoes on a square plinth.

The Robed Infantryman (figure 51) wears only a knee-length robe, neck-scarf, short trousers and a belt. His legs are bound in cloth. Again, he stands in square-tipped shoes on a square plinth. His deportment suggests that he carries a spear.

The Cavalryman (figure 52). The cavalryman wears a pillbox hat,

Charioteer Armour

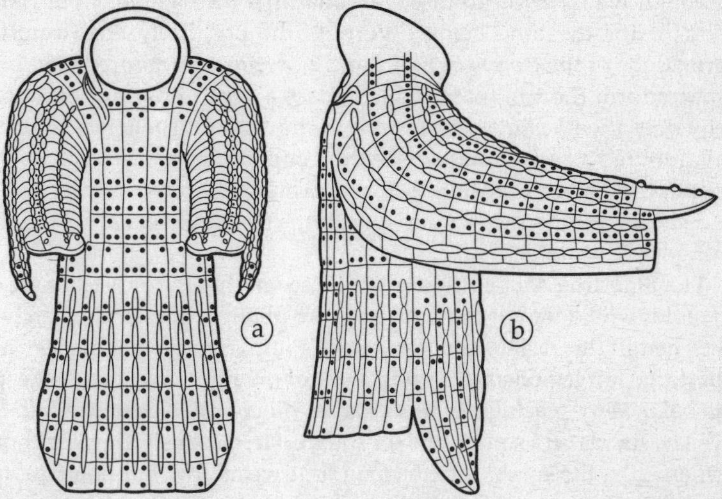

Figure 53. (a) Chariot-driver armour with protective sleeves. (b) Chariot-warrior armour.

neck-scarf and light body armour to the front and back. His shoes are soft and round at the toes so as not to injure his mount.

The Charioteer (figure 53). Charioteers' armour comes in two styles, one for the driver, with extra protection for the outstretched arms and hands that controlled the reins of the horses, and a lighter-duty version for the spear-carrying charioteer who required more mobility and freedom. The driver wore a helmet giving protection to the back of the neck.

The Kneeling Archer (figure 44a and plates 12 and 13). The kneeling archer is the most admired of the warriors. He kneels on his right knee with, ostensibly, a crossbow at the ready. His heavy armour covers the chest, back and shoulders, and his hair is gathered high in a bun on his head. High leather boots provide the firm foothold essential for pulling back the bowstring to rearm.

The missing corner on the plinth tells us that, for some (as yet) unknown reason, the kneeling archer is the most special of the ranks, and here we are mindful that the missing corners of the Amazing Lid of Palenque held the key to decoding the hidden stories concealed in the lid. The missing corner of the kneeling archer thus holds the key to understanding the real purpose and message of the terracotta warriors, although we have yet to discover what that message may be. Here, though (for the time being), we note the peculiarly anachronistic formations of the troops in Pits 1 and 2, where unarmoured standing archers form the vanguard, which raises a very important question: why does the kneeling archer, who wears armour, shelter behind the unarmoured standing archer (see the troop formations in plate 7), the first in the line of fire? Surely, the unarmoured archer should kneel, and shelter behind the armoured archer, who should stand first in the firing line?

The Standing Archer (figure 44b). It seems that the only example of a soldier who does not stand on a square plinth is the standing archer, sketched in figure 44b; and yet we note, importantly, that his legs are apart, the left leg one full step in front of the right, and that he keeps his balance by placing his right foot at ninety degrees to the left. So even he stands on a square, the set-square. He, curiously, fights without armour like the robed infantryman, but wears low cut boots to aid rearming of the bow. The specimen sketched in figure 44b stands as though ready to fire a bow.

The Secrets in the Hair

Hairstyles fall into three groups. The first type incorporates plaiting of the hair at the back of the head; this was then integrated with hair on one side of the head to form a bun. A second style involved the formation of a bun on the top of the head; plaits from the back of the head and from each temple were then stitched to the back of the head and secured to the bun. A third style involved production of a bun at the top of the head which was then covered by a cloth cap that was secured to the underside of the chin by a ribbon.

The hairstyles are indeed curious and elaborate and immediately raise suspicions. Why would a heavily armoured fighting force go into battle with heads unprotected? Where would the 8,000 or so hairdressers stay before the battle? Or are we to suppose that the soldiers all stood in a circle, each attending to the hair of the soldier in front before the battle commenced?

Of course, there must be more to the hairstyles than meets the eye. And, after all, we have been told to look at the soldiers in the tunnels carefully to hear the story of the sun and God.

To understand the secrets in the hairstyles we need to travel to the ancient Mayan city of Copan in Honduras, Central America, which is around 550 kilometres (342 miles) south-east of Palenque.

The Maya were master stonemasons, and Mayan sites are scattered with millions of carved blocks that, for the most part, nobody understands (Appendix 4 explains how many may be decoded).

In 1905 archaeologists discovered a curiously carved block of stone (a stela) which they named Stela J of Copan. The carving (figures 54 and 55) is unusual in that the picture-writing of the Maya, the glyphs, do not run in columns either vertically or horizontally. The glyphs are arranged diagonally. As though this were not perplexing enough, the glyphs forming the first part of the sentence begin as shown in figure 54b, in positions marked as 0, 1 and 2.

Early-twentieth-century scholars who analysed the carving noticed that instead of proceeding in any kind of logical fashion, the sentence then ducked beneath the adjacent glyph to re-emerge in position numbered 3 and then twisted in the opposite direction, to the glyph numbered 4. It eventually became clear that the glyphs followed the numerical sequence set out in figure 54 (see also plate 11). Stela J has perplexed every investigator since it was discovered. Another curiosity of the carving is that all the corners are missing. Again, we are mindful that the omission of information accommodates the encoding of information. When the front weave and back weave are opened like a book (plate 11), the full extent of the mat is revealed (figures 54 and 55). Counting the crossover junctions it becomes clear that the first horizontal row of crossovers contains four junctions, the next six, the next five and so on as listed in the column on the left in figure 55. The centre horizontal row contains five crossovers and the centre crossover, of the five, radiates outwards towards the corners at thirty-six degrees. The angle between the top two radii hence amounts to 72 degrees, as does the angle between the bottom two, a total of 144 (representing the 144,000 from the Book of Revelation in the Bible).

The left-hand vertical column of figures contained in Stela J, the numbers 4, 6, **5**, 6, 5, 6, **5**, 6, 5, 6, 5, 6, 4 appear, which when rearranged either side of the 5 by order of value gives 4, 55, 666 (the procession of numbers leading the reader to 666, the number of the beast from Revelation). The symmetrical column of figures can then be rationalised either side of (and inclusive of) the central number **5** (emboldened and underlined, above) so that each group amounts to

Maya Coding Using the Weave Technique; Stela J of Copan

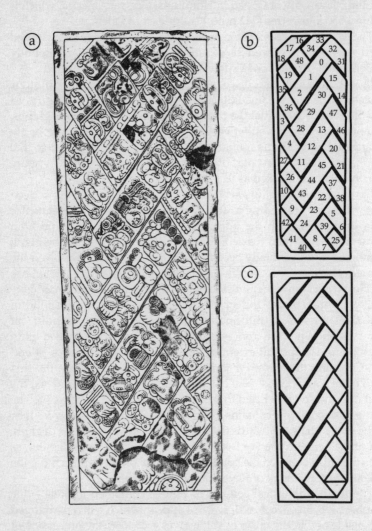

Figure 54. (a) Stone stela from the Mayan site of Copan, Honduras, about 550 kilometres (342 miles) south-east of Palenque, Mexico. The carved glyphs (writing characters) follow an unusual plaited pattern. (b) Detail of the ostensible weave on the front face of the stela (see also plate 11). The hieroglyphic message follows the numbered sequence. (c) Ostensible weave from the reverse side of the stela.

Maya Coding Using the Plait Technique;
Stela J of Copan (Angular and Numerical Analysis)

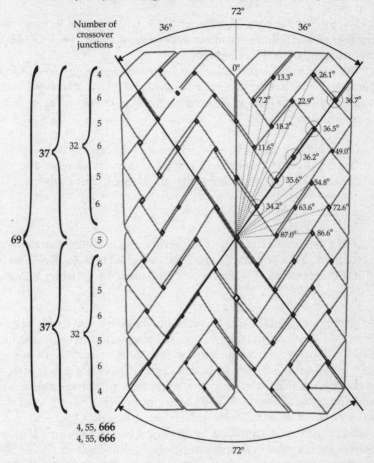

Figure 55. The vertical column of digits, 4, 6, 5, 6, 5, 6, 5, 6, 5, 6, 5, 6, 4, indicates the number of crossover junctions *(diamond shapes)* when the weave pattern is examined horizontally, from left to right. The number in the centre of this vertical column, 5 *(circled)*, calls attention to the row of five junctions *(circled in the weave pattern)* distributed 36 degrees clockwise from perpendicular and its corollary *(36 degrees to the left of perpendicular)* that together add up to 72 degrees *(indicated by the angular marker)*. The same applies to the bottom two quadrants. The top and bottom quadrants together amount to 144 degrees. The number 37, the rotational duration, in days, of the solar pole, and the number 666 (from the Book of Revelation) can also easily be found, as can the interchangeable 69, inviting the onlooker to turn 666 into 999.

37 at the top, and again 37 at the bottom (representing the duration of one revolution of the sun's polar magnetic field – on the solar surface – in days).

The total of the column adds up to 69, which brings to mind the numbers 6 and 9 that once again refer to the numbers 666 – of hell – and its corollary, 999 – of heaven.

This shows that information has been encoded in the weave and perhaps explains how the holy book of the Maya, *The Popol Vuh*, acquired its name. The 1947 written version of the book begins with the expression:

The Popol Vuh cannot be seen any more . . . the original book written long ago existed, but its sight is hidden from the searcher and the thinker (*The Popol Vuh*, University of Oklahoma Press, 1947, p. 79).

And ends:

And this was the life of the Quiche, because no longer can be seen the book of the Popol Vuh which the kings had in olden times, for it has disappeared (*The Popol Vuh*, University of Oklahoma Press, 1947, p. 235).

At the beginning of the eighteenth century a Dominican monk, Father Francisco Ximenez, lived within the confines of a convent located at Chichicastenango in the Guatemalan highlands, about 320 kilometres (200 miles) up the River Ucamacinta from Palenque. He was a wise and virtuous man who won the confidence of the Indians while attempting to convert them to Christianity. In return, they related the stories of their own traditions in their native tongue, Quiche.

Father Ximenez stumbled upon an ancient manuscript hidden behind loose stones in the parish church at Santo Thomas, Chichicastenango. The crumbling pages of the manuscript had been written by a Quiche Indian, whose name is unknown, in around AD 1550, in an attempt to set down the ancient traditions of his people. This told of the earlier book that had been 'lost' and had probably been written down from memory by the author versed in the history of the Maya.

Father Ximenez translated the document into Spanish under the title *Historias del Origen de los Indios esta de Guatemala*, which was later republished in 1857 in Vienna by Carl Sherzer, a European explorer who had chanced upon the book buried beneath piles of dust and cobwebs in the library at the University of San Carlos, Guatemala.

In 1861 another European explorer, Charles Etienne Brasseur de Bourborg, published his own French translation in Paris entitled *Popol Vuh, le Livre Sacré et les Mythes de l'antiquité Americaine, avec les Livres Héroïques des Quiches* that also contained a facsimile of the original Quiche text.

A Spanish version of the book, prepared by Adrian Recinos, was released in Mexico in 1947 and later translated into English by Delia Goetz and Sylvanus G. Morley, who say in the introduction that the original book, said to be 'lost' (pp. 18 and 19) could not have been a document of set form and permanent literary composition, meaning that it was unlikely the book had ever been written down in book form on paper.

The 1947 version of the book says this of the founding fathers of the Quiche:

They were endowed with intelligence; they saw and instantly they could see far, they succeeded in seeing, they succeeded in knowing all that there is in the world. When they looked, instantly they saw all around them, and they contemplated the arch of the heavens and the round face of the earth. The things hidden (in the distance) they saw all, without first having to move; at once they saw the world . . . Great was their wisdom.

It is worth noting here, for reasons that will become evident later, another passage from the book:

Great were the descriptions and the account of how all the sky and Earth were formed and divided into four parts; how it was partitioned, and how the sky was divided; and the measuring cord was brought, and it was stretched in the sky and over the earth, on the four angles, on the four corners [the four cardinal points] as was told by the creator and the maker, the mother and father of life, of all created things, he who gives breath and thought, she who gives birth to the children, he who watches over the happiness of the human race, the wise man, he who mediates on the goodness of all that exists in the sky, on the earth, in the lakes and in the sea (*The Popol Vuh*, Delia Goetz and Sylvanus G. Morley).

In regard to the passing away of the founding fathers, the book continues with the farewell speech of Balam-Quitze:

> We are going away [to die], we have completed our mission here. Then Balam-Quitze left the symbol of his being: 'This is a resemblance which I leave for you. This shall be your power . . .' He left the symbol whose form was invisible because it was 'wrapped-up' and could not be unwrapped: 'the seam did not show because it was not seen when they wrapped it up . . .' (*The Popol Vuh*, Delia Goetz and Sylvanus G. Morley).

Another manuscript, the *Titulo de los Señores de Totonicapan*, provides more information about the 'bundle of majesty': 'This gift is what they feared and respected . . . the gift was a stone, the stone of Naczit [Quetzalcoatl; Lord Pacal]', suggesting that the stone was the Amazing Lid of Palenque. Hence the opening and closing expressions of *The Popol Vuh*: *The Popol Vuh* cannot be seen any more; it has been hidden from the searcher (in the Temple of Inscriptions) and the thinker (it has been encoded). That this is so is now confirmed by this new interpretation of Stela J of Copan; the literal translation of the words '*Popol Vuh*' mean '*book of the mat*'. Stela J is the book of the mat, which is woven and has four missing corners. Stela J contains secret information. The words 'Popol Vuh' hence refer to the stone of Lord Pacal as '*the book which has been encoded like Stela J of Copan*'. Again, we note that Stela J has four missing corners, like the Lid of Palenque (which has only two missing corners – until the transparency is produced, when it then has four missing corners).

Which brings us back to the woven hairstyles of the terracotta warriors. Stela J hence provides the clue of where to begin our enquiries.

The first thing to notice about the head of the terracotta warriors is that, unlike the hands, it is not *fixed* to the body (plate 13a). It can thus be removed or turned to the side, or back, thereby accommodating examination of the hairstyles.

Examining the weave of one example (figure 56), three skeins of hair separate at the nape of the neck and coalesce into a plait. These three skeins produce a two-lane plait. The same is done to the hair around each temple. In this way the $3 + 3 + 3$ (9) become $2 + 2 + 2$ (6). In this way the esoteric number 9 may be converted to the esoteric

The Secrets in the Hair (I)

9 ⇄ 6

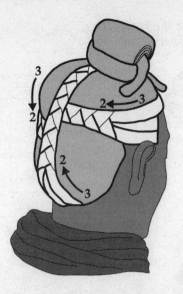

Figure 56. (a) One of several examples of a hair plait design showing how three skeins of hair from the nape of the neck become a two-lane plait. Another three skeins originate above the left ear to become a two-lane plait. Another three skeins originate above the right ear to become a two-lane plait. This means that the 3 + 3 + 3 skeins (= 9) resolve into 2 + 2 + 2 plaits (= 6). In this way the figure 9 is transformed into the figure 6 or, looked at another way, the figure 6 becomes the figure 9.

number 6 and vice versa. This suggests that good people can become bad people, just as bad people can become good people.

Figure 57a shows another style. This time the temple plaits confluence with the nape-of-the-neck plait, forming characteristic knots in the vertical plait that characterise the formation of sunspots on the sun's surface (aii). These then develop in the previous style (figure 57b) into full-blown sunspot loops.

The four unequal quadrants produced by sectioning the head by the hairstyle (figure 58a) emulate the four unequal quadrants of the solar wind radiated by the sun towards earth (figure 58d).

The highly elaborate and complex plaiting seen in figures 59a and 59b resemble the male scrotum and penis. The various hairstyles hence connect the warriors with the sun and with the fertility-controlling attributes of the sun. (Appendix 3 explains how the twenty-eight-day revolving sun showers the earth with particles that regulate the production of fertility hormones in females.)

The cloth cap in 59b, like a loincloth, provides a modicum of modesty to the genitalia.

That this is a reasonable interpretation of the evidence is supported by the golden mask of Tutankhamun (figure 59c). The rear of the mask is shaped in the style of a penis, the distinctive shape of the

119

The Secrets in the Hair (II)
Sunspots

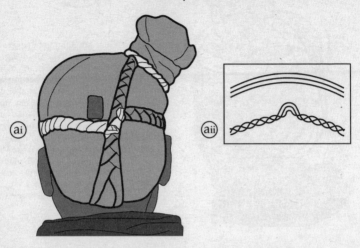

Figure 57. (ai) This style shows the confluence between a simple twisted pair, originating above the left ear, and a two-lane plait rising from a three-skein gathering at the nape of the neck. (aii) Schematic showing corollary magnetic activity on the sun; below the sun's surface magnetic field lines become tangled by the turbulent plasma and erupt, bursting through the solar surface as a magnetic bubble (bi, bii and biii; see also figure A14).

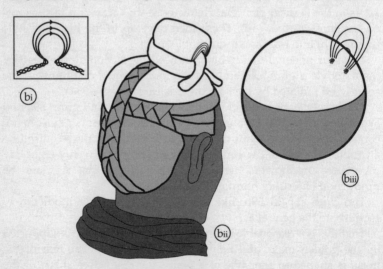

The Secrets in the Hair (III)
The Solar Wind

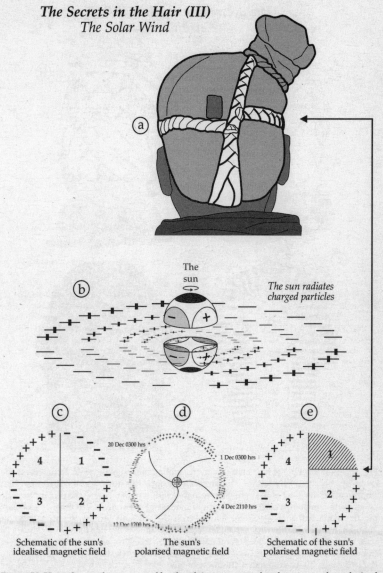

Figure 58. Here, the quadrants created by the plaits are unequal and represent the polarised solar magnetic field (d), as determined by *Interplanetary Spacecraft No. 1*, 1962, and (e), which shows a schematic of the same field, distorted to give two equal quadrants, one enlarged quadrant and one reduced quadrant (see also figure A3).

The Secrets in the Hair (IV)
Fertility

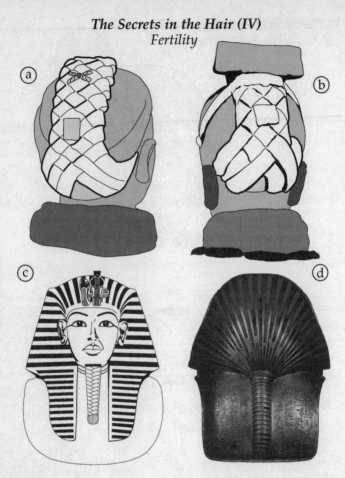

Figure 59. (a) Example of hair plait design resembling human male genitalia that carry the cross of the sun. (b) Another similar plait design, this time terminating in a bun (representing the head of the penis) beneath the cloth cap. In this way the cap, in the style of a simple loincloth, affords a modicum of modesty. Plait styles a and b hence associate the terracotta warriors, and their leader, with the sun and fertility. (c) Face mask of Tutankhamun which likewise associates hairstyle with fertility; this illustration shows 28 solar rays that depict the 28-day rotational rate of the sun's equatorial magnetic field (when measured from earth). (d) Rear of Tutankhamun's mask showing 26 rays of the sun, depicting the 26-day rotational duration of the solar equator, when measured on the surface of the sun. The rear view also depicts the shaft and head of a penis, associating Tutankhamun (the Egyptian sun-king) with the sun and fertility, as with the case of the terracotta warriors above. Note the presence of the cross and the square in a, and the square in b.

head revealed by the withdrawn foreskin and fed by the central vein up the centre. The rear of the mask contains 26 golden rays (the rotational duration of the sun's equatorial magnetic field, in days, when measured on the sun's surface). The front of the mask contains 28 rays (the rotational duration of the sun's equatorial magnetic field when measured from earth). Tutankhamun's treasures (figure A56), like the hairstyles of the terracotta warriors just examined, also explain that the solar wind affects life on earth.

Earlier examination revealed that the terracotta warriors either took up their positions on square plinths or else steadied themselves (in the case of the standing archer) by positioning one foot forwards at right angles to the other (the feet again positioned as a set-square in relation to each other).

Analysis of the hairstyles (in figures 57a and 59a–b) shows that the soldiers also carry a square-shaped mark on the back of the head in addition to characteristics detailed so far. The squares in figures 59a and b are offset by approximately 90 degrees from the square formed by the weave in the underlying hair. Figure 59a also features another separate cross, the arms of which resemble string or cord, emulating the above passage from *The Popol Vuh* that refers to the measuring cord that points to the four corners (the cross and the square). This time, the arms of the cross align with the cross pattern of the square in the hair weave. The square shape, given its frequent appearance on the heads of the warriors, clearly carried some importance in Chinese belief and thought. The symbolism of the square, therefore, cannot be underestimated or its importance overstated.

The Secrets of the Squares

It is uncertain who compiled *The Book of Great Learning*, one of the Chinese classics. Some believe that the chapters were written by Confucius or by the sage Tsang Shan as recorded by his disciples. Others say that K'ung Chi, the grandson of Confucius, conceived them. The first-century scholar Chia K'wei noted:

When K'ung Chi was living and in straits, in Suing, being afraid lest the persons of the former sages should become obscure and the principles of the ancient sovereigns and kings fall to the ground, he therefore made the Great Learning as the warp of them, and the

Doctrine of the Mean as the woof (Legge, *Chinese Classics*, Vol. 1, Chapter III, Section III). (The warp refers to the lengthways threads in a loom, and the woof – sometimes called the weft – to the horizontal cross-threads.)

The general consensus seems to be that the words at least arose from the school of Confucius if not from the great philosopher himself.

The teachings proposed that good government arose from self-disciplined and virtuous men. Legge comments:

... the book defines itself in its opening paragraph: 'The Great Learning teaches us to illustrate virtue; to love the people and to rest in the higher excellence.'

Legge's view is that the aim of the writer is clear: on the one side stand the people – the masses of the empire – and on the other those whose work and duty were divinely delegated by heaven through a single man, 'the Son of Heaven', the sovereign. The belief was that the lessons of virtue would diffuse, fragrance-like, through a nation, leading to happiness and tranquillity. Cultivation of the person was thus seen as the prime consideration and of the utmost importance to every man, be he sovereign or peasant.

Virtue could be pursued by the pursuit of knowledge, the acquisition of knowledge, sincerity of thought, purity of mind, body and spirit, sociological order and governmental control.

The chain of causation flowed synergistically; the cultivated individual becomes peaceful, which leads to a harmonious and loving family life, which in turn promotes a loving society. From its civility the whole state becomes courteous; well-governed states lead to a peaceful empire.

The Book of Great Learning then explains the golden rule, the *measuring square*. The application of the measuring square is that a ruler should treat others as he would have others treat himself. This sets out the ground rules for a relationship between two parties, as a measuring square sets into stone a relationship between two sides. The *square* in China was therefore *the mark of the virtuous man* and the mark of the *knowledgeable* man. This explains why the square is revered today in the West by esoteric societies, who regard themselves as being 'on the square'. This is also the reason why schoolteachers, in the West, wear a square hat – the mortarboard – that is fashioned to rest on a circularised cap which connects it to the head of the wearer. The cap personifies the circularised pole of the sun (the four peaks of the cap explicitly recognise the missing four bubbles of equatorial magnetic field; figure A6a). The tassle on the square, which is free to move around the square, mimics the rotational possibilities of the sun's pole, which revolves around the solar equator. In this way, esoteric societies pride themselves with virtue and knowledge and, moreover, as guardians of the super-science of the sun. This also explains the derivation of the expression 'fairly and squarely', used in relation to virtuous business transactions in the West.

There are other squares in China that refer to and contain the super-scientific knowledge of the sun and also, at the same time, the higher spiritual knowledge. Figure 60 shows an example of such a square, a numerological magic square of China. The original wooden board, from which these numbers were obtained, is today kept in the museum of Xian. The caption accompanying the exhibit explains that squares like this were often placed beneath the foundation stones in houses to bring good luck and fortune.

Analysis of the numbers in the square reveals that the six columns and six rows contain all the numbers from 1 to 36. The numbers in each of the columns add up to 111, as do the numbers in each of the horizontal and diagonal rows. The sum of all the vertical columns amounts to 666. The figure occupying the top right-hand corner of the square contains the number 10, a decimal number. The sum of the horizontal rows similarly amounts to 666. These numbers, 666 *decimal* 666 (666.666), when multiplied by the quantity of squares vertically (6), horizontally (6) and diagonally (6), amount to (666.666 x 6 x 6 x 6 =) 144,000 (143,999.9 – which covers both the 144,000 and the 999 intentions of the encoder).

This analysis of the numbers in the magic square encourages the transformation from the number of the beast in Revelation (666) to the number of those destined for the promised land in Revelation (144,000) but only by the man who has the wisdom to count the number ('. . . let he who has wisdom count the number of the beast: for it is the number of a man; and his number is six hundred three score and six' Revelation xiii, 18). A life of iniquity may thus be transformed into one of virtue. Whoever initiated the practice of

The Magic Square of China (I)

$$111 + 111 + 111 + 111 + 111 + 111 = 666$$

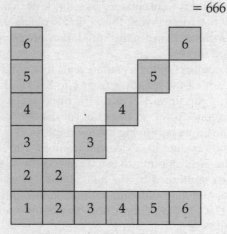

28	4	3	31	35	10	111
36	18	21	24	11	1	+ 111
7	23	12	17	22	30	+ 111
8	13	26	19	16	29	+ 111
5	20	15	14	25	32	+ 111
27	33	34	6	2	9	+ 111

$$= 666$$

$$666.666 \times \boxed{6} \times \boxed{6} \times \boxed{6} = 144{,}000 \ (143{,}999.9)$$

Figure 60. Each line of numbers in this magic square from Xian museum adds up, horizontally, vertically and diagonally, to 111. Hence the six horizontal rows amount to 666, the mark of the beast, as do the vertical rows. Taken together, 666.666 x 6 x 6 x 6 (*as shown above*) amount to 144,000 (the chosen few who will go to heaven). Magic squares like this were often placed under the foundation stones of houses in China to bring good luck.

The Magic Square of China (II)

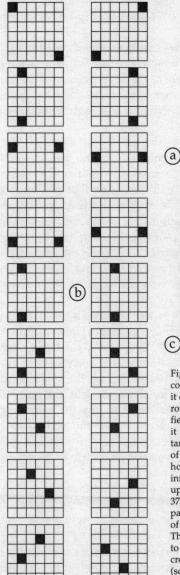

28	4	3	31	35	10
36	18	21	24	11	1
7	23	12	17	22	30
8	13	26	19	16	29
5	20	15	14	25	32
27	33	34	6	2	9

(a)

28					10
	18	21	24	11	
	23	12	17	22	
	13	26	19	16	
	20	15	14	25	
27					9

(b)

(c)

Figure 61. (a) The magic square of China contains only 36 numbers (1–36), and although it contains the important solar number 26 (the rotational duration of the equatorial magnetic field in days as measured on the solar surface), it cannot, therefore, contain the other important solar number 37 (the rotational duration of the solar poles in days). Analysis shows, however, that 18 pairs of figures (poles), infilled in black in the matrix array (b), add up to the missing number 37. Moreover, 18 x 37= 666. (c) When the diagonally juxtaposed pairs of black squares are discounted, a pattern of a white square on a black cross is revealed. This means that only squares that are square to each other produce the magic square on the cross. In this way only those who are virtuous (square) become the square (virtuous) on the cross (the sun).

placing stones inscribed with magic squares beneath the foundations of houses as totems of good luck knew this, and whoever included the mark of the square on the terracotta warriors must have known it too.

Further analysis (figure 61) shows that the squares contain only 36 numbers (from 1 to 36 inclusive), which is perplexing. The two most important numbers – to those aware of the super-science of the sun – are the numbers 26 and 37, the duration of the rotational rates, in days, of the sun's equator and poles respectively (as measured on the solar surface; see Appendix 3i).

Of the two figures, the square contains only one of the numbers, 26, and stops critically short (36) of accommodating the inclusion of the second. Closer inspection shows, remarkably, that opposing pairs (poles) of figures do indeed appear in the matrix that add up to the missing number 37, and these are shown in figure 61b as pairs of black infilled squares in each of the mini-matrix array. Assimilation and reintegration of each of these pairs (excluding the diagonally juxtaposed pairs) into the master matrix (figure 61a) reveals a digitised pattern of a white square on a black cross (which explains the presence of the square on a cross in the hair weave of the terracotta warriors), all contained within four corners.

Appendix 4 explains how each of the Supergods ruled the four corners of the sky, the heavens. The magic square of China thus, on the one hand, contains the numerology that pertains to the super-science of the sun (which explains that the sun revolves every 26 days at the equator and every 37 days at the poles) and on the other hand it exemplifies the spiritual understanding that God, light (the sun), rules the four corners of the heavens. The fact that only the squares (the virtuous) that are square with each other produce the 'square-on-the-cross' pattern indicates that those who are not 'square with each other' (the non-virtuous) do not produce a square on the cross, do not go to the sun and, therefore, do not go to heaven.

We have seen how the first emperor referred to himself as the Son of Heaven, like the Yellow Emperor before him, who was, legend says, born through an immaculate conception when a bright star lit up the sky.

The decoded treasures of the terracotta warriors reveal that Shi Huangdi understood the super-science of the sun, just like the other Supergods. When we examine his achievements, among them the construction of the Great Wall of China, ostensibly the greatest feat of *human* civil engineering ever accomplished, and the creation of his army of terracotta warriors at Xian, it might be fair to argue that he, like the other Supergods, performed miracles during his lifetime on earth.

The stories of Ssu-ma Ch'ien say that when Shi Huangdi died his body was laid to rest (inside his pyramid at Mount Li) in a lake of mercury. Why mercury?

The answer to this question may lie in the Tibetan–Nazi connection, featured in the book *The Black Sun* by the conspiracy theorist Peter Moon. (I should mention here that my own analysis of the facts – and the subsequent conclusions I reach – differ from those of Peter Moon. However, in fairness to the author, I could not have reached those conclusions without his well-researched and informative contribution.)

Moon explains how, in around 1926, Adolf Hitler's German Nazi Party believed themselves to be descendants of the Aryans who lived around 200 BC in a land located between Europe and Asia. They later migrated to India and Persia to the east and south-east, and to Europe to the west and north-west. Hitler adopted the notion and propagated the myth that the Aryans were the blond-haired, blue-eyed, fair-skinned master race, genetic precursors of the Germans.

Hitler's spiritual teacher, Karl Haushofer, was a Bon priest (of the indigenous shamanistic religion that precursed Buddhism in Tibet) who groomed Hitler for a messianic mission in accordance with certain Bon precepts.

At first the Nazis embraced the esoteric philosophies, believing that as descendants of the Aryans their antecedents dated back to the ultimate source of divine knowledge on earth: Hermes, Thoth and Osiris (thought by many to be different incarnations of the same spiritual energy). To esoterically illustrate their grasp of the secret higher knowledge (the super-science of the sun) they arrogantly adopted the mark of the radiating solar wind (figure 58d), the swastika, as their emblem – knowledge of which escaped modern science until 1963 with the advent of the *Mariner II* space mission. With nonchalant smugness the Nazis adopted the raised arm gesture of the Egyptian pharaoh Akhenaten, as a symbol of allegiance to the sun and, as a final defiant statement of consummate superiority, marched with the goose-step, their straight legs emulating the esoteric compasses of the great architect of the universe, God.

In the early 1920s a secret brotherhood was established within the Nazi Party known as the Thulian Society, the esoteric head of which was the Austrian occultist and educationalist Rudolf Steiner, who formulated his own mystic and spiritual method of teaching called anthroposophy, which rejected materialism and instead sought to develop the whole being intellectually, socially and spiritually. Hitler, threatened by Steiner's gaining popularity and powers, persecuted the mystic who, fearing for his life, fled to refuge in Switzerland and died shortly thereafter in 1925, (some say) from a broken heart.

Nineteen twenty-nine was to be a watershed for Hitler's ambitions. In that year seven senior Thulists were assassinated by Communists. Sympathy with the Thulists, and empathy with their aspirations of German supremacy, inspired a purge of Communism throughout Germany. The political vacuum that followed was one of the factors that facilitated the opportunistic rise of Hitler as head of the Thulian Society and his political takeover of the country.

Realising the extraordinary powers latent in esoteric understanding, Hitler gave up the idealistic and benevolent pursuits of Thule and instead pursued the hidden powers of the universe for his own ends: to elevate the German people as the chosen race in preference to the Israelites, who had been given that mandate by Moses. He then embarked on an extermination programme to wipe out the Jews, who stood in the way of his objective. The Nazis became a regime obsessed by megalomania and ethnic cleansing.

Heinrich Himmler, Hitler's Reichsfuhrer in the SS (the Schutz-Staffel, which means 'protective squadron'), was, like Hitler, interested in the powers of occultism for his own ends. He was especially interested in the runes, the secret inscriptions of the oldest German script that originated in Denmark in the third century. Runes were scratched on wood, metal, bone or stone and were, legend has it, given to mankind by Odin, the king of the gods. Odin, in German mythology, was the one-eyed god of battle, magic, inspiration and death, the supreme and oldest of the gods. To obtain the gift of wisdom, Odin sacrificed one eye to the well of Mimir, a renowned sage – from which arises the metaphor *let thine eye be single* in the Bible:

> The light of the body is the eye: if therefore thine eye be single, thy whole body shall be full of light (Matthew xi, 22).

Hence the allegorical portrayal of Odin as the one-eyed god of wisdom.

In 1939 Himmler purchased a derelict castle at Wewelsburg, near Paderborn in Westphalia, and renovated it as the most sacred temple of the SS in reverence to the order of warrior-knights, the Templars (of the twelfth and thirteenth centuries in England), who possessed the higher sacred teachings and committed themselves to a life of military service against non-believers (the Saracens and other non-Christians).

Underneath the temple at Wewelsburg was a room Himmler designated the Holy of Holies and inside that an altar of black marble decorated with two silver runes inscribed with 'SS'. On the marble rested the Holy Grail – or at least a replica – the cup used by Jesus at the Last Supper that was thought to be imbued with supernatural powers. According to one story, the blood of Jesus was collected in the Grail by Joseph of Arimathea at the Crucifixion, who carried it to England where, allegedly, he built the first church at Glastonbury. According to Arthurian legends, developed by Geoffrey of Monmouth, Chrétien de Troyes and the Norman writer Wace in around the twelfth century, Arthur was born at Tintagel in Cornwall in around the sixth century AD and was buried in Glastonbury. His life was spent in a quest to find the Holy Grail and acquire the supernatural powers it ostensibly contained.

Himmler and his compatriots adopted the title of the Order of the Black Knights and, like Hitler, at first pursued the higher esoteric principles. In a quest to acquire ever-higher levels of divine knowledge involving the possibilities of telepathy and out-of-body experiences (both useful during times of war), Himmler actively pursued the recovery of the Holy Grail and also the fabled Ark of the Covenant. (The Nazi sojourns into archaeological antiquity were popularised by the motion picture *Raiders of the Lost Ark* by the producer and director Steven Spielberg.)

The Ark of the Covenant, in the Old Testament, was the chest built by the Hebrew leader Moses that contained two stone tablets engraved with the Ten Commandments given to him by God on Mount Sinai. Himmler believed that whoever possessed the Ark and the tablets of Moses would become, by default, the chosen people.

Today the location of the Ark is unknown. After its appearance it was carried though the desert by the Israelites. King David took it to Jerusalem, where it was subsequently laid to rest inside the oracle known as the Holy of Holies, a perfect cube of solid gold encrusted in jewels that stood in the centre of the courtyard of Solomon's Temple. The temple, the finest ever constructed, was reportedly built by magic by Solomon's architect, Chiram Abiff, who possessed the higher secret knowledge handed down from the pyramid builders. It was destroyed in around 587 BC, probably by an earthquake.

Himmler authorised several archaeological expeditions to various countries in pursuit of both the Grail and the Ark without success. With Hitler at the helm and Himmler in command, the Thulian Society degenerated into a fraternity of racial bigotry.

The name 'Thule' was adopted by the Nazis to esoterically describe their society, which worshipped the super-science of the sun and with it the sacred numbers 666 and 999. 'Thule' is derived from the word 'thulium', a rare-earth element, discovered in 1886 by the French chemist Paul Lecoq de Boisbaudran. It was given the name to describe the invisible rays (X-rays) it emitted. The number of protons in the centre of the atom (referred to as the atomic number) of thulium is 69. Hence the atom thulium esoterically described the society that worshipped the numbers 6 and 9. (The word 'Thule' had also been used earlier by the Greek explorer Pytheas to describe the dark land (the place of darkness) six days' sailing from the north of Britain.)

This suggests that Thulian Nazis, the Black Knights who worshipped the black sun and 69, the atomic weight of thulium, were fully aware of the super-scientific numerological symbolism *at atomic level* as well as at an *astronomical* level.

But what has this got to do with mercury? Thulium is a silvery-white metal which is both malleable and ductile, the rarest of the rare-earth metals and poisonous. Thus it shares almost all the characteristics of the liquid metal mercury. This might explain why the ancient Chinese would wish to bury their Son of Heaven in thulium but, given the rarity of the metal, settled for the next best silvery-white, poisonous and malleable metal – mercury. And there is more to mercury than this: the atomic number of mercury is 80.

The first emperor was, therefore, when submerged in the mercury, object number 81, which was associated with the monkey, whose

The Silk Road

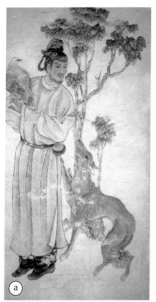

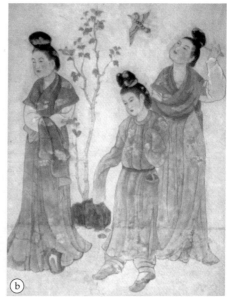

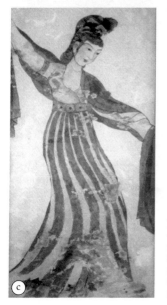

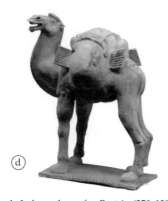

Plate 1. Independence for Bactria (250–139 BC), on the Persian plateau, connected the caravan trading routes from the eastern Mediterranean ports to China. Silk wall banners like these (a–c), and the clothing they depict, were transported as early as the Han dynasty by horse and Bactrian camel (d) from China to the West.

1

The Feathered Snake, the Stag and the First Emperor

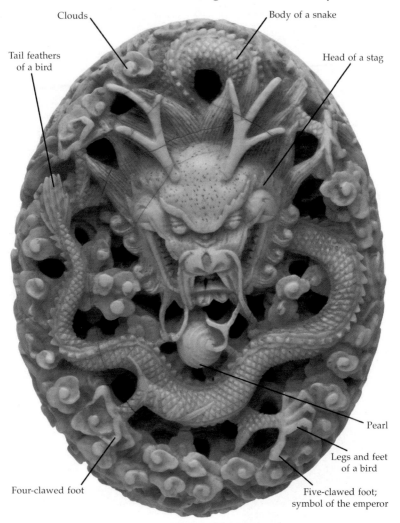

Clouds

Body of a snake

Tail feathers of a bird

Head of a stag

Pearl

Legs and feet of a bird

Four-clawed foot

Five-clawed foot; symbol of the emperor

Plate 2. Fourteenth-century mutton-fat jade carving of a dragon, the favoured personification of the first emperor. The mythological creature was part bird, part snake and part stag; a feathered snake and a stag. The bird represents the divine spirit in the sky and the snake the physical body on the ground that sheds its skin (reincarnation). The stag represents fertility and rebirth (see Appendix 4, iv). The asymmetry of the feet follows the convention used by the South American sun-king Viracocha (figure A60a).

The Feathered Snake and the Stag of Central America; Lord Pacal

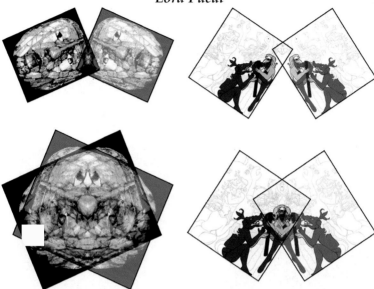

Angle of rotation: each transparency is rotated by 66.6 degrees.

Angle of rotation: each transparency is rotated by 33.3 degrees.

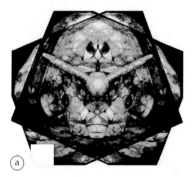

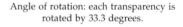

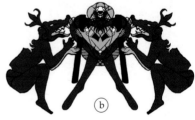

Plate 3. (a) Decoded composite picture from the Mosaic Mask of Palenque showing Lord Pacal (the image on the mask) as the feathered snake (a snake's head with wings on the forehead), Quetzalcoatl. To see this composite scene, each transparency is rotated by 66.6 degrees.

(b) Decoded composite picture from the Mural of Bonampak (see also Appendix 4, iv) showing Xipe Totec, the Mayan god of fire, sacrifice, rebirth and fertility, in his emanation as Camaxtle, lord of the stags. He carries two sticks, to rub together to make fire. In this final scene, from this epicentre series, he bows (curtsies) before two stags, who applaud the end of the performance. In order to see this scene, the transparencies need to be juxtaposed by 66.6 degrees.

The Stag, the Sun and the Dragon

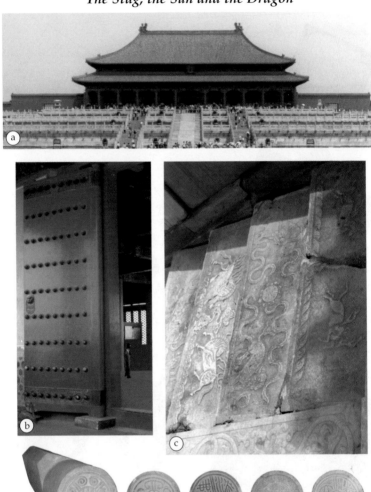

Plate 4. (a) The Hall of Great Harmony in the Forbidden City, Beijing, c. AD 1420, used by Ming and Ch'ing emperors for ceremonies marking the lunar new year and winter solstice. (b) Timber doors studded with 9x9 bronze studs representing the 81 obstacles to be overcome before entry into heaven. (c) Steps carved with two stags (top step) and four dragons around a solar symbol (second step) adjacent to the ceremonial ramp that leads to (a). (d) Roof ridge-end tiles featuring solar symbols from the mausoleum of the first emperor, c. 220 BC

The Underground Army of the First Emperor, Pit Number 1

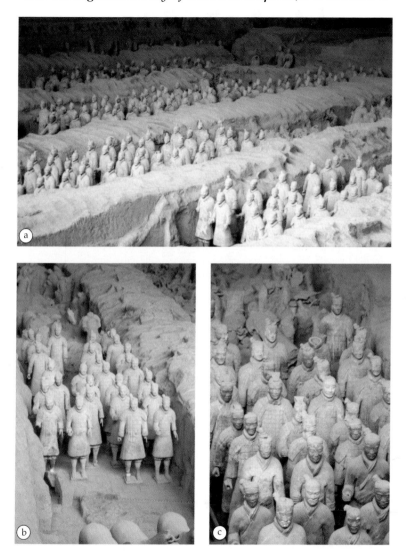

Plate 5. (a) Panoramic view of terracotta warriors in the corridors of Pit Number 1. (b) Armour-clad charioteers followed by infantrymen behind a (missing) chariot pulled by horses. (c) A group of robed infantrymen, to the fore, with armour-clad infantrymen behind.

Battle Formations, Pit Number 1

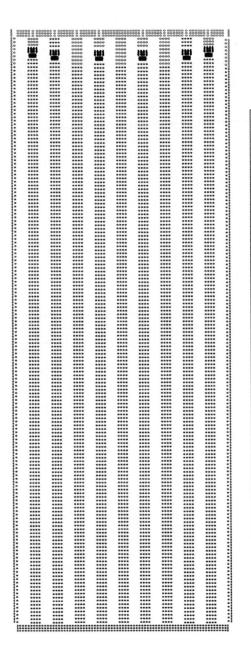

●●●● Armoured	○ Unarmoured	●●● Armoured	○ Unarmoured	Chariot
●●●● infantrymen	○ infantrymen	●●● archers	○ archers	containing
	○	●●●	○	officers

Battle Formations, Pit Number 2

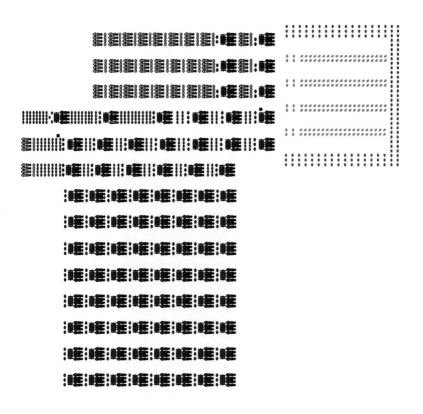

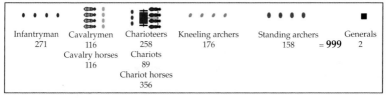

Infantryman	Cavalrymen	Charioteers	Kneeling archers	Standing archers	Generals
271	116	258	176	158	2
	Cavalry horses 116	Chariots 89		= **999**	
		Chariot horses 356			

Plate 7. Excavation of Pit Number 2 began in 1976. The first detachment, firing towards the east, consisted of two parallel rows of 30 standing archers (red) flanked on either side by two blocks of 48 standing archers (red). These protected 4 blocks of 40 kneeling archers and 4 blocks of 2 kneeling archers (green) to the rear.

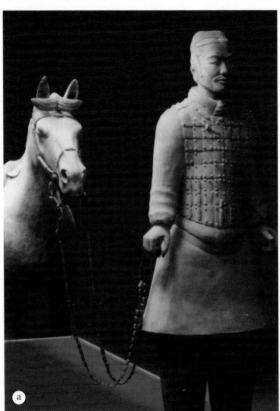

Cavalryman and Horse, Pit Number 2

Plate 8. (a) Terracotta cavalryman with saddled battle steed. The saddle was laid on top of a soft blanket and secured by a single girth. (b) Bridle arrangement of cavalry horse. (c) Terracotta cavalry horse (the tail of this one has become detached and is missing). The horse stands around 1.72 metres (5.64 feet) in height and 2.03 metres (6.6 feet) in length.

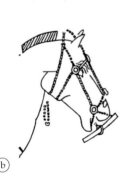

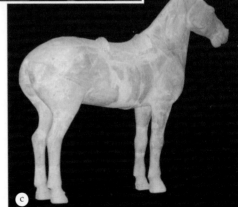

Pit Number 3

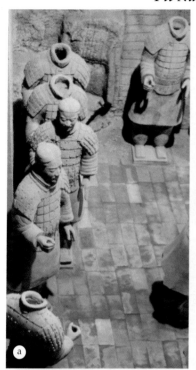

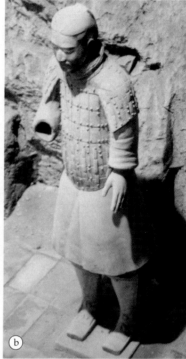

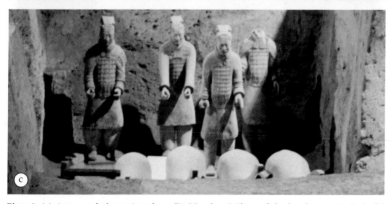

Plate 9. (a) Armour-clad warriors from Pit Number 3 (four of the heads are missing). (b) Detail of a warrior with a missing hand. Heads were made separately. Hands were fashioned separately, attached to the body and fired. (c) Charioteers and horses from Pit Number 3.

Infantry Armour and Weaponry

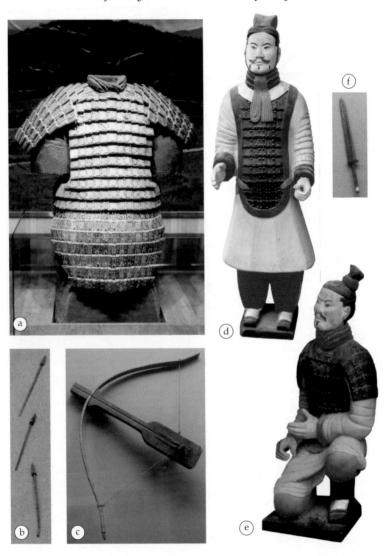

Plate 10. (a) Iron armour found buried near Pit Number 1. (b) Bronze crossbow bolts. (c) Wooden crossbow with bronze trigger mechanism. (d) Painted reconstruction of a standing infantryman and (e) a kneeling archer. (f) Bronze spearhead.

The Secrets in the Weave of Stela J of Copan

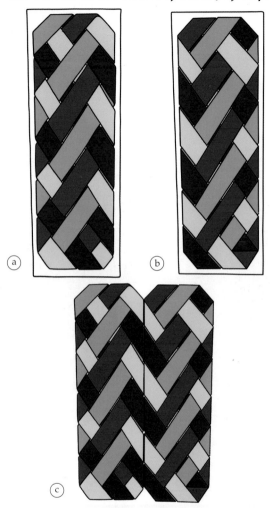

Plate 11. The absence of corners on Stela J, from Copan, like the absence of corners on the Amazing Lid of Palenque, suggests that secret information is encoded into the artefact (see Appendix 3). (a) Weave pattern on the front side of the carving, coloured for identification purposes. (b) Weave pattern on reverse side. (c) Front side hinged to back (see figures 54 and 55 for analysis). The literal translation of *The Popol Vuh*, the sacred book of the Maya, is *Book of the Mat*. Stela J hence explains that *Book of the Mat* refers to *the book (with the missing corners) that is encoded*. Hence, the Amazing Lid of Palenque is the *encoded book*, the *Book of the Mat*, *The Popol Vuh*.

Kneeling Archer

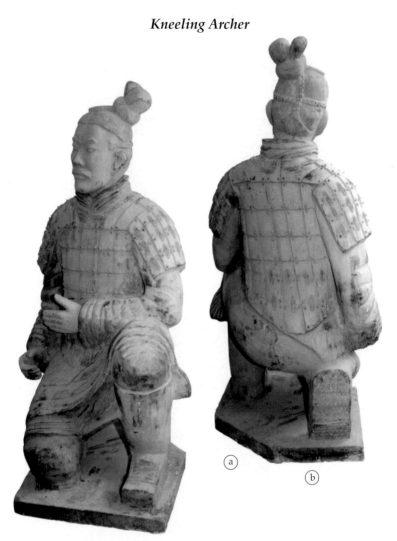

Plate 12. Kneeling terracotta archer from Pit Number 3. The archer was the first in the firing line and therefore the first of the soldiers that should be *looked at* (in accordance with the instructions revealed from analysis of the ten face shapes in Chapter 1). The first thing to note is that (a) the missing corner on the base. This tells us that, like the missing corners of Stela J from Copan and the Lid of Palenque, secret information is encoded into the artefact. The main text explains how information was encoded into: the face shapes, the hairstyles, the hands, the tunic dots and the battle formations in the trenches. (b) The underside of the foot reveals a tread pattern made of small (solar) circles.

Kneeling Archer (side views)

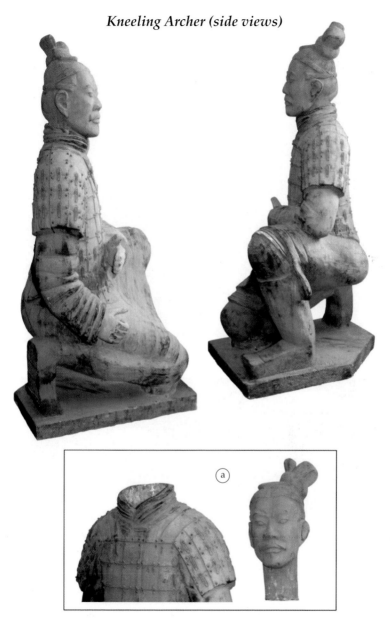

Plate 13. Kneeling archer, side views. (a) Detachable head shown separated from the body.

The Bronze Funerary Chariots and Horses

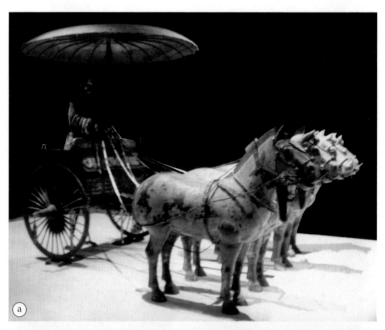

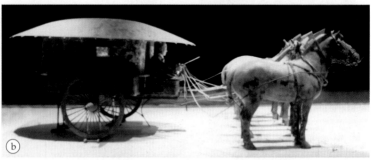

Plate 14. Two bronze chariots, each pulled by four bronze horses, were found buried 20 metres (65 feet) west of Shi Huangdi's mausoleum (see figure 2a). (a) The escort chariot carries a circular bronze (sun-shaped) umbrella canopy and is ridden by a standing bronze charioteer armed with a sword, a crossbow and a quiver of 66 bronze bolts. (b) The rear chariot has an enclosed rear coffin compartment with a door at the back and windows – one on either side of the carriage and one to the front – beneath a squared-circular bronze canopy. The driver is seated.

The Jade Burial Suit of Prince Liu Sheng

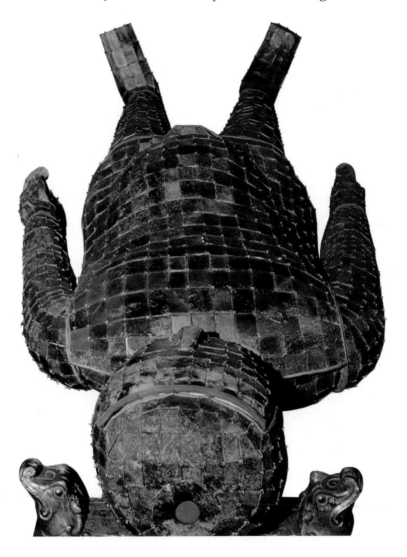

Plate 15. Jade burial suit of Prince Liu Sheng made from 2,690 pieces of green jade sewn together with gold thread. His bodily orifices were sealed with jade plugs (see figure 70). A bi (solar) disc on the top of his head allowed for the release of his soul.

The Jade Burial Suit of Princess Tou Wan

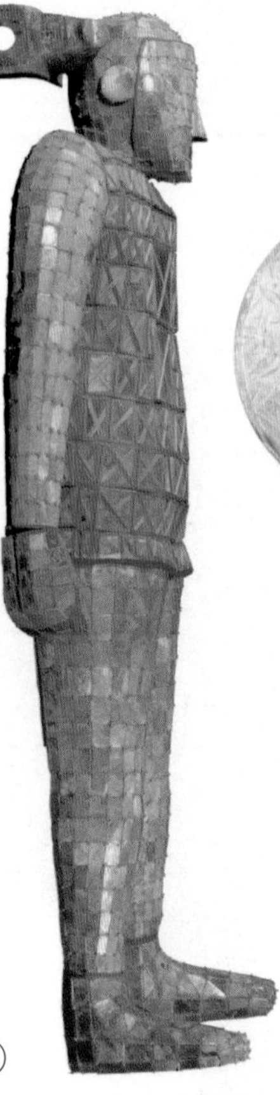

Burial Objects

Plate 16. (a) This 2,156-piece jade suit was stitched at the corners, like that of Prince Liu Sheng, except for the torso, which was made from differently sized pieces of jade strapped together by cross-shaped patterns of gold wire. The differences between the suits draws attention to the chest and back area, making them in some way special, inviting the observer to investigate the same areas (the dots on the armoured tunics of the terracotta warriors) more carefully – to reveal encoded information (*see main text*). (b) Astronomical jade bi discs, similar to those found in the tomb of Prince Liu Sheng, decorated with a granulated pattern. (c) A so-called tomb guardian, a terracotta anthropomorphic figure of a white man with a beard (c. AD 420–589) excavated from a tomb near Ankang. The serrated dorsal fin led to the decoding of the sun-shield of Monte Alban (figures A76–77), which carries a similar pattern.

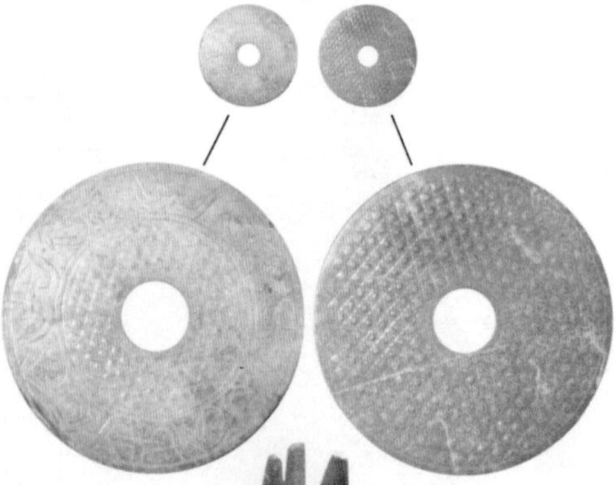

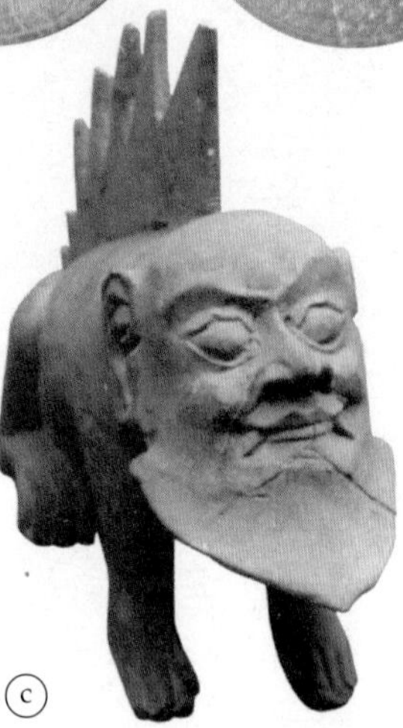

The Secret Sign of Vril

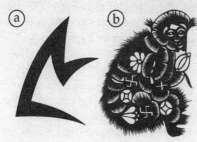

Figure 62. (a) Mark of the Vril Society used by the Nazis. Vril, a Tibetan word meaning the radiant energy of the sun, referred to angelic or godly energy – cherubs and seraphs etc. Compare this to (b), the Chinese paper-cut figure of the monkey eating a peach, the symbol of immortality. The pursuit of Vril by the Nazis was a quest for immortality through the control of the creative forces of the universe.

number, as we have seen, was 9 and had to complete 81 tasks (9 x 9) before entry into heaven. This means that the number of the first emperor, in the mercury, must have been 999.

Moreover, by burying their leader in a lake of mercury (9 x 9), the Chinese effectively sent their emperor straight to heaven. Correspondence again occurs here with the Egyptians. The Valley of the Kings is located between an uncharacteristic bend in the River Nile; its location is on a line taken by the virtual course of the Nile if the bend in the river did not exist. The Nile was regarded by the Egyptians as the Milky Way, in the heavens. Hence, by burying their beloved pharaohs in the Valley of the Kings, the Egyptians effectively buried their kings in the Milky Way, in the heavens.

Appendix 4 explains how ancient civilisations encoded their superknowledge into their treasures using numbers and pictures. The numbers themselves describe unchanging astronomical constants, such as the duration of sunspot cycles and precession (the slow backwards shift of the equinoctial points on the sun's path through the sky), spanning thousands of years into the future and the past, thus providing a common yardstick of measurement reference between inter-catastrophic epochs on earth.

It seems here, in the case of both thulium and mercury, that the ancients also used the nuclear constants contained in physical matter, the atomic weight of an element, to describe the same terms of reference and convey the same esoteric knowledge as did the Nazis. That this is so is confirmed by the fact that we live in a physical universe which is carbon-based. The carbon atom, not surprisingly, contains six protons (positive charges in the nucleus), six neutrons (that carry no known electrical charge) and six electrons (negative charges): 666, the mark of the beast, the physical universe. (The fact that the physical earth could be described in terms of 666 was the same conclusion that I reached in *The Tutankhamun Prophecies* and is explained again here in Appendix 3 (xv).)

The ancient Chinese must have been aware of the atomic number of thulium and aware of the physical similarities between thulium and mercury. In burying their leader in mercury, they further conveyed the message that they were aware of the atomic weight of mercury, the super-science of the sun and, additionally, the spiritual tenets of esotericism.

Study of the esoteric sciences could, occultists believed, lead to the activation of latent energies within the body (see also figure A30). Activation in turn would then allow access to techniques enabling the soul to leave the body at will to experience existence in other ethereal planes and other times (time travel). The power to manifest these energies was known in ancient Tibet as Vril, the activation of the god-like energy within.

No surprise that just after the war the Thulian Society in Germany was usurped by the Vril Society, who adopted the mark of Vril (figure 62). Vril was a Tibetan word which had an accompanying glyph meaning *chi*, life force or angelic vibration. Hence the pursuit of Vril was a quest to harness the creative power of the universe – God.

Placing the mark of Vril next to the picture of the paper-cut monkey, it becomes clear that the Vril mark is a stylised form of the monkey, suggesting that both derived from the same source.

Peter Moon, in *The Black Sun*, calls on Lord Bulwer-Lytton's view set down in *The Coming Race*. He describes the original progenitors of the human race as Vril-ya, who spoke the original language of Vril-ya:

> . . . a non-polluted language that suffered no amalgamation with other cultures. The language is based upon monosyllables which emanate from tonal vibrations.

Bulwer-Lytton offers Chinese as a splendid example of a language based on sound where certain sounds are repeated in different forms to give different meanings:

The idea is that the language of Vril-ya is much closer to describing original language, and the Chinese language is the best example of that in our current world.

We are here mindful that the first emperor was associated with the monkey, the monkey with the Tibetan mark of Vril, Vril with *chi* (the godly energy) and *chi* with Ch'in, the clan of the first emperor who spoke in a language similar to Vril-ya, the original language of divine beings. This correspondence, in turn, suggests that the first emperor of China was indeed a descendant of the original divine inhabitants of our planet, 'the Sons of Heaven' who understood the secret science of the sun and the higher orders of spirituality.

This account also explains, for the first time, the reason why the inside of Lord Pacal's sarcophagus was painted with red cinnabar, the powdered form of the liquid metal mercury. Like Shi Huangdi, his number was 81. It also explains why the pearl in the seashell, found at the foot of the stairs in the Temple of Inscriptions at Palenque (figure A71), is filled with cinnabar, the powdered form of mercury; referring to the fact that Lord Pacal was reborn as Venus (the white planet), the pearl in the heavens (in the mercury powder; 9 x 9).

The Secrets in the Hands

The deportment of the warriors suggests that they once carried weapons. But few weapons have been found. Archaeologists have thus assumed that the weapons must have been stolen when the tunnels were ransacked by the rebel leader Xiang Yu in around 206 BC. But this is by no means certain. The absence of the weapons may well, like the missing corners, refer to encoded information yet to be revealed (more on this later).

Careful examination of the hand shapes reveals that some soldiers have clenched fists, others have slightly opened fists, as though to carry a spear, and others have various combinations of extended fingers and thumbs or folded fingers and thumbs. Examination of the possibilities shows that a clenched fist depicts the number 'nothing'. A slightly open fist, where the thumb and index finger together form a circle, represents zero. Unfolding of the fingers, beginning with the thumb, then reveals the digits 1, 2, 3, 4, and 5. A flattened hand thus amounts to 5. This, in conjunction with a similar

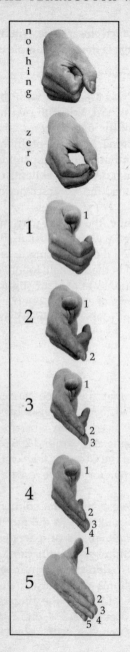

The Secrets in the Hands (I)

Figure 63. The shapes of the hands were fashioned (so archaeologists say) to accommodate the shapes of wooden-handled weapons ostensibly carried by the soldiers. However, closer inspection shows that the hand shapes contain a secret numerical code, as shown below.

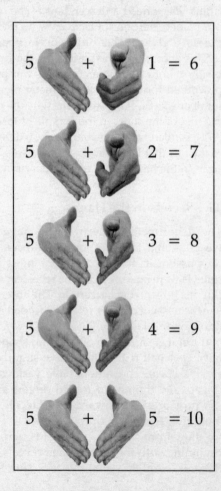

The Secrets in the Hands (II)
(Hand Variants)

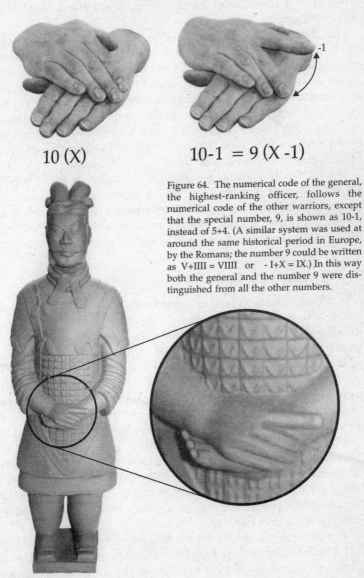

10 (X)   10-1 = 9 (X -1)

Figure 64. The numerical code of the general, the highest-ranking officer, follows the numerical code of the other warriors, except that the special number, 9, is shown as 10-1, instead of 5+4. (A similar system was used at around the same historical period in Europe, by the Romans; the number 9 could be written as V+IIII = VIIII or - I+X = IX.) In this way both the general and the number 9 were distinguished from all the other numbers.

137

algorithm applied to the left hand, yields digits 6 through 10, as shown in figure 63. This means that the kneeling archer's number is 6 (plate 12a), five on the left hand (5) plus the extended thumb (1) on the right hand.

That this must be so is confirmed by examination of the general's hands (figure 64), which adopt a variation on the rule. His hands are crossed, indicating the number 10, but one index finger is raised and points away from the hands. 10 minus 1 hence equals 9. The general, as the highest-ranking officer, was thus number 9. This departure from the convention in figure 63 is all the more remarkable when we consider that a similar (dualistic) system was in use at the same time by the Romans in Europe. The number 9 could be written as VIIII (5 plus 4) or as IX (minus 1, plus 10).

The archer thus kneels because his number 6 is lower than the general's higher number of 9, which explains why the archer is kneeling – but, referring to our earlier enquiry, does not explain why he shelters behind the unarmoured standing archer in Pit Number 2. This unanswered important question will be addressed again later.

The Secrets in the Tunic Dots

One of the first things to notice about the dots on the tunics is that they are all different combinations of the same possibilities. Ostensibly, the dots depict the heads of rivets used to keep the (iron, or alternatively leather) armour platelets in position. But surely there must be an optimum way of connecting a platelet to a tunic, one single best way, whether it be by using 1, 2, 3, 4, 5, 6, 7, 8 or 9 rivets. Clearly, there is an upper limit to the number of rivets that could possibly be used, constrained by the size of the rivet head and the available platelet area to which it will be stapled. But the warrior tunics do not adopt a stitching sequence that in any way could be seen as logical; some tunics, for example, have no rivets whatsoever. If platelets are capable of remaining fixed to tunics without the use of rivets, then why use rivets on other tunics at all? Given that rivets are not essential in attaching the platelets to the tunics, they must, therefore, have an entirely alternative function.

Dot patterns are used in the modern world by blind people (figure 65). The dots take up their position in a framework of cells within each platelet, in a similar way to the dots on the tunics of the terracotta

The Secrets in the Dots (I)
Braille (the Raised Dot Mnemonic Code of the Blind)

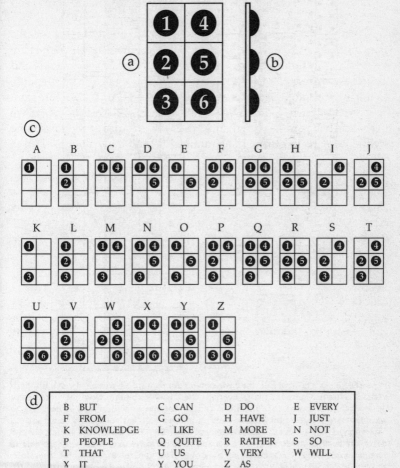

Figure 65. (a) Front view of Braille dot matrix showing the maximum number of squares occupied by the maximum number of dots. (b) Side view of Braille dot matrix showing raised relief of dots. (c) Combinations of dots used in Braille to represent letters of the alphabet. (d) Table showing how letters of the alphabet may also be used, in Braille, to represent whole words. (Single letters used in this way are called *Simple Upper Wordsigns*, *Simple* because they occupy only one cell, *Upper* because they have a dot on the top line, and *Wordsigns* because they are words.)

The Secrets in the Dots (II)

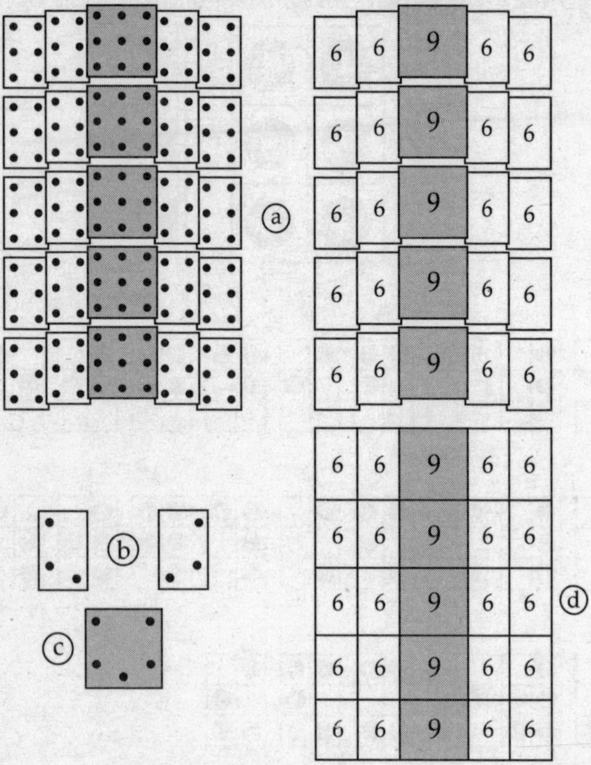

Figure 66. (a) As a general rule, the basic armour dot patterns are arranged vertically. Each vertical column of armour plates overlaps the adjacent column, from the front centre outwards. This means that the front central column is widest and hence able to accommodate a maximum of nine dots. Narrower adjacent columns accommodate a maximum of only six dots. This arrangement also means that the central vertical column down the back of the tunic is (as a general rule) narrower and likewise hence able to accommodate only a maximum of six dots. The general arrangement, therefore, accommodates vertical groups of either 66666 or 99999 down the centre front. Clearly, variations in the patterns depend on the number of combinations of dots. There are 720 possible combinations of a 6-dot pattern and 362,880 possible combinations of a 9-dot pattern. In addition, horizontal misalignment of dots produces more combinations (although exceptions to the general rule appear infrequently). (b) In this example the *horizontal alignment* of dots varies in the narrow columns. Where this occurs, the wider central column appears to synthesise the two mirror-image dot patterns, producing the resulting composite pattern (c). Variants, clearly, greatly increase the number of combination possibilities. Higher horizontal rows of plates also overlap lower horizontal rows to produce a final matrix as shown in (d).

The Secrets in the Dots (III)
The Quipu of Peru and the Tunic Dots of the Warriors

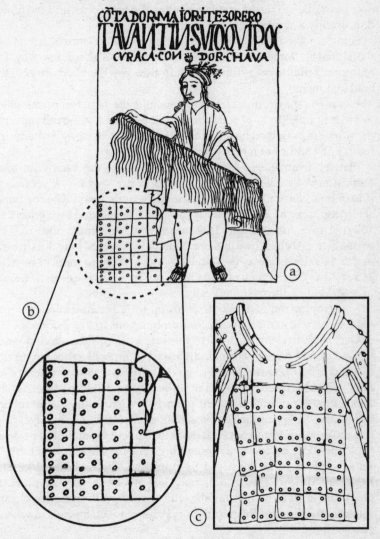

Figure 67. (a) Sixteenth-century drawing by Guamán Poma de Ayala showing the quipu of the Inca. (b) Detail of quipu nomenclature. (c) Tunic of a terracotta warrior showing the ostensible rivets fastening armour to breastplates.

warriors. Each cell in Braille is assigned a cell reference number, digitally delineating each of the various combination possibilities. The dots in Braille are raised in relief just like the tunic dots, and the tunic dots occupy a similar cell matrix.

Some combinations of Braille dots represent individual letters of the alphabet. Some words are also adapted, in a shorthand way, to represent actual words (figure 65d). In this way the blind are able to read by touch.

Figure 66a shows tunic platelets containing the *maximum* permissible number of dots (from observation of the warriors), although none of the warriors examined has been found to contain so many; patterns in figures 66b and c are more typical).

Platelet arrangement begins in the centre of the back with one vertical row. Platelets are then attached to the lowest row on either side of this. Naturally, the last platelet to be added would be the front centre top, after all the horizontal rows have been fitted to overlap the adjacent row and column. This means that the centre front row is wider than all other rows and can contain as many as nine dots, if cell matrix position is always maintained. The maximum number of cells in a fixed-cell arrangement must therefore be either the esoteric 66666 or 99999, down the front vertically.

Rearranging the patterns produces up to 720 combinations from a 6-dot pattern or as many as 362,880 combinations from a 9-dot pattern.

Occasionally, the cell matrix framework is abandoned and instead out-of-line dots form individual patterns, like those in figure 66b and c. In this case – and it seems that this is a general rule where dots are misplaced from cells – the centre front platelet is an amalgamation of each adjacent pattern, a mirror image. Clearly, in these cases the combination possibilities are infinitely massive, just like the number of accents of dialects in a given population. The dots must therefore be *telling* us something. The message in its simplest sense appears to be conveyed by numbers. The numbers, like the Peruvian quipu (figure 67), may simply be a way of storing quantifiable data, which for the quipu concerned numbers representing quantities of the population, bales of wool, bushels of wheat etc.

To definitively determine the meaning of the dot codes would entail examination of every single tunic. No doubt if every dot pattern of every soldier were entered into a computer database, the message encoded in the dot patterns would be revealed, but such an investigation is beyond the resource of a single individual. Suffice to say, the tunics, like the pits, the hairstyles and the hands, reveal the numbers 666 and 999 and, additionally, must contain further information.

The Bronze Horses and Chariots

Two teams of magnificent bronze horses and chariots (plate 14) were excavated 20 metres (65 feet) west of the pyramid in 1980, although the vehicles might better be described as carriages rather than chariots. They were certainly not for use in battle. The two-thirds (.666) life-size teams were replicas of those used by Shi Huangdi on his frequent sojourns around the country searching for the elixir of immortality. When found, the horses and carriages were all facing west towards the setting sun. They are haltered in silver and gold and carry a silver bit between the teeth. Some fellow British travellers at Xian, who own horses and therefore understand equine tack, pointed out – when I asked about the authenticity of the replicas – that the horses could not possibly have coped with the bit between their teeth (as they were shown) for long. The distressed expressions on the horses' faces were probably due to the ill-fitting bits that would not normally have been used on horses with 'wolf teeth', those late-developing teeth at the front of the mouth usually extracted from modern horses destined to carry a bit. Their view was that a horse could survive only a single journey wearing such a bit before suffering great pain.

A twenty-two-spoked circular bronze umbrella-style canopy covers the smaller carriage. A standing driver, armed with a sword, two bronze shields, a crossbow and a quiver containing sixty-six bronze arrows, grips the reins between his delicate fingers. The mark of 'battalion number nine' (out of twenty) is written on his headgear.

The attention to detail on the carriage and driver is remarkable. This team precedes the other in the burial pit. The rectangular carriage measures 1.26 metres (4.1 feet) wide and 0.70 metres (2.3 feet) long.

A single axle supports two thirty-spoked wheels. The number of radiating spokes in the bronze umbrella-canopy (22) multiplied by the number of spokes in the wheel (30) amounts to 660, not quite reaching the esoteric number 666. Could this be a mistake? We can check by working backwards from the desired answer; the esoteric number we would expect to find (666) divided by 22 (the number of spokes on the

The Squared Circle and the Sunspot Cycle

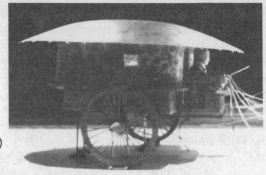

(a)

Figure 68. (a) The squared-circular spoked canopy of the bronze funerary chariot. The 33 spokes describe the path of the earth around the sun (see main text). (b) The Amazing Lid of Palenque's sub-transformer also reveals that the 'squared circle' shape represents the sun (see figure A74). Here the 20 spokes (18 spokes + 4 half (narrow) spokes) represent the 20 sunspot cycles that subsist within one solar neutral sheet reversal period of 1,366,040 days.

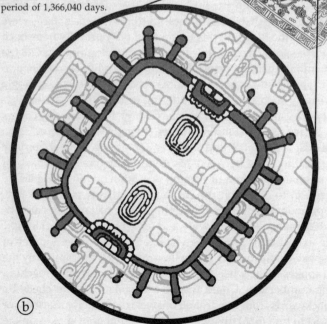

(b)

144

umbrella-canopy) amounts to 30.2727. But it is not possible to have 0.2727ths of a spoke in the canopy. We might be tempted to settle the argument by saying that 22 is the closet *whole* number to the right answer. But this is not how the ancients worked. The ancients did not make mistakes, and everything was done for a reason. This means that they deliberately intended to emphasise the remainder, 0.2727, which happens to be 1 divided by 3.66. The numbers 3.66 *are* astronomically significant; there are 366 days in one solar leap year (the earth takes 366 days to make one such revolution around the sun). No other whole number would describe the same event. The 22-spoke circular bronze umbrella is hence a metaphor to describe the radiating sun.

The second carriage has a fully enclosed rear compartment with a door at the back and windows on either side and one to the front, beneath a squared-circular bronze canopy. The carriage, capable of carrying a coffin, measures 3.17 metres (10.4 feet) long and 1.06 metres (3.47 feet) high. Like the first, it has a single axle with two thirty-spoked wheels. The seated driver wears a robe and a hat and carries a sword at the waist. The bronze roof on this one (like the seated driver) has descended on to the carriage itself, an allegory suggesting that the sun has set and the emperor has died.

This canopy has 33 spokes; 33 multiplied by the number of spokes in the wheel (30) amounts to only 990. Here we encounter the same problem as we did earlier, and not surprisingly we come up with the same solution: the desired esoteric number 999, divided by 33 (the number of spokes in the canopy) amounts to 30.2727. As before, for the number to be esoterically significant, the canopy would require 30.2727 spokes which, as before, is not possible. Again, this tells us that the squared-circular bronze canopy likewise represents a model of the sun, this time a sun that has gone down, set.

Esotericists believe that the squared circle symbolises the holy spirit, God, incarnate on earth, the soul (the sun or the circle) inside a body (the earth) which the Chinese represented as a square.

That the shape does represent the sun is confirmed by one of the decoded stories from the Amazing Lid of Palenque. The particular picture is unusual in that it can be seen only using a *second derivative* decoding process. This simply means that the Amazing Lid of Palenque firstly needs to be sliced, as shown in figure A74. As before, a mirror image is taken. This time the two pieces are buttressed together as shown, rather than overlaid. This produces another new abridged version of the Lid of Palenque, a *Sub-Transformer*.

Figure 68 shows the squared circle from the centre of the Sub-Transformer. This one, though, has only 20 spokes (18 full-size spokes and 4 half-width spokes, a total of 20), unlike the chariot that carries 33. But these also represent the sun, in a different way: the 20 sunspot cycles that subsist during one solar neutral sheet reversal period (1,366,040 days). This composite picture is obtained by rotating each transparency by 1.36 degrees. This confirms that the canopy of the bronze funerary chariot (plate 14) hence represents the sun.

Further analysis confirms interpretation of the information; a composite picture is present at the same time as the squared circle (figure A75a). This shows Xolotol ('shol-o-tol') the blind dog, carrying bones in his teeth. Xolotol was the Mayan name for the god that represented Venus in the evening (Venus as the evening star). Legend says that Xolotol cried so much that his eyes fell from their sockets. Because he was blind he was chosen to accompany Quetzalcoatl into the underworld, the place of darkness, to collect the bones to make mankind in the fifth and final age of the sun. This depiction shows Xolotol with tears falling from his eyes carrying bones in his teeth. Either side of his face a small face confirms that Xolotol is indeed a *twin*, one of the emanations of Venus. The god of ice, Venus in the morning, appears at the bottom of the composite with an ice dagger on each cheek. The daggers refer to ice crystals that form in the morning – hence the association with the morning star. Again, twins flank the god of ice, confirming interpretation of the picture.

Astronomically, Venus appears either as the morning or evening star, relative to the sun, which is in the centre. The squared circle therefore *must* represent the sun. Here, the squared circle becomes the face of Viracocha of Tiahuanaco (figure A75b), who holds a bird in each hand, confirming that the bas-relief carving of Viracocha, from the Gateway of the Sun (figure A76c and d) at Tiahuanaco, likewise depicts the sun – i.e. Viracocha *is* the sun (see also Appendix 5).

The engineering of this bronze chariot is again of the highest order. Spokes in the wheels are a perfect precision interference-fit with the pre-heated hub, eliminating the need for additional fastening. Both teams of horses and carriages are painted with sky-blue paint (faded to light grey) showing cloud patterns, one-legged dragons known as Kui and phoenix birds.

Shi Huangdi was reported to have made five nationwide tours during his reign. His retinue was said to consist of 81 sets of chariots and horses with the emperor's own chariot at the centre.

To be sure, the allegorical significance of the bronze horses and carriages is clear: they were intended to be used for a single journey only (inferred from the badly fitting bit between the wolf teeth), the most important journey Shi Huangdi would ever make. When he died they carried him through the clouds (hence the cloud patterns painted on the horses and carriages) to the sun, to become the centre of the heavens (81, 9 x 9).

If we recall, the names of 80 workmen were engraved on the weapons of the terracotta warriors, and Shi Huangdi was number 81 (9 x 9). And he was buried in mercury, the atomic weight of which is 80; he was number 81 (9 x 9) in the mercury. Moreover, the circular canopy of the leading carriage, which is high in the sky, is replaced by the squared-circular canopy of the second carriage. In this way the circle is squared, an esoteric metaphor that implies that the sun becomes the earth, that a spiritual teacher takes on the body, implying that Shi Huangdi was a Son of Heaven on earth. Shi Huangdi was a Supergod who came to teach us the story of the sun and God.

CHAPTER FIVE

The Battlefield of Xian

The Lost Tombs of Liu Sheng and Tou Wan

The brief reign of Er Shi brought to an end the rule of the Ch'in in 207 BC. The vision of Shi Huangdi and his sweeping reforms had created the greatest nation on earth. The introduction of a common written language and common systems of currency, weights and measures brought accelerated growth through economies of scale and comparative advantage. Organised labour, diverted to capital projects like the Great Wall, brought safety to the peasant farmers. Construction of the great canals brought improved irrigation as well as a nationwide transportation system. China had successfully negotiated its own infancy; it had learned to talk, to walk and to measure. But in so doing the Ch'in dynasty had exhausted itself. It had grown up, matured and decayed within the development phase of the new great nation.

Er Shi was succeeded by Gaodi, of the Western Han dynasty. Huidi succeeded Gaodi and then came Lu Hou, who was followed by Wendi and his son Wudi (141–87 BC). On accession he bestowed on his elder brother, Liu Sheng, governance of the kingdom of Chung-shan in the north-east, where he ruled with his wife, Princess Tou Wan, for almost forty years until his death in 113 BC. This practice of enfeoffment was common at the time and recorded by Ssu-ma Ch'ien:

All the sons of the Emperor Ching by his five concubines were

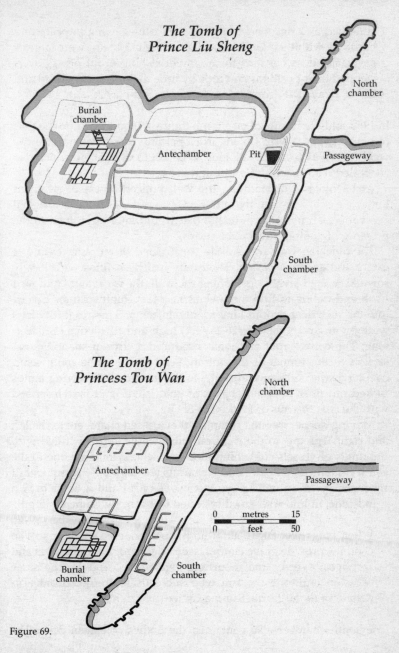

The Tomb of Prince Liu Sheng

Burial chamber

North chamber

Antechamber

Pit

Passageway

South chamber

The Tomb of Princess Tou Wan

North chamber

Antechamber

Passageway

Burial chamber

South chamber

| 0 | metres | 15 |
| 0 | feet | 50 |

Figure 69.

149

enfeoffed as kings. Some fulfilled their duties living in peace and harmony with their kind and, whether their domains were large or small, acted as bastions to the imperial house. But others overstepped their positions and little by little their power declined and faded away (*The Records of the Historian*, Ssu-ma Ch'ien).

In 1968 soldiers stumbled on a tomb (figure 69) quarried into the hills of Lingshan, near Man Ch'eng in Hopei province. The entranceway was blocked by a stone wall, long since lost to vegetation, which had concealed it so successfully through the ages.

Archaeologists dismantling the wall noticed layers of stratified limestone debris around the entranceway, workings from the original excavation left by tomb builders, that would later alert them to the presence of another royal tomb nearby.

The blocking wall was solidly constructed of an outer casing, a cavity and an inner casing. The cavity had been filled with locally smelted molten lava. Demolishing the wall, the excavators removed earth and debris to find themselves in a long high corridor carved into the rock deep within Ling Mountain, some 8 metres (26.25 feet) wide by around 8 metres (26.25 feet) high and 51 metres (171 feet) long. The convex roof and walls produced a circular-shaped cross-section to the tunnel at the entrance-end that became more semi-circular as the corridor widened. On the floor, their flickering lamps picked out lines of small objects of gold, silver and jade inscribed with the coat of arms of Prince Liu Sheng.

Moving deeper into the complex, they passed chambers to the left and right. The one to the right ran northwards and was filled with hundreds of vessels containing food and wine, while the one to the south contained 16 horses and 6 chariots (16 x 6 = 96, the number of magnetic cycles in one 187-year sunspot cycle) and a horse-drawn grindstone, in line with an edict issued in 148 BC by Emperor Jingdi:

> When kings die, an imperial household grandee shall be sent to condole, provide grave clothes, sacrificial food, funeral horses and carriages, oversee the mourning ceremonies, and on the same occasion enthrone the son who succeeds to the kingdom (*The Records of the Historian*, Ssu-ma Ch'ien).

The south chamber also contained the bodies of eleven dogs. The

Chinese had their own view of the underworld that was said to consist of ten levels (ten hells), each of which was governed by a king who specialised in the punishment of specific sins. These fell within the jurisdiction of the Jade Emperor, who in turn delegated duties to the Emperor of the Eastern Peak on earth.

It was the job of the king of the first hell to sort the bad souls from the very bad souls as they arrived. Good deeds were weighed against bad ones, and those with a positive deed account were returned to earth immediately for another try at purification (earth being the eleventh hell). The rest were sent on to the other nine hells for punishment before rebirth on earth. The king in the tenth hell had to decide whether rebirth on earth would be in animal or human form and on the degree of happiness that the soul could expect in the next life, which depended on the amount of accumulated karma from the past lives. The soul was then made to drink a special broth, to wipe out all memory of past lives, before it was cast into a red river that carried it back to earth. This ancient belief might explain away the *number* of dogs (eleven) that were found in the south chamber but not the *presence* of the dogs (as against cats or birds etc.).

Dogs accompanied the dead in tombs both in Egypt and South and Central America. Mexicans believed that the underworld consisted of nine separate levels, each of which had to be successfully negotiated before moving on to the next. The first level consisted of a swift-flowing river. The deceased would hold on to a dog that would carry its master across the river who could then progress on the journey to the next level. The significance of both the *quantity* and *presence* of dogs in the south chamber suggest that the Chinese may have shared similar beliefs: 11 x 9 = 99 (the number of heaven and the Supergods).

Just beyond the north and south chambers archaeologists took care not to fall into the booby-trapped pit that was once covered in fibre matting. Hugging the walls, they continued westerly until they arrived in a massive chamber measuring around 15.24 metres (50 feet) long, 12.2 metres (40 feet) wide and 7.62 metres (25 feet) high. The floor was littered with all kinds of treasures, including bronze urns and bowls, lacquerware and ceramics. The chamber had once been curtained, the walls timber panelled and the roof lined with tiles. It was divided into several levels and smaller chambers. At the far end, straight ahead above a platform, a wall made of massive stone blocks had been sealed with molten iron. This had to be the burial chamber of the enigmatic prince, Liu Sheng.

With the wall removed, the crypt revealed its secrets. Inscriptions on many of the treasures bore the name of the royal household, 'Chung-shan nei fu . . .', referring to the kingdom of Chung-shan, south-west of Beijing, that had a population of 600,000. Other inscriptions revealed that:

On 27 July 154 [BC] the Emperor Ching decreed that his imperial sons Liu Tuan be established as king of Chiao-hsi and Liu Sheng as king of Chung-shan and granted to the common people one step in noble rank.

On the floor of the sarcophagus they found a bronze incense burner fashioned to represent clouds swirling around mountain peaks, thought to represent those of the fabled Mount Tai in Taishan, the stopping-off place for the soul before it progressed to the ten hells. Round the top of the burner, tigers and stags look out from behind the five fabled peaks of the mountain.

Before his death, Shi Huangdi built the magnificent Erpang palace south of the Wei River, which, for the Chinese, represented the Milky Way in the sky. The palace was laid out to reflect the star patterns in the sky, and the main reception hall faced south towards Chung-nan shan mountain. The belief was that a trap door at the top of the mountain led to the heavenly apex star. One day the emperor would pass through the trap door at the top of the mountain, pass through Taishan and on to the land of immortals. A 40.2-kilometre (28-mile) covered walkway connected the palace to the foot of the mountain to accommodate the emperor on his final journey.

A bronze wine vessel inlaid with gold and silver dragons, a collection of knives and swords and two magnificent seated golden leopards sporting black spots (like the dark spots on the golden face of the sun – sunspots) were all found on the floor. In all, more than 2,800 objects were discovered, including gilt-bronze mirrors, silks and jade pieces. In the centre of the sarcophagus lay a lacquered coffin containing the collapsed jade suit of the king.

If we are to believe the historical documents, Liu Sheng was not the most popular of Jingdi's thirteen sons:

Liu Sheng loved to drink and was very fond of women so that, with all his offspring and their families, his household numbered 120 persons. He was always criticising his elder brother, the king of Chiao-hsi, saying: 'Although my brother is king, he spends all his time doing the work of clerks and officials. A true king should pass his days listening to music and delighting himself with beautiful sights and sounds.' His brother replied: 'The king of Chung-shan fritters away his days in sensual gratification instead of assisting the Son of Heaven to bring order to the common people. How can someone like that be called bastion of the throne?' (*The Records of the Historian*, Ssu-ma Ch'ien).

But the fact that he was buried in a jade suit bestowed on him not only the status of a member of the royal household but also that of a Son of Heaven.

More than forty jade suits have been found in royal tombs, giving rise, together with the historical documents, to the belief that Shi Huangdi would almost certainly have been buried in one.

Various accounts are given in regard to the construction of the suits (figure 70). One says that the suit 'contains 2,498 small plaques pierced at the four corners' (*Mysteries of Ancient China*, edited by Jessica Rawson), but this cannot possibly be the case, given that, for example, the piece of jade at the top of the head (plate 15) is circular and hence does not have corners. Moreover, other pieces, notably in the hands and feet, are triangularly shaped with only three corners. In *New Treasures of the Past*, Brian Fagan quotes 2,160 pieces. In *Princes of Jade* (by Edmund Capon and William MacQuitty) Edmund Capon cites a figure of 2,690. Brian Fagan's account does mention that each of the jade pieces was numbered by the artisans who manufactured the suit, which means that his number *should* be the right one, although, having said that, he might be confusing the number of pieces with that of the jade suit of Princess Tou Wan (discussed later), which MacQuitty says has 2,156 pieces. In any case, the number of pieces, and the number of microscopic holes drilled into the pieces, will, without doubt, be of numerological significance in the esoteric sense, although what these figures will turn out to be remains to be seen.

The suit measures 1.88 metres (6.16 feet) long and the individual pieces vary in size from between 1.5 by 1 centimetres (0.59 by 0. 39 inches) up to 4.5 by 3.5 centimetres (1.77 by 1.38 inches). The circular

*The Secret Codes of
Prince Liu Sheng's
Burial Suit (c. 141 BC)*

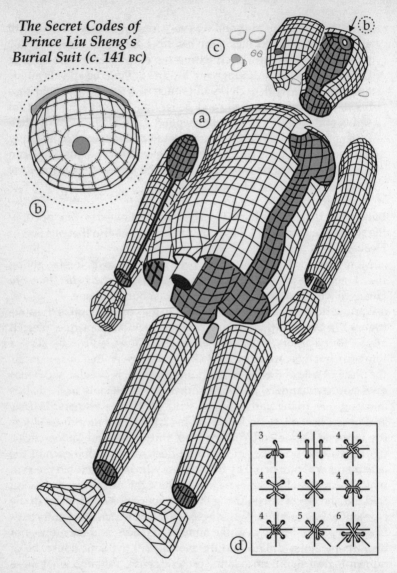

Figure 70.   (a) The twelve sections of the jade suit. (b) Top of the head of the jade suit showing circular disc (360 degrees). (c) Jade body plugs: eye covers, nose plugs, ear plugs, mouth plug and *(pelvic area, lower suit)* anal plug and genital cylindrical cap cover. (d) Nine types of knots, distributed between four configurations of holes (3, 4, 5, 6) made from gold thread, were used to stitch the jade pieces together (3 x 4 x 5 x 6 = 360).

disc at the top of the head allowed for the escape of the soul, the *chi* energy, also known as *hun*. That this is so is confirmed from figure A71, one of the pictures from Lord Pacal's decoded Amazing Lid of Palenque, which shows the soul of Lord Pacal leaving his body through a hole in the top of the head, carried away in the tail feathers of the rising quetzal bird. The circular bi disc thus represents rebirth, the process of spiritual rebirth at death. The bodily orifices – ears, nose, mouth and anus – were plugged with pieces of jade, and a jade cap sealed the genitals to prevent the soul leaving from those parts of the body. Several jade bi discs decorated with dragons were placed by the side of the prince in his sarcophagus.

Ideas of what remains after physical death of the body changed over time. The oldest beliefs refer to the existence of two souls, the *hun* and the *po*. On physical death the *hun* (light), the inner spark that gives life, leaves the body through a hole in the top of the head and travels to heaven (the stars) as *shen*. The body-soul, *po*, animates the body when alive and stays with the body for as long as three years, according to Taoist belief, providing the correct funerary offerings are made at the time of burial; otherwise it turns into a *gui*, a malevolent ghost. Hence, the orifices were plugged with jade to keep the *po* in the body for as long as possible and thus postpone any conversion to ghost.

It was this belief that inspired relatives of the deceased to provide lavish burials where tombs were furnished with all kinds of offerings.

After the three-year period the *po* moved on to purgatory, the place where sins are purged.

Although the stars were seen as the final resting place for good souls, there were also two halfway paradises for earthly souls. These were Mount Kun Lun in Turkestan to the west, home of the everlasting jade, the substance that was believed to confer immortality when consumed, and the mythical Isles of Penglai, off the east coast. These islands were reputedly inhabited by immortals whose good actions had earned them a period in paradise before rebirth on earth or prior to progression to a higher state of existence.

Ssu-ma Ch'ien, in his *Historical Records*, names three islands of Penglai: Penglai, Fang Chang and Ying Chou, in the Gulf of Chihli. Accounts say that beyond these lie as many as five or ten mythical islands of Penglai which are difficult, if not impossible, to reach. Legends say that boats approaching the mythical islands are driven away by strong offshore winds. Other stories say that the mythical islands disappear into luminous cloud whenever mariners sight them.

A few years ago a tourist filming out to sea from the Penglai Pagoda, a tourist attraction on the north-east coast of China, captured a line of mushroom-shaped mountains shimmering on the horizon. The islands were in fact mirages, illusions caused by refraction of light from layers of air. The film and sightings have persuaded some scholars that belief in the mythical mountains must have arisen from the same phenomenon in antiquity.

Some accounts say that several heroes did overcome all the obstacles to reach the islands successfully and returned to tell the tales of their discoveries: palaces of gold and silver; white men and women; white beasts and birds that ate the herb of life and drank from the fountain of life; of the great mountains of jade which spewed forth magic streams of heavenly water, which when mixed with the 'fungus of immortality' that grew nearby, produced an elixir that when consumed, conferred everlasting life.

It was on one such expedition, searching for the elixir of immortality, that Shi Huangdi took ill and died.

The 666 of Prince Liu Sheng

The nine types of knot, used to tie the thousands of jade pieces together, were made from 1.1 kilogrammes (3.3 pounds) of gold wire, some of which was made from twelve individual strands of thread. These stitched together (figure 70d) either three, four, five or six pieces of jade at a time; there are six variations of the four-hole knot, one example of a three-hole knot, one example of a five-hole knot, and one example of a six-hole knot.

In regard to the three- and five-hole varieties: 3 divided by 5 = 0.6; alternatively, 3 x 5 = 15 (and 1 + 5 = 6). In this way the nine knots contain the esoteric number 666. Or, put another way, the number 666 is contained in the 9 (figure 71). There had to be a reason for the elaborate bindings.

Examination of the top of Liu Sheng's suit (figure 70b) shows a complex arrangement of platelets, the lines of which correspond to the schematic of the solar wind impinging on the earth's magnetosphere (figure 72). (A similar depiction can be found encoded into the design of the scarab brooch worn by Tutankhamun between the

The Secrets in the Knots of Prince Liu Sheng's Jade Suit

type of knot	number of holes		
1st	4 holes		
2nd	4 holes		
3rd	4 holes		
4th	4 holes	$}$	$} = 6$
5th	4 holes		
6th	4 holes		
7th	6 holes		$= 6$
8th	3 holes	$3 \div 5 =$	$.6$
9th	5 holes	or $3 \times 5 = 15\,(1 + 5 = 6)$	or $} = 6$

Figure 71. The nine types of knot, shown in figure 70d, consist of three-, four-, five- and six-hole types; six of the four-hole type, one of the three-hole type, one of the five-hole type and one of the six-hole type. (The three- and five-hole types are the odd ones out – they do not include the number six). However, simple manipulation of the numbers 3 and 5 produce the number 6, as shown. In this way the number 9 (nine types of knot) is transformed into the number 666.

bandages of his mummy; figure A56.) Hence the higher esoteric teachings and the super science of the sun were deliberately encoded into the jade burial suit of Liu Sheng. If the design of Shi Huangdi's suit follows the same pattern, then he, too, will have taken his secrets to his sarcophagus before his soul journeyed through the bi to Mount Tai in the heavens, land of the leopards (with their sunspots), the dragons and the stag.

Liu Sheng's head rested on a jade and gilt-bronze headrest that carried at each end a dragon's head – the insignia of the emperor – suggesting that heavenly ordained status had been conferred on the prince.

Less has been reported on the tomb of Princess Tou Wan found around 200 metres (656 feet) north of Liu Sheng's. Its layout (figure 69) is similar to that of his, except that the central procession was clear of the booby-trapped pit, and the burial chamber was orientated in a different direction, cut at right angles to the antechamber.

Like the prince's tomb, hers was stocked with all kinds of treasures – bronze, ceramics and jade – and she, too, was clothed in a jade suit (plate 16a).

Her suit differed from Liu Sheng's in several ways: the jade contained more iron and was hence more yellow than green; the lines of the platelets on the head followed concentric circles, unlike those of Liu Sheng which proposed the schematic of the solar wind; and her head rested on a jade headrest which was not decorated with dragons.

The most apparent difference in the design of the two suits is in the method of attachment of the jade pieces of the torso, which are *strapped* together with crossed loops of gold wire, not tied together through holes drilled in each piece. This distinguishing feature must have been included for a reason. Comparing the torsos of the two draws attention to the method of binding of the chest plates and also brings to mind the method used to attach the platelets on the tunics of the terracotta warriors. That, to the mindful enquirer, in turn draws attention to the rivets (tunic dots) of the terracotta warriors, inviting closer examination of the meaning of the dot patterns on the terracotta warriors.

Several simple circular jade bi discs, placed near the body, resembled those in Liu Sheng's tomb, except that they were not decorated with dragons.

It seems that the princess was not a Son of Heaven, because the dragons were absent from her headrest and the bi discs. Moreover, the absence of the solar wind pattern on the headgear suggests that she did not teach the super-science of the sun.

Plate 16c shows a terracotta anthropomorphic figure, part white man with a beard and part dragon, dating from between AD 420 and 589 from a tomb near Ankang (today kept in the Xian museum, not far from the magic square discussed in Chapter 4, which dates from the same period). Earlier, we saw how the magic square was an essential part of Chinese belief at the time the terracotta soldiers were made. The white man with the beard could well have likewise been enshrined in Chinese folklore at the same time. This figure wears an unusually shaped serrated dorsal fin, similar to one featured in the sun-shield of Monte Alban (figure A57d), down his back.

Further analysis of the sawtooth mark shows the shield is actually

The Secrets in the Headgear of Prince Liu Sheng

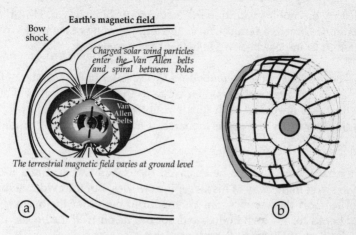

Figure 72. (a) The schematic of the earth's magnetosphere (from figure A3v), compressed on the sunward side by the solar wind, corresponds with (b) lines on the head of the jade suit, created by intersections between the jade platelets. The same scenario was encoded into the design of the scarab brooch of Tutankhamun (figure A56).

another Maya Transformer. The secret pictures obtained from decoding the sun-shield reveal (figure A76): a picture of the Gateway of the Sun, at Tiahuanaco, Bolivia, reflected in the waters of Lake Titicaca; the face of Lord Pacal regurgitating a pearl (figure A77a) and the face of Viracocha (figure A77b) and several other pictures not shown here.

Lord Pacal, the Viracochas and Tutankhamun were all known as the 'white man with a beard'. A jade figurine of a white man with a beard was found in the tomb of Lord Pacal at Palenque (figure A33h). A carving at Tiahuanaco, Bolivia, shows Viracocha as the white man with a beard (figure A68; the larger statue). Tutankhamun wears a beard made from the body of a snake which terminates in the tail feathers of a bird. Lord Pacal was also known as the feathered snake, the dragon, as was Viracocha of Tiahuanaco and Tutankhamun. These links offer further remarkable correspondence between the cultures of China, Mexico, Egypt and Peru.

The Legacy of Shi Huangdi

History has not been kind to the memory of Shi Huangdi. Historians denounce him as a tyrant who ordered the burning of the books in an attempt to impose his own beliefs on the population:

> The burning of the ancient books by the order of the founder of the Ch'in dynasty is always referred to as the greatest disaster which they sustained and with this is coupled the slaughter of many of the literati by the same monarch (*Chinese Classics*, Vol. I, James Legge).

Other accounts say that he enslaved thousands and executed those who stood in the way of his sweeping reforms. But the evidence does not support those views. Shi Huangdi did not order the burning of the books for his own kudos, and nor did he burn *all* the books.

The Book of Historical Records says this:

> In his thirty-fourth year [the twenty-first year, that is, after he had ascended the throne of the Ch'in as king – it was only the twelfth year of his reign as Emperor] the emperor, returning from a visit to the south, which had extended as far as Yueh, gave a feast in his palace at Hsien-yang, when the great scholars, amounting to seventy men, appeared and wished him long life. One of the principal ministers, Chau Ch'ing-ch'an, came forward and said: 'Formerly the state of Ch'in was only 1,000 li in extent, but Your Majesty, by your spirit-like efficacy and intelligent wisdom, has tranquillised and settled the whole empire and driven away all the barbarous tribes, so that wherever the sun and moon shine, all rulers appear before you as guests acknowledging subjugation. You have formed the states of the various princes into provinces and districts where the people enjoy a happy tranquillity, suffering no more from the calamities of war and contention. This condition of things will be transmitted for 10,000 generations. From the highest antiquity there has been no one in awful virtue like Your Majesty.'
>
> The emperor was pleased with this flattery. Then Shun-yu Yueh, one of the great scholars, a native of Ch'i, advanced and said: 'The sovereigns of Yin and Chau, for more than 1,000 years, invested their sons and younger brothers, and meritorious ministers, with

domains and rule and could thus depend on them for support and aid – that I have heard. But now Your Majesty is in possession of all within the seas, and your sons and younger brothers are nothing but private individuals. The issue will be that someone will arise to play the part of T'ien Ch'ang, or of the six nobles of Tsin. Without the support of your own family, where will you find the aid which you may require? That a state of things not modelled from the lessons of antiquity can long continue – that is what I have not heard. Ch'ing is now showing himself to be a flatterer, who increases the errors of Your Majesty, and not a loyal minister.'

The emperor requested the opinions of others on the representation, and the premier Li Sze, said: 'The five emperors were not one the double of the other, nor did the three dynasties accept one another's ways. Each had a peculiar system of government, not for the sake of contrariety, but as being required by the changed times. Now, Your Majesty has laid the foundations of imperial sway, so that it will last for 10,000 generations. This is indeed beyond what a stupid scholar can understand. And, moreover, Yueh only talks of things belonging to the three dynasties which are not fit to be models to you. At other times, when the princes were all striving together, they endeavoured to gather the wandering scholars about them; but now, the empire is in a stable condition and laws and ordinances issued from one supreme authority. Let those of the people who abide in their homes give their strength to the toils of husbandry, while those who become scholars should study the various laws and prohibitions. Instead of doing this, however, the scholars do not learn what belongs to the present day but study antiquity. They go on to condemn the present time, leading the masses of the people astray and to disorder.

'At the risk of my life, I, the Prime Minister, say: Formerly, when the nation was disunited and disturbed, there was no one who could give unity to it. The princes therefore stood up together; constant references were made to antiquity to the injury of the present state; baseless statements were dressed up to confound what was real and men made a boast of their own peculiar learning to condemn what their rulers appointed. And now, when Your Majesty has consolidated the empire, and distinguishing black from white, has constituted it a stable unity, they still honour their peculiar learning and combine together; they teach men what is contrary to your laws. When they hear that an ordinance has been issued, everyone sets to discussing it with this learning. In the court, they are dissatisfied in heart; out of it they keep talking in the streets. While they make a pretence of vaunting their master, they consider it fine to have extraordinary views of their own, and so they lead on their people to be guilty of murmuring and evil speaking. If these things are not prohibited, Your Majesty's authority will decline and parties will be formed. The best way is to prohibit them. I pray that all the records in charge of the historiographers be burned, excepting those of Ch'in; but with the exception of those officers belonging to the Board of Great Scholars, all throughout the empire who presume to keep copies of the Shih-Ching or of the Shu-Ching, or of the books of the Hundred Schools, be required to go with them to the officers in charge of the several districts and burn them; that all who may dare to speak together about the Shih and the Shu to be put to death and their bodies exposed in the market-place; that those who make mention of the past, so as to blame the present, be put to death along with their relatives; that officers who shall know of the violation of those rules and not inform against the offenders be held equally guilty with them; and that whoever that shall not have burned their books within thirty days after the issuing of the ordinance be branded and sent to labour on the Wall for four years. The only books which should be spared are those on medicine, divination and husbandry. Whoever wants to learn the laws may go to the magistrates and learn of them.'

The imperial decision was: 'Approved.'

The destruction of the scholars is related more briefly:

In the year after the burning of the books the resentment of the emperor was excited by the remarks and flight of two scholars who had been favourites with them, and he was determined to institute a strict enquiry about all of their classes in Hsie-yang, to find out whether they have been making ominous speeches about him and disturbing the minds of the people. The investigation was committed to the censors and, it being discovered that upwards of up to 460 scholars had violated the prohibitions, they were all buried alive in pits, for a warning to the empire, while degradation and banishment were employed more strictly than before against all who fell under suspicion. The emperor's eldest son, Fu Su, remonstrated with him, saying that such measures against those who repeated the words of Confucius and sought to imitate him would alienate all the people for the infant dynasty. But his interference offended his father so much that he was sent off from court, to be with a general who was superintending the building of the Great Wall.

What we find is that the emperor did not unilaterally order the burning of the books. He met his advisers – 'The emperor requested the opinions of others on the representation' – and approved only after discussion. Moreover, not all the books were burned; those on medicine, agriculture and divination were spared, permitting the continued development of the body and soul. Nor did it apply to the classics, which were in charge of the Board of Great Scholars. As Legge points out:

> There ought to have been no difficulty in finding copies when the Han dynasty superseded that of Ch'in, and probably there would have been none [no difficulty] but for the sack of the capital in 206 BC by Hsiang Yu, the formidable opponent of the founder of the House of Han. Then, we are told, the fires blazed for three months among the palaces and public buildings and must have proved as destructive to the copies of the Great Scholars as the edict of the tyrant had been to the copies among the people (*Chinese Classics*, Vol. I, James Legge).

Legge also points out that Shi Huangdi lasted only three years after the issuing of his edict and that 'the calamity inflicted on the ancient Books of China, by the House of Ch'in, could not have approached anything like *a complete destruction* of them' (author's italics). He later comments: 'The injury which they sustained from the dynasty of the Ch'in was, I believe, the same in character as that to which they were exposed during all the time of the Warring States.'

In regard to Shi Huangdi's ostensible tyrannical megalomania, the records show that 460 scholars acted illegally and were punished in accordance with the law of the land. I personally do not favour capital punishment, used today in ninety-two countries, among them the USA. But are we to describe the presidents of America as tyrants?

Ssu-ma Ch'ien, in defence of Shi Huangdi, notes:

> By the end of ten years the Ch'in people were acquiescent. Nothing lost on the road was picked up and pocketed, the hills were free from bandits, every household prospered, men fought bravely on the battlefield but avoided quarrels at home, and good government existed in both towns and villages (*The Records of the Historian*, Ssu-ma Ch'ien).

These gains were accomplished through the discipline of the individual and the discipline of the state. The evidence from the treasures of Shi Huangdi suggests that he was a spiritual leader who understood the true purpose of life on earth. He understood, like the other Supergods, that the purpose of this earthly existence is to purify the soul in preparation for the afterlife. The Supergods taught that purification comes through sacrifice. Every day, each individual must fight a battle within themselves in a never-ending struggle to reconcile life's imponderables. This is the true significance of the terracotta warriors that stand ready for battle.

A similar allegory is used in the Hindu holy book the Bhagavad-Gita, the Lord's Song, part of the epic poem the Mahabharata, which provides in its teachings a path of salvation for the spiritual aspirant in a discourse between the prodigy soldier Arjuna and Lord Krishna (God), who appears, to help Arjuna during his hour of need on the battlefield.

The ancient story begins with the King Dhrtarashtra (figure 73) sitting in his palace many miles from the battlefield of Kurukshetra, where his sons' armies are about to fight his nephews, the Pandavas. The king is anxious about the outcome of the battle because the location of Kurukshetra is a holy place which would favour the pious Pandavas rather than his own sons.

He summons his blind secretary, Sanjaya, who has spiritual vision (clairvoyance), to describe the events taking place on the battlefield. Sanjaya tells the king how the two armies are poised to charge against each other and then, as though time is stopping or slowing down, as is often said to happen during such moments of trauma, the leader of the Pandavas, the boy-soldier Arjuna, is overcome with despondency

The Battlefield at Kurukshetra

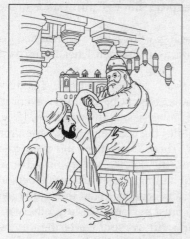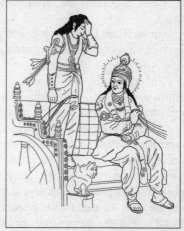

Figure 73. *(left)* Sanjaya tells the king of the events taking place many miles away on the battlefield of Kurukshetra. *(right)* The despondency of Arjuna (standing), accompanied by Lord Krishna, his spiritual guide, creator of the universe: 'My whole body trembles . . . my bow is slipping from my hand . . .'

at the thought of killing his relatives who stand before him: '. . . Rather would I content myself with a beggar's crust than kill these teachers of mine' (*The Geeta*, Shri Purohit Swami).

Lord Krishna, an incarnation of the highest of gods, creator of the earth (in Hindu belief), then descends to accompany Arjuna on his chariot as it stands between the armies. Krishna begins to describe to Arjuna his true purpose in life and the reason for his being on the battlefield at that moment. During the discourse Krishna explains the meaning of life and death and the purpose of the universe. This is the beginning of the Bhagavad-Gita.

Arjuna's lamentations, explains Krishna, are due to illusions (*Maya*). He is identifying his relatives with their physical bodies, thinking that if he kills their bodies he will be killing their very selves. Krishna explains the difference between the body and the soul; the body is merely a temporary home for the soul. The soul occupies many bodies before and after its present incarnation: '. . . as the soul experiences in this body infancy, youth and old age, so finally it passes into another. The wise have no delusion about this'. (*The Geeta*, Shri Purohit Swami).

165

The advice that follows is deeply philosophical and pragmatic, intended to help the enquirer obtain peace through purification of the spirit.

Arjuna hears that his past actions in past lives have determined his status as a soldier in this incarnation, as against a teacher, a merchant or a worker.

Krishna explains to Arjuna that each person must fulfil his duty and therefore he, as a soldier, must engage in battle. Every event in the physical world requires an *act*, an *actor* and an *instrument*. Here, the battle is seen as the act, the soldier the actor and the weapon the instrument that facilitates the act. These three inevitably lead to a preordained outcome. As an actor, the soldier suffers no adverse karma in performing his duty of killing. Providing each person performs his part, no adverse karma is generated. But the soldier (an allegory for an individual person) must perform his duty, otherwise karma will be generated causing future soul suffering to the individual.

If Arjuna wins the battle, he will enjoy the spoils of war on earth, as King of India; should he lose, his soul will be released to enjoy the spoils of the Kingdom of Heaven, because he has fulfilled his duty. The lesson is that the outcome of the battle is irrelevant. It is how the battle is fought that determines the accumulation of karma and the future suffering of the soul. Having recognised our duty, it must be carried out irrespective of any inherent danger or promise of gain. Instead of weakness, cowardice and pusillanimity, the dutiful soldier braces himself for the battle ahead. He who turns and flees, who runs away with fear, is lost.

The complex arguments (that cause battles to rage within us) are not always easy for the aspirant to grasp. At one point, duty is distinguished from truth; we must always be truthful, but where truth and duty conflict then duty must rule. (The following example illustrates reconciliation of such a dichotomy – given the complexity of the arguments. A schoolteacher confronted by a knife-wielding maniac asking for Sally Smith should not reveal that the pupil is sitting at her desk but instead should say that Sally Smith has left to catch the bus. Thus, the teacher dishonestly answers the maniac but fulfils her duty to protect her pupil. In this way the teacher generates no karma from the dishonesty.)

It is every person's duty to prevent people from hurting others and to stop them hurting themselves (the actor) from dishonest acts, because those acts will generate karma that will ultimately destroy the actor and others.

With regard to the body, Krishna compares the five senses of touch, taste, sight, sound and smell to a team of five horses. The rider in the chariot is compared with the soul that must control the horses using the reins (the intellect) lest the horses bolt, smashing the chariot and hurting the soul.

Desire is seen as the overriding enemy to defeat, because desire leads to frustration (when we cannot get what we want), frustration leads to anger, anger to delusion and delusion to destruction of the self and others. It is the body, the senses, that desire. It is the soul that suffers.

The terracotta soldiers, standing in formation, poised, before the battle begins, reflect on the discourse that took place on the battlefield at Kurukshetra between Krishna and Arjuna. The troops are disciplined and virtuous (on the square). They do not need weapons because love, as personified in their expressions, is the greatest weapon of all.

God, as their armour, protects them from harm. He has bestowed on them wisdom (an understanding of the super-science of the sun and the higher orders of spirituality), in preparation for the battle ahead. The chariots are in formation, the horses bridled, yoked and restrained. The charioteers (souls) are peaceful and in control.

Which brings us back to the anachronistic formations of archers in Pit 2. Figure A53a tells us that the man who carried the cross 'aimed at the heart'; Jesus came to purify the hearts of others. Figures A53b–d show that the Supergods, Lord Pacal, Viracocha, and Viracocha Pachacamac also 'aimed at the heart'. And so it is with the enigmatic kneeling archer, the most revered of the terracotta army. It is he, and only he, who occupies the square with the missing corner. It is he who holds the key to the secret of the terracotta warriors – and the man who left them behind. This is the message 'the most revered man carries the cross (bow) and aims at the heart'. Like the other Supergods, Shi Huangdi, the most revered, carried the cross and aimed at the heart.

But the kneeling and standing archers have more to say. They tell us that firing arrows at the hearts of *others* purifies the hearts *of others*. But if we are to purify *our own* heart then we must *stand exposed* (without armour) and allow the arrows of others to pierce and purify our own heart. Which explains why the unarmoured archers stand first in the firing line in Pits 1 and 2, ready to take the arrows of others. Theirs is the quest for purification. This brings sense to the anachronistic rules of the 'ball game' of the Maya, where the *winners* were killed (to enjoy the kingdom of heaven) after the game, and the losers were left to play, and fight, again (and again and again and again) in this battlefield of hell.

Shi Huangdi, like the first founding fathers of the Maya – who could see the past the present and the future – came to tell us the story of the man who would come later and die on the cross (as did the Mural of Bonampak which appeared in Mexico 700 years later).

Our journey of discovery leaves us with three questions:

- What is the significance of the total number of troops in the pits at Xian?
- Why were there two generals, instead of just one, as expected, in Pit Number 2?
- Whatever happened to the missing general, the sixty-ninth soldier, from Pit Number 3?

Analysis of troop numbers reveals:

	Troops	Generals	
Pit 1	7,029	1	
Pit 2	999	2	(1 general too many in this pit).
Pit 3	68	0	(1 soldier too few in this pit – and no general).

Clearly, one general from Pit 3 must have been visiting Pit 2 at the time of the analysis. The missing soldier from Pit 3 must, therefore, have been the extra general present in Pit 2. Moreover (adjusting the figures):

	Troops		Generals		
Pit 1	7029	+	1	=	7,030
Pit 2	999	+	1	=	1,000
Pit 3	68	+	1	=	69
			Total	=	8,099

This total number of soldiers, 8,099, means little esoterically. However, the lesson we learned from the missing soldier of Pit 3 was that whenever a featured number (68) makes no sense then we need to be mindful that 'one might be missing'. Further analysis confirmed that the true figure of 69 could be reached by including the surplus general from Pit 2. In the same way, here, again, the number 8,099 means little esoterically, suggesting that one more *general* must still be missing; that general must, of course, be the commander-in-chief himself.

No life-size terracotta figure of the first emperor was ever found (the one featured in figure 25 shows a miniature replica, made by the museum in Xian). The inclusion of Shi Huangdi, as the commander-in-chief, increases the ostensible total from 8,099 to the esoteric 8,100, taking us from 81 (9 x 9 – the number of a Supergod, and heaven) to 00 (0 x 0, the number of God). The most important figure is, once again, the piece that is missing: Shi Huangdi, the man in the mercury whose number was 81. He came to tell us how to win the greatest battle of all, the battle of life.

Like Krishna, he explained the paradigm of existence about the sun and God (set down in Appendices 3 and 4) and in so doing explained the purpose of life. Like the other Supergods, he encoded the super-science of the sun and the higher orders of spirituality into his treasures, his terracotta army, to help those on the narrow path of virtue. Shi Huangdi was the Son of Heaven.

Table of Chinese Dynasties

Dates	Dynasty
2852 BC	*Furshi*
2737 BC	*Shernnurng*
2697 BC	*Huarngdih*
2597 BC	*Shauhhauh*
2513 BC	*Chuanshyuh*
2145 BC	*Yaur*
2042 BC	*Shuhn*
1989–1557 BC	Hsia *(Shiah)*
1557–1049 BC	Shang or Yin *(Shang)*
1049–313 BC	Chow *(Jou)*
	722–481 BC Ch'un Ch'iu, Spring and Autumn period
	403–221 BC Warring States period
221–207 BC	Ch'in *(Chirn)*
207 BC–AD 23	Western Han *(Hahn)*
AD 9–23	Xin *(Shin)* – Wang Mang interregnum
AD 25–220	Eastern Han *(Hahn)*
AD 220–280	Three Kingdoms
	AD 221–264 Shu *(Shuu)*
	AD 220–265 Wei *(Weih)*
	AD 222–280 Wu *(Wur)*
AD 265–316	Western Chin *(Jihn)*
AD 317–590	AD 317–590 Southern Dynasties
	AD 317–419 Eastern Chin *(Jihn)*
	AD 420–479 Sung *(Suhng)*
	AD 479–501 Ch'i *(Chir)*
	AD 502–556 Liang *(Liarng)*
	AD 557–589 Ch'en *(Chern)*
	AD 386–581 Northern Dynasties
	AD 386–535 Northern Wei *(Weih)*
	AD 534–550 Eastern Wei *(Weih)*
	AD 535–556 Western Wei *(Weih)*
	AD 550–577 Northern Ch'i *(Chir)*
	AD 557–581 Northern Chou *(Jou)*

Figure A1a. Common Wade–Giles (phonetic) spellings followed by Peiping (national language) spellings in italics.

Dates	Dynasty	
AD 581–618	Sui (Sueir)	
AD 618–907	T'ang (Tarng)	
AD 907–960	Five Dynasties	
	AD 907–923	Later Liang (Liarng)
	AD 923–935	Later T'ang (Tarng)
	AD 936–947	Later Chin (Jihn)
	AD 947–951	Later Han (Hahn)
	AD 951–960	Later Chou (Jou)
AD 907–1125	Liao (Liaur)	
AD 960–1126	Northern Song (Suhng)	
AD 990–1227	Hsi-hsia (Shishiah)	
AD 1127–1279	Southern Song (Suhng)	
AD 1115–1234	Chin (Jin)	
AD 1279–1368	Yuan (Yuarn) (Mongol)	
AD 1368–1644	Ming (Mirng)	
AD 1644–1911	Ch'ing (Ching) (Manchu)	
AD 1911–	People's Republic of China	

Figure A1b. (Note: Different dynasties ruled simultaneously in different regions where indicated.)

APPENDIX 2

Table of Chinese Emperors

Emperor	Years of Reign	From	Emperor	Years of Reign		From
Yaur	100	2145 BC	Woo-ting	59	1	1273 BC
Shuhn	50	2042 BC	Tsoo-kang	11	1	1214 BC
			Tsoo-kea	33	1	1203 BC
HSIA DYNASTY			Fung-sin	4	1	1170 BC
Yu	8	1989 BC	Kang-ting	8	1	1166 BC
K'e	16	1978 BC	Woo-yih	35	1	1158 BC
T'ae-k'ang	4	1957 BC	Wan-ting	13	1	1123 BC
Chung-k'ang	7	1951 BC	Te-yih	9	1	1110 BC
Seang	28	1942 BC	Te-sin	52	1	1101 BC
Usuppation	40	1914 BC				
Sh'aou-k'ang	21	1874 BC	**CHOW DYNASTY**			
Ch'oo	17	1851 BC	Woo	6	1	1049 BC
Fun	44	1832 BC	Ching	37	1	1043 BC
Mang	58	1788 BC	K'ang	26	1	1006 BC
Sëe	25	1729 BC	Ch'aou	19		980 BC
Puh-këang	59	1701 BC	Muh	55		961 BC
Peen	18	1642 BC	Kung	12		906 BC
Kin	8	1621 BC	E	25		894 BC
K'ung-këa	9	1,611 BC	Hëaou	9		869 BC
Haou	3	1600 BC	E	8		860 BC
Fa	7	1595 BC	Le	26		852 BC
Kwei	31	1588 BC	Seuen	46		826 BC
			Yew	11		780 BC
SHANG DYNASTY			P'ing	51		769 BC
T'ang	12	1557 BC	Hwan	23		718 BC
Wae-ping	2	1545 BC	Chwang	15		695 BC
Chung-jin	4	1543 BC	Le	5		680 BC
T'ae-këa	12	1539 BC	Hwuy	25		675 BC
Yuh-ting	19	1527 BC	Sëang	33		650 BC
Sëaou-kang	5	1508 BC	K'ing	6		617 BC
Sëaou-kea	17	1503 BC	K'wang	6		611 BC
Yung-ke	12	1486 BC	Ting	21		605 BC
T'ae-mow	75	1474 BC	Këen	14		584 BC
Chung-ting	9	1399 BC	Ling	27		570 BC
Wae-jin	10	1390 BC	King	25		543 BC
Ho-t'an-këa	9	1380 BC	King	44		518 BC
Tsoo-yih	19	1371 BC	Yuen	7		474 BC
Tsoo-sin	14	1352 BC	Ching-ting	28		467 BC
K'ae-këa	5	1338 BC	K'aou	15		439 BC
Tsoo-ting	9	1333 BC	Wei-lëe	24		424 BC
Nan-kang	6	1324 BC	Ngan *	26		400 BC
Yang-këa	4	1318 BC	Lëe *	7		374 BC
Pwan-kang	28	1314 BC	Hëen *	48		367 BC
Sëaou-sin	3	1286 BC	Shin-tsing *	6		319 BC
Sëaou-yih	10	1283 BC	Yin *			313 BC

* Warring States Years: 403–220 BC

Figure A2a. Dates of emperors according to the Bamboo Books

Emperor (after unification)

CH'IN DYNASTY

Qin Shi Huangdi	221–210 BC
Er Shi	210–207 BC

WESTERN HAN DYNASTY

Gaodi	206–195 BC
Huidi	195–188 BC
Lu Hou (Regent)	188–180 BC
Wendi	180–157 BC
Jingdi	157–141 BC
Wudi	141–87 BC
Zhaodi	87–74 BC
Xuandi	74–49 BC
Yuandi	49–33 BC
Chengdi	33–7 BC
Aidi	7–1 BC
Pingdi	1 BC–AD 6
Ruzi	AD 7–9
Wang Mang	AD 9–23

EASTERN HAN DYNASTY

Guang Wudi	AD 25–57
Mingdi	AD 57–75
Zhangdi	AD 75–88
Hedi	AD 88–106
Shangdi	AD 106
Andi	AD 106–125
Shundi	AD 125–144
Chongdi	A D144–145
Zhidi	AD 145–146
Huandi	AD 146–168
Lingd	AD 168–189
Xiandi	AD 189–220

THREE KINGDOMS PERIOD

Shu Dynasty

Xuande	AD 221–223
Hou Zhu	AD 223–263

Wei Dynasty

Wendi	AD 220–226
Mingdi	AD 227–239
Shaodi	AD 240–253
Gao Gui Xiang Gong	AD 254–260
Yuandi	AD 260–264

Wu Dynasty

Wudi	AD 222–252
Feidi	AD 252–258
Jingdi	AD 258–264
Modi	AD 264–280

Emperor (after unification)

PERIOD OF DISUNION

Western Chin Dynasty

Wudi	AD 265–289
Huidi	AD 290–306
Huaidi	AD 307–312
Mindi	AD 313–316

Eastern Chin Dynasty

Yuandi	AD 317–322
Mingdi	AD 323–325
Chengdi	AD 326–342
Kangdi	AD 343–344
Mudi	AD 345–361
Aidi	AD 362–365
Hai Xi Gong	AD 366–370
Jian Wendi	AD 371–372
Xiao Wudi	AD 373–396
Andi	AD 397–418
Gongdi	AD 419

Sung Dynasty

Wudi	AD 420–422
Ying Yang Wang	AD 423
Wendi	AD 424–453
Xiao Wudi	AD 454–464
Mingdi	AD 465–472
Cang Wu Wang	AD 473–476
Shundi	AD 477–479

Ch'i Dynasty

Gaodi	AD 479–482
Wudi	AD 483–493
Mingdi	AD 494–498
Dong Hunhou	AD 499–500
Hedi	AD 501

Liang Dynasty

Wudi	AD 502–549
Jian Wendi	AD 550
Yu Zhang Wang	AD 551
Yuandi	AD 552–554
Jingdi	AD 555–556

Ch'en Dynasty

Wudi	AD 557–559
Wendi	AD 560–566
Lin Hai Wang	AD 567–568
Xuandi	AD 569–582
Hou Zhu	AD 583–589

SUI DYNASTY

Wendi	AD 581–604
Yangdi	AD 604–617
Gongdi	AD 617–618

T'ANG DYNASTY

Gaozu	AD 618–626
Taizong	AD 626–649

175

Figure A2b (i).

Emperor (after unification)

T'ANG (continued)

Gaozong	AD 649–683
Zhongzong	AD 684
	AD 705–710
Ruizong	AD 684–690
	AD 710–712
Wu Zetian	AD 690–705
Xuanzong	AD 712–756
Suzong	AD 756–762
Daizong	AD 762–779
Dezong	AD 779–805
Shunzong	AD 805
Xianzong	AD 805–820
Muzong	AD 820–824
Jingzong	AD 824–827
Wenzong	AD 827–840
Wuzong	AD 840–846
Xuanzong	AD 846–859
Yizong	AD 859–873
Xizong	AD 873–888
Zhaozong	AD 888–904
Aidi (Zhaoxuan)	AD 904–907

FIVE DYNASTIES
Later Liang Dynasty

Taizu	AD 907–910
Modi	AD 911–923

Later T'ang Dynasty

Zhuangzong	AD 923–926
Mingzong	AD 926–934
Feidi	AD 934–935

Later Chin Dynasty

Gaozu	AD 936–944
Chudi	AD 944–947

Later Han Dynasty

Gaozu	AD 947–948
Yindi	AD 948–951

Later Chou Dynasty

Taizu	AD 951–954
Shizong	AD 954–960

NORTHERN SONG DYNASTY

Taizu	AD 960–976
Taizong	AD 976–997
Zhenzong	AD 998–1022
Renzong	AD 1022–1063
Yingzong	AD 1064–1067
Shenzong	AD 1068–1085
Zhezong	AD 1086–1101
Huizong	AD 1101–1125
Quinzong	AD 1126

Emperor (after unification)

SOUTHERN SONG DYNASTY

Gaozong	AD 1127–1162
Ziaozong	AD 1163–1190
Guangzong	AD 1190–1194
Ningzong	AD 1195–1224
Lizong	AD 1225–1264
Duzong	AD 1265–1274
Gongzong	AD 1275
Duanzong	AD 1276–1278
Bing Di	AD 1279

YUAN DYNASTY

Khubilai (Shizu)	AD 1279–1294
Temur Oljeitu (Chengzong)	AD 1294–1307
Khaishan (Wuzong)	AD 1308–1311
Ayurbarwada (Renzong)	AD 1311–1320
Shidebala (Yingzong)	AD 1321–1323
Yesun Temur (Taiding)	AD 1323–1328
Tugh Temur (Wenzong)	AD 1328–1329
	AD 1329–1332
Khoshila (Mingzong)	AD 1329
Toghon Temur (Shundi)	AD 1333–1368

MING DYNASTY

Hongwu	AD 1368–1398
Jianwen	AD 1399–1402
Yongle	AD 1403–1424
Hongxi	AD 1425
Xuande	AD 1426–1435
Zhengtong/Tianshun	AD 1436–1449
	AD 1457–1464
Jingtai	AD 1450–1457
Chenghua	AD 1465–1487
Hongzhi	AD 1488–1505
Zhengde	AD 1506–1521
Jiajing	AD 1522–1567
Longqing	AD 1567–1572
Wanli	AD 1573–1620
Taichang	AD 1620
Tianqi	AD 1621–1627
Chongzhen	AD 1628–1644

CH'ING DYNASTY

Shunzhi	AD 1644–1661
Kangxi	AD 1661–1722
Yongzheng	AD 1723–1735
Qianlong	AD 1736–1795
Jiajing	AD 1796–1820
Daoguang	AD 1821–1850
Xianfeng	AD 1851–1861
Tongzhi	AD 1862–1874
Guangxu	AD 1875–1908
Puyi	AD 1909–1911

Figure A2b (ii).

APPENDIX 3

The Sun and God

(i) How the Sun Determines Personality; the Astrogenetic Theory

This theory brings together many of the accepted scientific discoveries of the twentieth century.

Figure A3i shows a schematic view of the sun's idealised magnetic fields; the black areas illustrate the magnetic field between the poles (the vertical polar field). Four more 'bubbles' of magnetism exist around the equator (the equatorial field). Figure A3ii shows a cross-sectional view of the four bubbles of magnetism.

The sun spins on its axis, causing the equator to revolve once every 26 days (28 days when observed from the moving earth) while the more slowly moving polar regions take 37 days to complete one revolution (40.5 days when observed from the moving earth). The resulting turbulence showers the distant earth with charged particles.

These particles were first detected by the *Mariner II* spacecraft in 1962 and given the collective name of 'the solar wind'. The concentric girdle of particles shown schematically here (figure A3i) was mapped by the *Interplanetary Spacecraft No. 1* (IMP 1) throughout the month of December 1963 (figure 58d). The polarity of particles can be seen to coincide with the rotating equatorial magnetic field sectors of the sun at that time. The girdle hence shows *the sectored structure of the solar wind*.

In 1979 British astronomer Professor Iain Nicolson discovered that

How the Sun Determines Personality

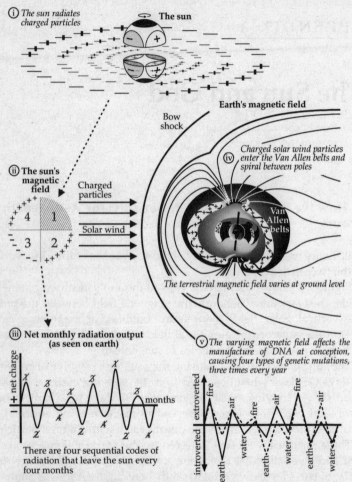

(i) *The sun radiates charged particles*

The sun

(ii) **The sun's magnetic field**

Charged particles

Solar wind

Earth's magnetic field

Bow shock

(iv) *Charged solar wind particles enter the Van Allen belts and spiral between poles*

Van Allen belts

The terrestrial magnetic field varies at ground level

(iii) **Net monthly radiation output (as seen on earth)**

There are four sequential codes of radiation that leave the sun every four months

(v) *The varying magnetic field affects the manufacture of DNA at conception, causing four types of genetic mutations, three times every year*

(vi) *The 12 genetic mutations every year correlate with the 12 signs of the zodiac (above graphs from two studies by Jeff Mayo and Professor Hans Eysenck, London Institute of Psychiatry). The positive 'signs' are extroverted; the negative 'signs' are introverted. This suggests that the sun is responsible for the determination of personality (sun-sign astrology) through genetic mutations beginning at the moment of conception*

Figure A3.

bombardment of the Van Allen radiation belts, which encircle the earth (figure A3iv), by the solar wind causes changes in the earth's magnetic field: 'Variations in the solar wind produce changes in the earth's magnetosphere that are reflected in the terrestrial magnetic field at ground level.' (*The Sun*, I. Nicolson, Mitchell Beazley, 1979).

In 1986 (figure A3iii) I showed that the differential rotation of the sun (the interaction of its magnetic fields) results in the release of twelve different monthly bursts of radiation from the sun throughout the year. From this, it becomes clear that the twelve types of radiations from the sun will result in twelve bursts of magnetic activity from the Van Allen belts during the same twelve-month period.

The final piece of the puzzle appeared two years earlier, in 1984. A team at the Naval Medical Research Institute at Bethesda, Maryland, USA, led by Dr A. R. Lieboff, had been experimenting on test-tube babies when they noticed that magnetic fields, from electric lighting in the laboratory, were causing genetic mutations in their experiments. Studying the phenomenon more closely, they discovered that magnetic fields, just like these, affected the manufacture of DNA in tissues, causing genetic mutations in developing foetuses. The team's experiments were performed with human cells called fibroblasts. The lowest level of magnetic field used was lower than that of the earth and still it had an effect, proving that the earth's field is strong enough to have the same effect.

Figure A3v shows two superimposed graphs, the results of two personality studies undertaken by astrologer Jeff Mayo, under the aegis of Professor H. J. Eysenck of the London Institute of Psychiatry. The first study involved 1,795 subjects (broken line) and the second 2,324 subjects (solid line). Both show that the so-called 'positive' astrological signs Aries, Gemini, Leo, Libra, Sagittarius and Aquarius are predominantly extroverted, while the so-called remaining 'negative' signs are predominantly introverted. In summary, the astrogenetic model suggests that personality is genetically determined at the moment of conception. Twelve types of personality result from twelve types of solar radiation. Astrogenetics also shows that the position of the planets, at conception and birth, can affect both the moment of birth and the moment of labour in pregnant females and modify the development of personality (see *The Tutankhamun Prophecies*, Appendices 1xvii and xviii).

Fertility Hormone Production (I)
(a three-stage process)

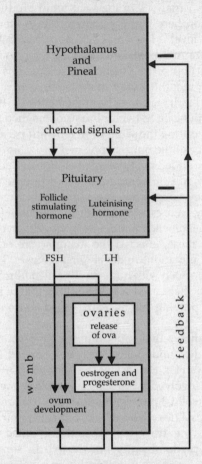

Figure A4. Summary of hormonal control of the ovarian function. The hypothalamus gland sends chemical signals to the so-called master gland, the pituitary. The pituitary manufactures and releases two hormones, the follicle-stimulating hormone (FSH) and the luteinising hormone (LH), both of which are essential for the release of eggs from the ovaries. Ovaries stimulate the production of oestrogen and progesterone. When sufficient levels of these have been produced, a feedback signal to the pituitary, hypothalamus and pineal switches off the production of FSH and LH. The solar hormone theory (figure A8) suggests that solar-inspired magnetic modulations in the first instance stimulate the hypothalamus and the pituitary, causing menstruation and ovulation to vary with variations in solar emissions (see also figure A5).

(ii) How the Sun Controls Fertility in Females

In 1987 Dr Ross Aidey, White House Chief Medical Advisor for the Reagan administration, published a scientific paper ('Cell Membranes, Electromagnetic Fields and Intercellular Communication') announcing:

... about 20 per cent of pineal cells in pigeons, guinea-pigs and rats respond to changes in both direction and intensity of the earth's magnetic field ... causing variation in the peptide hormone melatonin, which powerfully influences circadian rhythms.

The biological rhythm cycle had already been determined by others as lasting 28 days in humans, which corresponds exactly with the sun's 28-day period of rotation, as seen from the earth. It became clear that the sun's radiation not only determined personality but controlled behaviour of the human organism after the moment of birth; the sun's radiation is converted by the Van Allen belts into modulating magnetic fields (Nicolson) which affect the endocrine system directly (Aidey), causing the pineal gland to regulate the production of the timing-hormone melatonin throughout the 28-day period. At least, that was the inference, but how to prove it? Measuring variations in melatonin against corresponding changes in behaviour is difficult if not impossible to do, given the subjective nature of behaviour. It seemed unlikely that a link between the two could ever be proven.

But this raised a more general question: was there a direct link between the sun's radiation and endocrine activity in humans? This was easier to answer. It would be more straightforward to compare the sun's radiation with the 28-day human menstrual cycle; the production of fertility hormones is well documented and understood. If the sun could be seen to regulate these hormones, then it would support the hypothesis that the sun bioregulates behaviour through regulation of the endocrine system and variations in melatonin production.

Figures A4–A8 demonstrate how the endocrine system is regulated by solar radiation; Figure A4 shows how the hypothalamus, a tiny gland within the brain, in conjunction with the pineal gland, sends chemical signals to the pituitary gland, which responds by manufacturing the follicle-stimulating hormone (FSH) and the luteinising hormone (LH), both of which are necessary for the release of the

Fertility Hormone Production (II)
(functional analysis)

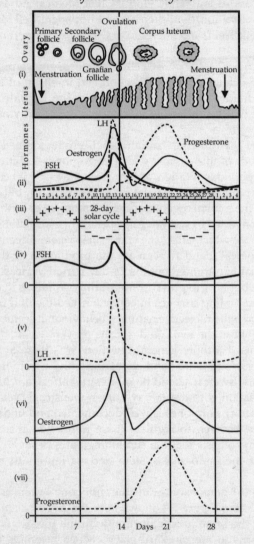

Figure A5. (i) A menstrual cycle in which fertilisation does not occur. (ii) Graphs showing the production of fertility hormones during one cycle. (iii) Solar cycle radiation (SCR). (iv–vii) Function-by-function analysis of hormone activity.

Solar Hormone Regulation (I)
(graphical analysis)

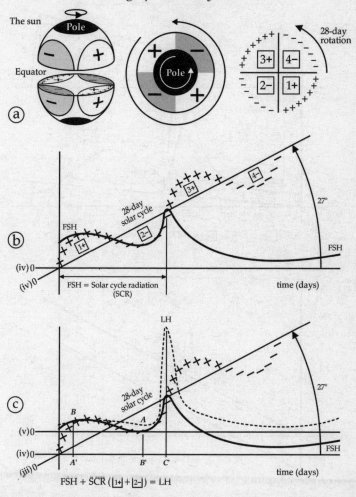

Figure A6. (a) Cross-sectional representation of the sun; the polar field is shown in black and the equatorial field quadrants are numbered 1, 2, 3, 4. The radiation emissions (solar cycle radiation–SCR) from each quadrant are polarised either negatively or positively, as indicated. The four quadrants of solar cycle radiation are shown graphically in (b); FSH correlates with SCR during quadrants 1 and 2, switches off on day 14, and decays exponentionally. (c) FSH + SCR (quadrants 1 and 2) together give rise to a pulse of LH on day 14 of the cycle.

Solar Hormone Regulation (II)
(graphical analysis)

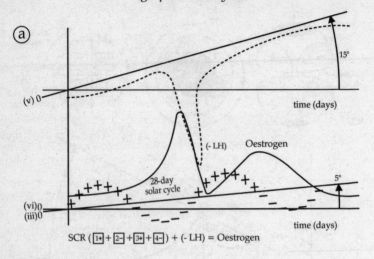

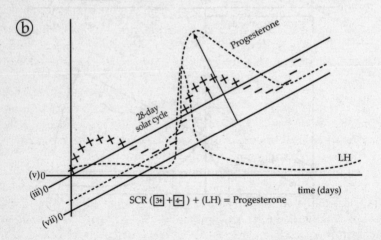

Figure A7. (a) Oestrogen production begins on day 1 of the cycle and grows exponentionally before being suppressed by the massive pulse of LH on day 14. (b) A surge in LH on day 14 causes an increase in progesterone production, which peaks approximately 24 hours after the peak in solar radiation (third quadrant) and then falls, tracking the solar cycle to the peak of the fourth quadrant of SCR.

follicle from the ovary and for womb implantation of the zygote (early foetus). The ovaries in turn produce the sex hormones oestrogen and progesterone which, when sufficient levels of FSH and LH have been produced, shut off the supply to the hypothalamus, pineal and pituitary, thereby switching off the cycle of hormone production.

Figure A5i shows the 28-day behaviour of fertility hormones when fertilisation does not occur. The events taking place within the pituitary, ovary and uterus are precisely synchronised. A5ii details in graphical form the variations in fertility hormones which take place within the body over the same time (source: after *Principles of Psychology*, Price, Glickstein, Horton and Bailey, Holt, Rinehart and Winston, 1982).

A5iii shows the 28-day solar cycle made up of positive and negative days of radiation. Beneath this, the graphs shown in A5 are individually separated in order to compare each to the solar cycle radiation cycle.

At first none of the fertility hormones appears to share the graphical signature of the solar cycle waveform, which switches from positive to negative every seven days, suggesting that the solar cycle does not play a part in hormone production or regulation. However, on closer inspection (figure A6b), we note that when the solar cycle radiation waveform is rotated through 27 degrees, a perfect correlation between the two waveforms becomes evident. A6b shows that the follicle-stimulating hormone takes three days to grow to a measurable (detectable) amount. It then tracks the solar cycle, exactly, until day 14, when the cycle changes polarity. At this time FSH decays exponentially, as one would expect of a chemical decay process. This suggests that the hormone FSH is regulated by the sun's radiation.

We can now compare the *combined* behaviour of FSH plus the solar cycle radiation with variations in the production of LH (figure A6c).

FSH *plus* solar radiation from (solar) quadrants 1 and 2 (first seven-day period and second seven-day period) become additive between points A′ and B′. At A′, solar radiation begins to fall, as does FSH against the y axis. Because *both* FSH *and* solar radiation are falling, LH falls from B to A, between A′ and B′. At B′, *both* FSH *and* solar radiation are rising, against the y axis. This leads to an increase in LH. LH rises rapidly at point C′ and peaks at 14 days, switches off and decays exponentially at the end of quadrant 2.

Figure A7a shows that although solar radiation triggers exponential growth in oestrogen at the start of the cycle, the massive pulse of LH suppresses and inhibits further oestrogen production, which recovers gradually, as LH decays, to track the remainder of the solar cycle.

Meanwhile (figure A7b) progesterone, previously inhibited (by oestrogen) from day one, is now allowed to increase, as LH pulses (suppressing oestrogen). At the same time, solar radiation rises, to peak in its third quadrant, allowing progesterone to peak twenty-four hours after the peak in the solar cycle. Thereafter progesterone falls, tracking the solar radiation cycle to the peak of the fourth quadrant negative cycle.

This analysis shows that the sun's radiation affects the hypothalamus and pineal gland in humans and in so doing regulates fertility hormones. In summary (figure A8), the sun's radiation is converted to magnetic modulations by the Van Allen belts. These then act on the hypothalamus and pineal glands which, in line with Ross Aidey's experiments on rats, pigeons and guinea-pigs, convert the magnetic modulations into chemical variations in the endocrine system. The expression 'electrochemical transduction' denotes this magnetic-to-chemical conversion process. Hence the 28-day solar cycle regulates menstruation and fertility in females. This is why ancient sun-worshipping civilisations like the Maya and Egyptians worshipped the sun as the god of fertility.

There are exceptions to this general 28-day rule:

(i) The duration of the cycle will vary when the polar magnetic field of the sun interferes with the equatorial magnetic field of the sun. This means that the cycle will vary (quite naturally) from between 24 to 32 days long (28 days +/- 4 days, with the average duration amounting to 28 days).

(ii) Menstruation is affected by each individual's biological clock, which begins at the moment of conception (just like astrological personality determination covered earlier). For this reason females will *not* all menstruate at the same time, because each individual's clock began at a different time.

This can be illustrated using the carousel analogy (figure A9): Imagine that for every revolution of the carousel the horses and riders rise to the top of their respective pole and then descend to the floor once. Each passenger queues to alight the carousel at point 'A'. One passenger mounts the first horse and the carousel moves forward slightly. The first passenger rises from the floor of the carousel as the horse rises. The

How the Sun Regulates Hormone Production, and hence Fertility, in Females

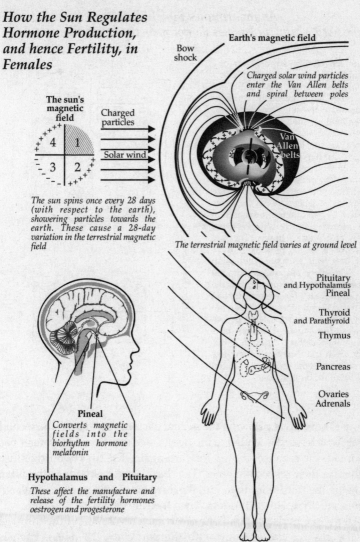

Bow shock

Earth's magnetic field

Charged solar wind particles enter the Van Allen belts and spiral between poles

The sun's magnetic field

Charged particles

Solar wind

The sun spins once every 28 days (with respect to the earth), showering particles towards the earth. These cause a 28-day variation in the terrestrial magnetic field

Van Allen belts

The terrestrial magnetic field varies at ground level

Pituitary and Hypothalamus
Pineal

Thyroid and Parathyroid

Thymus

Pancreas

Ovaries
Adrenals

Pineal
Converts magnetic fields into the biorhythm hormone melatonin

Hypothalamus and Pituitary
These affect the manufacture and release of the fertility hormones oestrogen and progesterone

The endocrine system converts the modulating magnetic field into chemicals (hormones). This magnetic-to-chemical conversion process is termed 'electrochemical transduction' (Astrogenetics, 1988). The 28-day magnetic variations regulate menstruation in females. Research suggests that longer cycle variations (12-year cycles) trigger puberty and menopause (12 years and 48 (4 x 12) years after conception)

Figure A8.

Asynchronous Synchronicity
(the reason why all females do not menstruate simultaneously)

Figure A9. Here a carousel analogy explains why women menstruate every 28 days on average and yet do not menstruate simultaneously; the four quadrants of the sun's magnetic field (figure A6a) are shown as the roof of a carousel *(the shaded sector has been omitted to simplify the illustration).* Imagine that the carousel revolves once every 28 days, corresponding to the revolutionary period of the solar equatorial field. Before the carousel ride begins, the passengers mount the horses at point 'A', at different moments in time, as each horse reaches the lower extremity of vertical travel. The ride begins once all the passengers have taken their seats. Each horse moves up and down every 28 days, as indicated by the sinusoidal waveform beneath the carousel, but each horse moves up and down at different times. The horses are all synchronised to the 28-day period. Females all menstruate at different times because they alighted the earth at different times and their biorhythms, like the mounting of the horses, commenced at different moments in time.

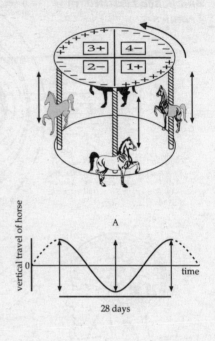

carousel now stops, allowing the second passenger to mount the second horse, which has descended to the floor. Once the second passenger has mounted, the carousel moves forward again. The first two riders rise higher up their respective poles. The third horse descends to the floor, allowing the third rider to mount the third horse, and so on until all the horses are occupied with riders. Then the ride begins.

All the riders rise and fall once with each revolution of the carousel (in the case of the analogy with the sun every 28 days). Each is synchronised to the sun's 28-day rotation. But each rises and falls at a different moment in time. This is because they each took their respective seats at different moments in time. The rise and fall of each rider relative to the next is therefore 'asynchronous'. Women do not all menstruate at the same time because each was conceived (alighted the earth) at a different moment in time. Hence biorhythms (and endocrine activity) commence at a different time for each female. But each endocrine system is locked into the 28-day biorhythmic solar clock.

(iii) Anything that affects the biorhythm or metabolic rate will cause variation in duration of the cycle. These agents could be stimulants like coffee or tobacco, or artificial hormones, or anything that interferes with the biorhythmic signal from the sun, such as overhead power cables or electromagnetic interference (Appendix 3vii).

(iv) Females radiate hormones as a natural bodily emission. These radiated emissions, if stronger than the sun's emissions, will cause females in close proximity to synchronise menstruation for as long as the interference continues.

(v) Scientific evidence shows that females placed under ground, shielded from the sun's radiation, will stop menstruating and their biological clocks will malfunction, as the following article from *New Scientist* (June 1989) illustrates:

Stefania Follini, an Italian interior designer, emerged from isolation last week after four months in a cave in New Mexico. Italian scientists watched how her waking days lasted 35 hours and were punctuated by sleeping periods of up to 10 hours. She lost 17 pounds and her menstrual cycle stopped. Follini believed she had spent two months under ground, not four.

These results dismiss the notion that the moon is the prime mover in regard to fertility, which it never could be: its cycle of periodicity amounts to 29.5 days, not 28. More important, it becomes clear that fertility on earth is dependent on the sun's radiation: no radiation = no babies.

Solar radiations play a crucial role in the procreation of humans on earth. Could they likewise play an important and crucial part in the procreation of animals, birds, reptiles, fish, insects (note that the silkworm reproductive cycle, detailed in Chapter 2, follows both the 7-day field sector and 28-day solar cycle) or viruses? If this is the case, for viruses, then the implications are far-reaching: for example, placing AIDS sufferers under ground would disrupt the procreational ability of the virus, preventing further replication. The fact that bright sunshine causes spontaneous replication of a virus is not news to any cold-sore sufferer who has spent too long on the beach.

Sunspots and the Rise and Fall of Civilisations

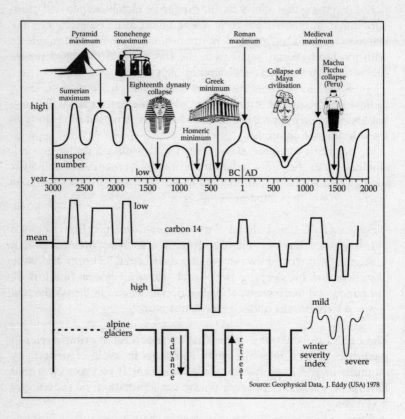

Figure A10. A series of graphs showing that the rise and fall of civilisations correspond with the rise and fall of radiation from the sun. The top graph shows a long-term envelope of sunspot activity derived from the centre graph of carbon 14. More carbon 14 is absorbed in the growth rings of trees during sunspot minima. Sunspot minima also correlate with mini-ice ages (lower graph) and a winter severity index (based on a mean for Paris and London for the period shown). Reduced radiation results in reduced fertility on earth; the eighteenth dynasty of Tutankhamun collapsed during a massive minimum, as did the civilisation of the Maya 2,000 years later. The Inca city of Machu Picchu, occupied by the Virgins of the Sun from around AD 1450, was abandoned when the sun's radiation returned to normal levels in around AD 1520, long before the Conquest.

(Appendix 3v also shows a known link between sunspots and the influenza virus.)

(iii) How the Sun Regulates the Rise and Fall of Civilisations

The bristlecone pine tree, from the west coast of North America, lives for as long as 4,000 years. Its tree rings contain information of past climate and solar activity since the year it was planted. Very old bristlecone pines, which have long since turned to coal, provide records going back 8,000 years or so. From this we know that the level of solar radiation varies substantially over great periods of time.

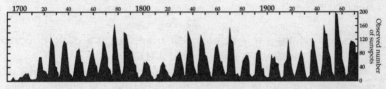

Figure A11. The (approximate) 11.5-year sunspot cycle, from observation since 1680.

American researcher John Eddy collected geophysical data on the bristlecone pine and from it derived an envelope of variations in the sunspot cycle going back 5,000 years (figure A10), showing that the amount of solar radiation indeed varies with sunspot activity. If the solar hormone theory is correct, then fertility on earth should also have varied with the level of solar radiation throughout history.

Eddy's graphs proved that not only had the sun's radiation fluctuated greatly over the past 5,000 years but radiation minima led to mini ice ages on earth. Professor Iain Nicolson (*The Sun*, Mitchell Beazley, 1979), in addition noted that Eddy's graphs, for some unknown reason, seemed to follow the rise and fall of civilisations throughout history. As Nicolson says: '. . . the data is persuasive, but not completely conclusive.' The solar hormone theory explains away the enigma: as radiation from the sun reduces, populations decline in numbers (figure A10).

(iv) Solar Radiation and Sunspot Activity

Throughout history, civilisations have catalogued the presence of

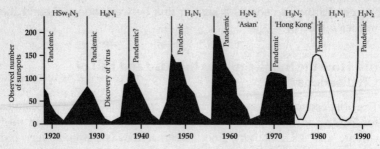

Figure A12. A remarkable coincidence exists between peaks in the 11.5-year sunspot cycle (when solar activity is at a maximum) and the occurrence of influenza pandemics associated with antigenic shifts of the virus. Solar radiation appears to mutate the virus every 11.5 years. The record up to 1971 is from Hope-Simpson (solid graph); the line graph shows the situation for the period 1971–89. (Source: after *Nature*, 275.86, 1978).

black spots on the sun's surface which appear in a cycle peaking approximately every 11.5 years (figure A11).

In the middle of these mini-cycles as few as perhaps five pairs of spots might be visible (through tinted plastic). At cycle maxima perhaps 100 pairs of spots may appear on the surface. From 1645–1715 no sunspots at all were recorded.

Magnetic disturbances associated with spots vary enormously, from around 0.4 Gauss (Gauss being a measure of magnetic field strength; the earth's field strength is 0.6 Gauss) at minima, to around 4,000 Gauss at maxima. This 6,000-fold cyclical increase plays havoc with the sun, which showers off 6,000 times more particles in the solar wind. These in turn bombard the earth, disrupting not just fertility but also human behaviour through variations in biorhythmic hormones (and other hormones known to cause schizophrenia).

(v) How Sunspots Cause Schizophrenia

A link has already been established between sunspots and virus pandemics on earth. In 1978 *Nature* magazine published the research of R. E. Hope-Simpson (*Nature*, 275.86, 1978, R. E. Hope-Simpson) which showed a remarkable coincidence between peaks in the 11.5-year sunspot cycle and influenza pandemics associated with antigenic shifts in the virus (figure A12). The virus mutated to a different variety with each successive sunspot cycle, showing that the sun's radiation can disrupt replication of a virus.

In 1991 the *Daily Telegraph* reported that scientists had found a direct link between schizophrenia and influenza (3 July 1991). Professor Robin Murray of the London Institute of Psychiatry said his research

... showed that there was an 88 per cent increase in the number of babies, who later developed schizophrenia, born in England in the spring of 1958 following the massive influenza pandemic (sunspot maximum) of 1957. The correlation is conclusive from 1939 onwards.

Putting these two reports together, Hope-Simpson shows a link between sunspots and viruses, and Murray shows a link between viruses and schizophrenia. It becomes clear that radiation from the sun is causing variations in hormones, leading to schizophrenia. This electromagnetic view also explains away another enigma perplexing scientists who cannot understand why rates of schizophrenia in West Indian immigrants is higher in England compared with figures for the indigenous population of the West Indies and higher than those of the progeny of West Indians born in England. This is quite simply due to biorhythmic desynchronisation: whenever an organism is removed from its place of birth (to a different geographical point on the surface of the earth) it is subjected to a different combination of magnetic fields from the sun *and* the earth (together), because the earth's field will have changed (this is how the homing pigeon finds its way home). This different magnetic field, through the process of electromagnetic transduction, disrupts hormone levels throughout the endocrine system. In its simplest sense we call this 'homesickness'. The body, like the pigeon, simply wishes to return to the geographical place on the earth's surface where it was conceived, where its endocrine system was in equilibrium. Homesickness is a biochemical response, like jetlag, to a shift in magnetism affecting the endocrine system. The higher incidence in schizophrenia can be ascribed to the same phenomenon. (The picture is slightly more complicated in the case of the homing pigeon, which appears to have an 'erasable, programmable memory', enabling it to re-'home' to new geographical locations.)

(vi) How the Sun Controls Biorhythms

Figure A3i shows a moment in time where the radiation sequence from the sun conforms to a code 234, field number 1 being disturbed (at that instant) by the differential rotation of the polar field. Clearly there are three other sequences – 123, 124, 134 – when field numbers 4, 3 and 2 are each neutralised respectively by the polar field each month. These four codes give rise to four distinct types of of astrological personalities, known to astrologers as fire, earth, air and water signs. Once born, these infants will grow and respond favourably to radiation patterns that were instrumental in their creation at conception and adversely to variant patterns. On good radiation days they will be more alert and responsive and on bad radiation days sluggish and more accident-prone, as the sun's radiation affects the operating performance of the brain.

(vii) How the Sun Causes Cancer

In 1967 biologist Janet Harker undertook experiments on cockroaches to ascertain which part of the brain was responsible for awakening the cockroaches at midnight and sending them to sleep at 6 a.m. Using an electron-microscope, she was able to locate areas of the cockroach's brain responsible for time referral. When she removed this part of the brain the cockroaches lost all sense of time and stayed awake continuously until they died. To make sure that this part of the brain was indeed a biological 'clock', Harker swapped the same part of the brain between an Australian cockroach and a British cockroach. Each adopted the previous rhythms of the other: the British cockroach went to sleep at midnight and awoke at 6 a.m., proving the clock was 'ticking' away after the transplant.

Since then, Ross Aidey's experiments have established that the sun affects the manufacture of the timing hormone melatonin. The sun's radiation hence synchronises and periodically recalibrates Harker's biological clock. In effect, there are two clocks, an astronomical one and a biological one. Coordination of both ensures endocrinological harmony; disruption to either causes chaos.

Janet Harker continued her experiments on cockroaches. She implanted one cockroach with two clocks, one Australian, the other British. Both cockroaches developed cancer every time the experiment was carried out, and died. This suggests that cancer is connected to de-synchronisation of the body with its internal biological clock. Consider the case of a human radiated with a radiation pattern of, say, 123 at the time of conception. Its biological clock will be regulated by that sequence thereafter. Figure A13a describes the theoretical relationship between the solar clock (biorhythmic signal) and the biological system (clock); the 123 radiation pattern generates a 123 magnetic modulation that flows across the pineal gland. This and other glands release hormones into the body triggering cell division in the healthy body. Cells divide and grow. Systems develop, and the body grows. The metabolic system adopts the periodicity of the solar clock and cells divide and multiply to the periodicity of the 123 clock. The 'healthy' system sends a *stop* signal back to the body cells. The cells stop dividing. The organism is healthy.

Figure A13b shows an unhealthy situation. Here the same correct radiation pattern of 123 again flows across the pineal gland. Again cells divide and multiply. But this time the metabolic rate is influenced by an outside carcinogen, like tobacco or coffee. The carcinogen causes the metabolic rate to shift to a different rhythm, say 134. The two comparator clocks can now never agree; one is counting 123 from the sun, the other 134 from the metabolic rate. The *stop* signal will never be sent to stop cells dividing. Cells divide and multiply, divide and multiply over and over again. This is cancer. Put two clocks in one body and, like Harker's cockroaches, the result is chaos.

Introduction of artificial hormones will influence the body and the endocrine system directly. This is why oestrogen in the contraceptive pill causes cancer. Anything that interferes with either the autonomous endocrine system or the solar clock will cause biorhythmic de-synchronisation and cancer. Overhead power lines cause cancer by 'blocking out' the solar clock. Again the metabolic rate loses parity, leading to cancerous activity in cells.

This also explains why chemotherapy, a modern chemical treatment for cancer, is only 25 per cent effective: one in four. If the treatment were scheduled to coincide with biorhythms, then the success rate might rise to perhaps 100 per cent by matching the treatment to the correct solar code of 123, 124, 134 or 234

(viii) How VDUs Cause Miscarriages

Visual display units, used in computer systems and television tubes, radiate electromagnetic radiation and X-rays (ionising radiations). These impinge on the pineal gland directly, affecting the amount of

How the Sun Causes Cancers

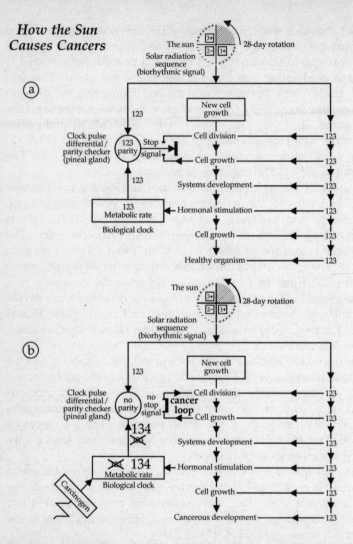

Figure A13. (a) Model of cell division and growth in a healthy organism. The biorhythmic signal and the internal biological clock share the same 'clock speed', which leads to cellular harmony. (b) Model of cell division and growth in a dysfunctional organism: the internal biological clock is disturbed with the introduction of a carcinogen into the system. The biological 'clock speed' now shifts to, say, 134. The differential/parity checker senses lack of parity. No stop signal is sent to the cell division mechanism. Cells divide and multiply uncontrollably. Like Harker's cockroach experiments, two clocks in one body result in cancer.

Solar Radiation and Sunspot Activity

The sun's polar magnetic field (infilled in black, below) revolves once around the sun's axis every 37 days (every 40.5 days when measured from earth). The equatorial region, which has its own magnetic field, revolves faster: every 26 days when measured on the sun's surface, 28 days when viewed from earth. The different rotational speeds of these two magnetic fields are known by scientists as 'the differential rotation of the sun's magnetic fields'. It is this magnetic interaction which causes charged particles to leave the sun's surface and bombard the earth

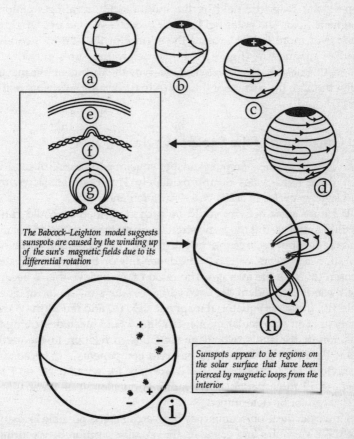

The Babcock–Leighton model suggests sunspots are caused by the winding up of the sun's magnetic fields due to its differential rotation

Sunspots appear to be regions on the solar surface that have been pierced by magnetic loops from the interior

Figure A14. Radiation from the sun is known to vary with changes in sunspot activity. In 1961 engineers Babcock and Leighton proposed that sunspots were caused by the winding up of the sun's two separate magnetic fields. Hence, radiation from the sun and fertility on earth can be expected to correlate with sunspot activity.

hormone production. This can lead to insufficient progesterone production during pregnancy, resulting in spontaneous miscarriage of the foetus.

(ix) The Cause of Sunspots

In 1961 a model was put forward by engineers Babcock and Leighton, who proposed that sunspots were caused by the winding up of the sun's polar magnetic field by the more quickly rotating equatorial magnetic field. The polar field slowly becomes wound up, wrapping itself ever more tightly around the surface of the sun in a coil-like field of magnetism (figure A14a–d). Below the sun's surface, the magnetic lines become tangled (A14e–f) by the turbulent plasma and burst through the surface of the sun (A14g), forming a sunspot pair (h and i).

(x) Calculation of the Sunspot Cycle

John Eddy's bristlecone pine sunspot envelope (figure A10) suggests that these mini-cycles of approximately 11.5 years subsist within longer-term cycles of 1,200 years' duration and more.

If future solar activity could be predicted, then so could future fertility patterns. But modern astronomers maintain, quite adamantly, that the sunspot cycle cannot be calculated. They agree that the *average* duration is 11 years, or 11.5 years, depending on the period of history chosen to make the average. The reason they believe this is because the cycle is dependent on *three* variables: the sun's polar magnetic field (P), the sun's equatorial magnetic field (E) and the earth (W). An analysis at any particular moment in time would mean describing the position of the sun's two magnetic fields in relation to the earth's field. Because the sun's field has two components *and* because its behaviour is 'cumulative' (i.e. it appears to 'wind itself up') *and* because all three variables are moving, calculation of the magnetic cycles cannot be determined.

However, these objections may be overcome. It *is* possible to analyse the three variables and calculate the angular position between them using a method I describe as 'rotational differentiation'. Because P and E are revolving at different speeds, there must come a moment in time when they both occupy the same angular position. This happens

The 187-Year (68,302-Day) Sunspot Cycle

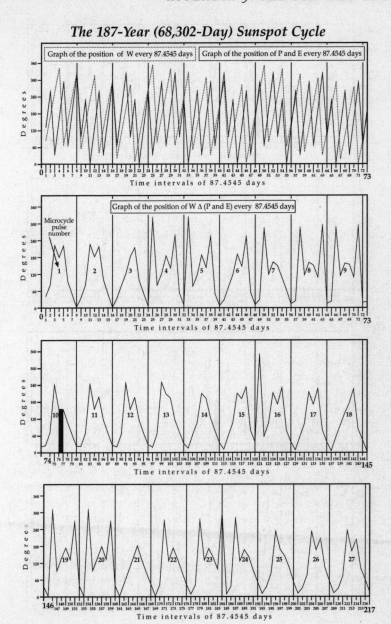

Figure A15a.

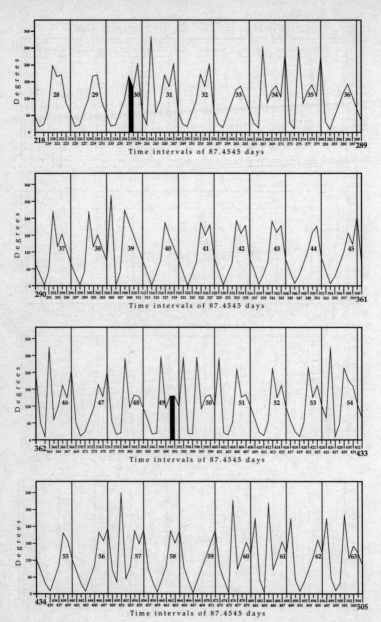

Figure A15b.

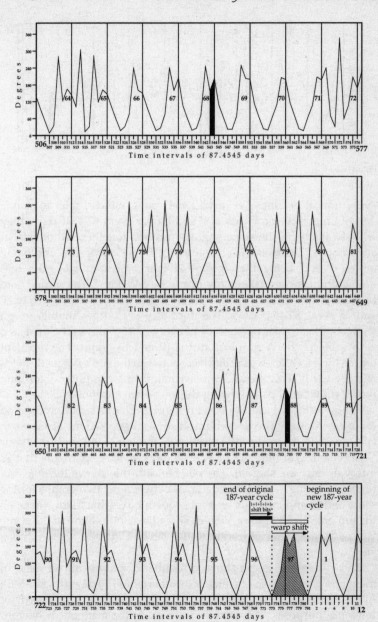

Figure A15c.

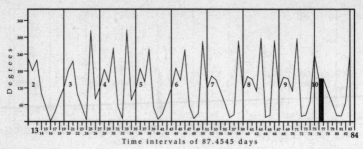

Figure A15d.

every time E overlaps P, every 87.4545 days, which I refer to as one 'bit' of time. If we now look at P and E only every 87.4545 days, they will always be in the same angular position together, although that angular position itself will change every 87.4545 days. This effectively 'glues' P and E together (provided that measurements from that moment in time are taken only every 87.4545 days). The second step in the calculation is to draw a graph of the combined position of (P and E) every 87.4545 days. The third step is to draw another graph showing the angular position of W every 87.4545 days. The final step is to subtract the W graph from the (P and E) graph. The resultant graph, therefore, shows the *difference* between the sun's magnetic fields and the earth. This method was written into a computer algorithm, which provided a plot showing the long-term sunspot cycle.

Figure A15a, top, shows two zigzagging graphs superimposed on top of each other. The dotted graph shows the positions of the earth (W), the solid line shows the position of the combined sun's magnetic field (P and E) at intervals of 87.4545 days (to save space, the first 73 intervals only are shown). The box beneath this shows the *difference* (denoted by the Greek letter delta, Δ) between the two graphs for the same period and intervals, and subsequent boxes that follow (beneath the top graph and figures A15b-d) show the continuation of the entire '*difference*' graph which continues far beyond interval 73, to interval 781.

The 'difference' graph shows a number of pulses (microcycles) of magnetic activity, each of which lasts for around 700 days (8 x 87.4545). In all, there are 97 pulses, each of which has been numbered for reference purposes. This enables us to study the magnetic behaviour of the earth against that of the sun. If, at one moment in time, the

The Hypothesised 11.49-Year Sunspot Cycle

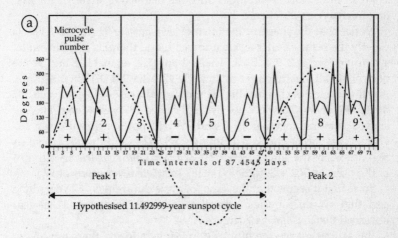

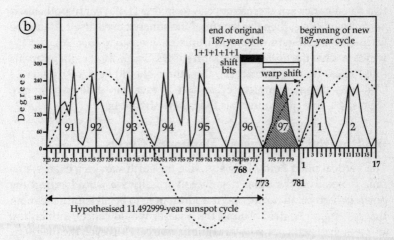

Figure A16. (a) The first 9 cycles of the 97-microcycle series of pulses that make up one 187-year sunspot cycle showing the hypothesised 11.49-year cycle (*dotted line*). (b) The last 7 cycles of the 97-microcycle series; the black horizontal space bar shows the end of one 187-year cycle (96 microcycles) shunted forward by 5 divisions from 768 to 773. Eight more divisions separate the old fundamental cycle (*white space bar above the words 'warp shift'*) from the new fundamental cycle, which begins after bit 781.

sun's polar field, equatorial field and earth are all aligned, then the difference between them will be zero. This is the start of the cycle. Then all three start revolving (notice the distinctive shape of the first few microcycles numbered 1–9).

Notice that the shape of the microcycle *following* 97 (figure A15c) is exactly the same as microcycle number 1, and that this is followed by a repeat of cycles 2, 3, 4, 5 etc. These shapes tell us that P, E and W are once again all together after microcycle 97, after 'bit 781' on the graph. Another cycle now begins. Bit 781 multiplied by 87.4545 days = 68,302 days, 187 years. The sunspot cycle is hence 187 years long. Having started rotating together P, E and W will not synchronise for 187 years. (This can be checked as follows: 68,302 ÷ 26 (P) = 2,627 *complete* revolutions of the equator. 68,302 ÷ 37 (P) = 1,846 *complete* revolutions of the pole. 68,302 ÷ 365.25 (W) = 187 *complete* revolutions of W.)

So at first it seems that the sunspot cycle duration is 187 years long and that six microcycles 'group' together to form one 11.49-year observed *fundamental cycle* (figure A16).

But at first glance the figures don't quite add up, there are one or two discrepancies: if six microcycles form one 11.49-year hypothesised *fundamental* cycle, then the length of the sunspot cycle itself should be 96 microcycles (some whole multiple of 6: e.g. 6 x 16 = 96), not 97, which is what the 'difference' graph shows. Secondly, if eight intervals (bits) make up one microcycle, then there should be 8 x 97 intervals (776 bits) in one complete cycle, but in fact the 'difference graph' shows 781, five more intervals than there should be.

(xi) How the Sun Causes Catastrophe Cycles

The vertical polar field of the sun, like the earth, carries a charge; one pole is positive, the other negative. Normally we would expect the north pole to be all north, and the south pole to be all south, meaning that the magnetic field around the equator would cancel, amounting to a region of zero, or neutral magnetic charge. However, the magnetic distribution of this area, from observation, is known to be 'warped' and 'tilted' (figure A17).

Examining figure A15, the five intersections of the warp show up clearly at microcycle pulse numbers 10, 30, 49, 68 and 88. These microcycles are nine bits wide, unlike all the others, which are only eight. This suggests that the differential rotation of the sun's magnetic

The Warped and Tilted Neutral Sheet of the Sun's Magnetic Field

Figure A17. This diagram shows the sun's magnetic field around the equator (which is neither north nor south polarity) to be distorted. This area of null magnetic activity is also tilted and hence is known more commonly to scientists as the warped, tilted, neutral sheet of the sun.

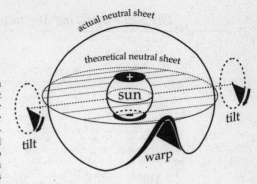

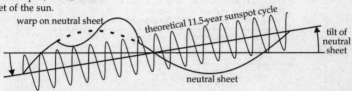

Figure A18. The smaller cycles represent a theoretical 11.5-year sunspot cycle. It is this that distorts the neutral sheet into its observed warped shape.

Modulation of the Sunspot Cycle by the Neutral Sheet

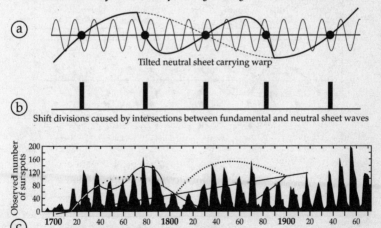

Figure A19 (a–c). The distorted neutral sheet amplifies and suppresses sunspot activity, leading to variations in the number of observed sunspots over time. The variations in numbers follow the shape of the neutral sheet.

The Sun's Twisting Magnetic Field

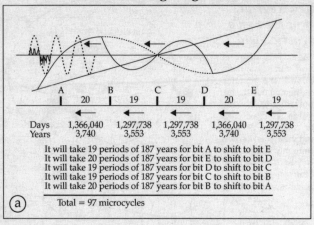

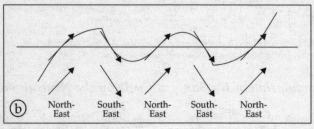

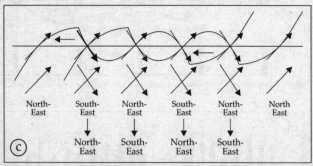

	A		B		C		D		E	
		20		19		19		20		19

| Days | 1,366,040 | 1,297,738 | 1,297,738 | 1,366,040 | 1,297,738 |
| Years | 3,740 | 3,553 | 3,553 | 3,740 | 3,553 |

It will take 19 periods of 187 years for bit A to shift to bit E
It will take 20 periods of 187 years for bit E to shift to bit D
It will take 19 periods of 187 years for bit D to shift to bit C
It will take 19 periods of 187 years for bit C to shift to bit B
It will take 20 periods of 187 years for bit B to shift to bit A

Total = 97 microcycles

Figure A20. (a) Schematic showing how the sun's neutral sheet slides to the left by a known amount every 187 years. (b) Neutral sheet showing field direction indicated by arrows. (c) Schematic showing the original position of the neutral sheet, with original direction arrows, compared with the new position of the neutral sheet shown after 20 periods of 187 years. The sun's neutral sheet effectively shifts direction, indicated by the arrows, compared with its initial field direction.

field distorts and twists the neutral sheet into its warped and tilted position. The extra bits arise whenever the two waves intersect (figure A18).

Plotting the shift bits along the entire length of the 187-year cycle, it becomes clear what is actually happening (figures A19a and b): the tilted warped neutral sheet can be seen to 'modulate' (squash and pull) the observed sunspot plot (figure A19c). The graph shows clearly that the warp interferes with the winding-up process of the sun's magnetic fields. Where the warp crosses the microcycles, the micro-cycles are shunted forward. The effect is to slow down the cumulative magnetic activity within the sun such that the 96-microcycle series becomes 96 plus an extra five interval- 'shift bits'. These 'bits' shift the entire 11.5-year cycle forward by one bit at every point of intersection (see figure A16b, black space bar).

Examination of figure A16b reconciles the ostensible error between the hypothesised 11.49-year cycle, which should be 16 x 8 (768) and the actual printout, which shows microcycle 96 ending at bit 773. The extra five shift bits shunt the cycle forward by five bits during the cycle, accounting for the 'error' between the two values.

Addressing the problem of 97 microcycles instead of 96: examination of figure A16b tells us that the new 11.5-year hypothesised cycle is displaced from the original 187-year cycle by eight bits (figure 16b, white space bar), one complete microcycle (number 97). It is the fundamental cycle that carries the warp. The graph is therefore telling us that the warp itself also moves, by eight shift bits, every 187 years. This means that shift bits must move by eight bits every 187-year cycle together with the neutral sheet, also by eight bits (one microcycle) every 187-year period.

Individual shift bits thus trickle along the microcycle sequence. For one shift bit to move through 97 microcycles will take 97 x 187 = 18,139 years. This is the duration of the long-term sunspot cycle. This means that if P, E, W and the neutral sheet all begin together, they will take 18,139 years to get back together again.

The analysis is even more revealing: shift bits will virtually collide as they shift along the sequence. For example, because there are twenty microcycles separating bit E from D, and because the warp shifts one microcycle every 187 years, it will take 20 x 187 years for bit E to 'collide' with the original position of bit D (figure A20). This period of twenty 187-year sunspot cycles (20 x 68,302) = 1,366,040 days. This

How the Sun's Twisting Magnetic Fields Destroy Life on Earth

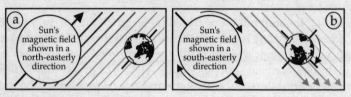

Figure A21. (a) The sun's and earth's magnetic fields are mutually coupled. (b) Analysis of sunspot activity shows that the sun's magnetic field shifts direction after 3,740 years (1,366,040 days). Magnetic shifts always bring infertility cycles through variation in the production of oestrogen and progesterone in females. The concomitant shifting of the earth's magnetic field allows an increase in harmful ionising radiation from the sun to enter the earth's atmosphere, causing increased spontaneous foetal abortion (miscarriages) and hence higher infant mortality. Sometimes, in a worst-case scenario, the earth flips on its axis, realigning its magnetic field to that of the sun. When this happens, catastrophic destruction frequents earth.

How the Maya Understood the Super-Science of the Sun

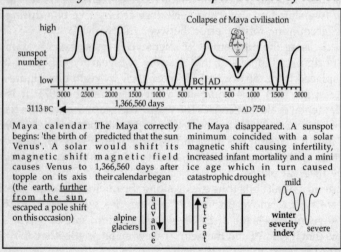

Maya calendar begins: 'the birth of Venus'. A solar magnetic shift causes Venus to topple on its axis (the earth, <u>further from the sun</u>, escaped a pole shift on this occasion)

The Maya correctly predicted that the sun would shift its magnetic field 1,366,560 days after their calendar began

The Maya disappeared. A sunspot minimum coincided with a solar magnetic shift causing infertility, increased infant mortality and a mini ice age which in turn caused catastrophic drought

Figure A22. The Maya worshipped the sun as the god of astrology (personality determination) and the god of fertility. They worshipped the number 1,366,560 as the mythological birthdate of the planet Venus, correctly predicting that their own civilisation would decline 1,366,560 days (one solar magnetic reversal) after their calendar began in 3113 BC. (The Mayan figure of 1,366,560 differs slightly from the computer-calculated value of 1,366,040. They used observations of the planet Venus to monitor the cycle; 2,340 revolutions of the Venus interval (figure A23), as seen from earth, amounts to 1,366,560 days.)

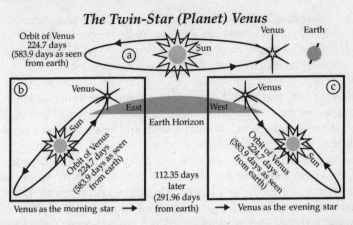

Figure A23. (a) The 224.7-day orbit of Venus falls between that of Mercury (not shown here). However, the interval between successive identical appearances of Venus, as seen from the moving earth, is 583.9 days. This means that Venus, in the position shown in (b), appears brightly illuminated in the dark morning sky. In position (c) the sun sets before Venus, which shines brightly in the darkening evening sky. Because of this, and because Venus is the brightest heavenly body, it is referred to as the 'morning star' and the 'evening star', the twin star. Brightness (light) is synonymous with purity; hence, several spiritually pure teachers, including Jesus, Tutankhamun and Lord Pacal, were associated with Venus (see figures A69–73).

was the number worshipped by the Maya. (The actual number worshipped by the Maya was 1,366,560 days. The Maya kept track of the cycle using complete numbers of Venus intervals, the position of Venus as seen from earth. 2,340 complete Venus intervals amounts to 1,366,560 days. For the Maya, this date was known as 'the birth of Venus', which coincided with the beginning of the Maya calendar in 3113 BC.) What does this mean?

We can mark the direction of the neutral sheet on top of the waveform using arrows (figure A20b), and again underneath (figure A20c). Then we can shift the warp along the sequence by twenty microcycle shifts so that bit E collides with bit D (figure A20c). What this shows is that the neutral sheet 'reverses' every 1,366,040 days. By worshipping the sacred number of 1,366,560 the Maya were trying to tell us that the sun's magnetic field reverses every 1,366,560 days.

When the sun's magnetic field shifts in this way, three things can happen:

(1) disruption in fertility occurs on earth;

(2) more harmful ionising radiations enter the earth's atmosphere, leading to increased infant mutations and higher infant mortality;

(3) if the magnetic twist is strong enough the earth will tilt (figure A21) on its axis (note: this does not happen every shift).

It seems likely that in 3113 BC the planet Venus (see figure A23), which is closer to the sun than the earth, toppled on its axis; but on that occasion the earth, which is more distant and hence less influenced by the diminished magnetic fluctuations, escaped 'pole-tilting' and destruction (which would explain why Venus is the only planet in our solar system that is upside down and why it spins in the opposite direction to all the other planets). The Maya knew (figure A22) that destruction would come again, 1,366,560 days after the last time, in around AD 627. Palaeomagnetic evidence, from Pearson (after Cox) in *Climate and Evolution*, and tree-ring data (Pearson, after Bucha, 1970) shows that the earth's magnetic field shifted at that time and that the shift followed the direction of the sun's neutral warp. The Maya knew that the sun's radiation would fail them for 187 years on either side of this period, from AD 440 to AD 814. In AD 750 the Maya disappeared. At the same time as the neutral sheet reversed, a sunspot minimum also failed their reproductive needs and led to a mini-ice age, which brought drought and destruction. Although there was no pole tilt, it was the end for the Maya. Other countries in higher latitudes survived the drought and the reduced fertility, and suffered less from the increased ionising radiations that bombard equatorial regions more perpendicularly and severely than their neighbours.

More than a thousand years ago, in the jungles of Central America, the Maya believed that the earth had been destroyed on four previous occasions; now we know why, and how.

They believed that the sun affects fertility and the rise and fall of civilisations; now we know how.

They believed in astrology, that the sun affects character, fate and fortune; now we know it does.

They believed we are now living in the fifth and final 'age of the sun', which they say will end on 22 December in the year 2012, although it is unclear, at this moment, how this will occur.

Perhaps we need to listen to what they have been trying to tell us.

What some people fail to appreciate is that if this method *is* wrong, then the Maya must have *guessed* the duration of magnetic reversals to be 1,366,560 days. It also means that the Maya Transformers (a few of which are featured in this book) do not contain encoded information; it means that the earth does not tilt on its axis periodically (which in turn means there is no reason why palm trees can't grow in the icy climate of Spitzbergen, no reason why oil deposits can't be found in Antarctica, and that frozen mammoths, buried beneath the tundra of frozen Siberia, survived on a diet of snow and, moreover, that the buttercups found clenched between their teeth are the imaginings of generations of explorers and excavators). It further means that modern man understands how cancer is caused but is unwilling to effect a cure, that he understands how pigeons navigate but refuses to say, that he believes the cause of homesickness to be emotional rather than biochemical, while at the same time accepts that modern science appreciates that the cause of jetlag is down to variations in the production of melatonin caused by time differences. It would also mean that the reason why trade unions around the world advise their female members not to use VDU screens when pregnant is because they are all mistaken and that all the miscarriages which have taken place never actually occurred. And it means, of course, that the orthodox scientific community is much cleverer than Tutankhamun, Lord Pacal and Viracocha, each of whom encoded the super-science of the sun into their treasures.

(xii) The Cause of Chinese Astrology

Six microcycles of magnetic activity on the sun's surface (figure A16) amount to: 6 x 8 x 87.4545 days = 4,197.8 days = 11.49 years. However, that duration (from figure A16) amounts to a preliminary analysis, exclusive of shift bit and neutral warp considerations. As figure A16 goes on to show, the neutral warp shift bits, and the neutral warp shift, extend the duration such that the cycles subsist for 11.69 years. The true position (explained in detail in *The Tutankhamun Prophecies*) is even more complex due to the *differential* nature of the variables. Exact analysis of the variables shows that the *differential* of the fundamental sunspot cycle period actually takes 11.97 years on average, which is very close to the 12-year astrological cycle recognised by the ancient Chinese.

The Chinese cycle of 12 years is itself one-fifth of a longer Chinese cycle of 60 years, after which time events repeat. In addition, analysis

The 12-Year Chinese Astrological Cycle

Sign						Correction days		
Rat	31	January	1900 to 18	February	1901	+18	Metal	(+)
Ox	19	February	1901 to 07	February	1902	−12	Metal	(−)
Tiger	08	February	1902 to 28	January	1903	−10	Water	(+)
Rabbit	29	January	1903 to 15	February	1904	+17	Water	(−)
Dragon	16	February	1904 to 03	February	1905	−13	Wood	(+)
Snake	04	February	1905 to 24	January	1906	− 11	Wood	(−)
Horse	25	January	1906 to 12	February	1907	+18	Fire	(+)
Sheep	13	February	1907 to 01	February	1908	− 12	Fire	(−)
Monkey	02	February	1908 to 21	January	1909	− 12	Earth	(+)
Rooster	22	January	1909 to 09	February	1910	+18	Earth	(−)
Dog	10	February	1910 to 29	January	1911	− 12	Metal	(+)
Boar	30	January	1911 to 17	February	1912	+18	Metal	(−)

Correction days from 1900 to 1912 = +17

	17	February	1912 to 04	February	1924	− 14		
	04	February	1924 to 23	January	1936	− 13		
	24	January	1936 to 09	February	1948	+16		
	10	Februar	1948 to 27	January	1960	− 14		
	28	January	1960 to 15	January	1972	− 12		
	16	January	1972 to 01	February	1984	+18		

Figure A24. The exact Chinese astrological years from 1900 to 1984 showing correction days for every 12-year cycle.

of the behaviour of the *magnetic microcycles* (from which the differential is obtained) shows that each year the *microcycles* change direction and hence correlate with the years of the Chinese cycle, which alternate in polarity each year. Each year of the Chinese cycle is also 'error-corrected'. Hence the Chinese year varies in length (marginally) together with its dates of commencement and completion.

The Exact Chinese Years, from 1900 to 1984

Examination of the Chinese astrological years (figure A24) shows that the Chinese apply an annual error correction. During the first 12-year cycle, this amounts to +17 days (the cycle begins on 31 January 1900 and ends on 17 February 1912). The next 12-year period is corrected by -14 days, the next by -13; then 16; and then -14, as shown. The absolute deviation of these correction periods (during one 60-year cycle) amounts to -17 + 14 + 13 + 16 + 14 = 74 days, which over 5 cycles amounts to plus or minus 14.8 days (plus or minus 0.02025 years), on average, each 12-year period.

This error, applied to the 12-year cycle, means that the duration of the Chinese cycle varies between 11.98 years and 12.02 years. The 12-year Chinese cycle is, therefore, almost identical to the solar radiation *differential* cycle of 11.97 years. This, though, is the average over only 60 years, not the 18,139 years of one great sunspot cycle.

So how did the ancient Chinese obtain their figure? How did they know that the sun had two distinct magnetic fields? How did they know that these rotated? How did they know that the speeds of rotation amounted to 37- and 26-day periods, and how did they manage the complex calculations to determine the duration of the differential?

Tutankhamun taught his people the super-science of the sun, as did Lord Pacal of the Maya, Viracocha, and Viracocha Pachacamac of South America. Each of these Supergods left behind their knowledge encoded into their treasures. Who brought the super-science of the sun to the ancient Chinese? Was it Shi Huangdi, the Son of Heaven, or did he inherit the knowledge from a succession of Sons of Heaven dating back to the Yellow Emperor in around 2697 BC? The secret message encoded into the ten face shapes of the first emperor's terracotta army (Chapter 1) instructed us to examine carefully the soldiers in the tunnels, to learn more about the sun and God. This completes the section on the sun and how it affects life on earth. We can now examine the world of God, as perceived by the ancients. This explains what God is, and what the soul is, which in turn explains why we live, why we die and why this has to be.

(xiii) The Four Bodies

Ancient civilisations believed that the human constitution may be broken down into four distinct areas (figure A25): the astral (spiritual), the physical, the intellectual and the emotional. They believed that these four bodies were created simultaneously and that on death the physical body returned to dust, taking with it the emotional body (an

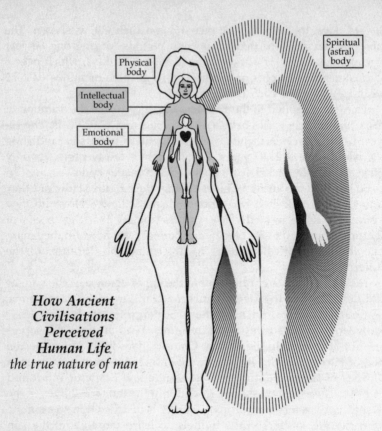

*How Ancient
Civilisations
Perceived
Human Life*
the true nature of man

Figure A25. The four bodies.

adjunct of the heart) and the intellectual body (an adjunct of the brain). Destination of the soul depended on the purity of the soul at the time of physical death; pure souls would journey to the heavens and become stars, everlasting gods. Impure souls would journey through the underworld and purgatory before reincarnating on earth for another try at soul purification through physical, emotional and intellectual suffering. It was for this reason that the Egyptians preserved only some of their internal organs (liver, lungs, stomach and intestines) in canopic jars on physical death. The practice was allegorical; there was no need to preserve the heart and brain – if they did reincarnate they would receive a new heart and a new brain, thereby remembering nothing of their previous emotional or intellectual lifetimes.

(xiv) The Three Worlds (the various destinations of the soul)

The archaeological evidence left to us by the Supergods suggests that three worlds exist (figure A26) that accommodate the physical and spiritual states of being. These are the God World, where resides the creator of the universe; the Physical World, which includes the stars, planets, trees, birds and all living and non-living tangibles; and the Soul World, the place where impure spirits subsist in between existence in either the Physical World or the God World.

(xv) The General Theory of Existence (incorporating the Theory of Divine Reconciliation)

Before we can progress towards a true understanding of the meaning of life (as put forward by the ancients) and our own place in the universe, we must first consider the religious argument for reincarnation which recognises that all the world's religions agree on certain propositions: in the beginning God the creator existed; God the creator was light (electromagnetic energy); God was good and God was love. Christianity adds that God made man in his own image.

We can now examine the religious argument: if God is good and God is love, then the only thing better than God must be more God. God's objective must therefore be growth, more God. This is the Theory of Divine Reconciliation, one part of an all-embracing General Theory of Existence (figure A27). The Bible tells us that God made man in his own image, and we know that man cannot grow (beyond a given limit) unless he sacrifices a part of his physical being, a sperm containing chromosomes, to produce more offspring. In the same way, a woman cannot grow unless she sacrifices an ovum containing chromosomes. This must mean that God cannot grow unless he likewise sacrifices a part of himself, throws a part of himself away, as it were. So in the beginning God, electromagnetic energy, must have detached a part of himself (figure A28), a portion of electromagnetic energy (light). Physicist Albert Einstein tells us that energy cannot be destroyed, only converted from one state to another; energy may be converted to mass (physical things), at least in a mathematical sense,

Figure A26. Decoded stories from the Amazing Lid of Palenque, the tombstone lid that covered the sarcophagus of Lord Pacal of the Maya (Appendix 4) explain how the souls of those who die at childbirth, in battle and in sacrifice migrate to the paradises, destinations of the dead, to enjoy heavenly bliss presumably before proceeding to the God World. Other pictures, from the same lid, explain how the soul leaves the body for either rebirth in the stars (the heavens and the God World) or rebirth on earth (reincarnation). The encoded stories describe the journey of the soul through the underworld and purgatory. The Maya, Egyptians and Peruvians all believed that there were nine levels to the underworld through which the departed soul had to travel prior to moving on, either to the God World or to reincarnation on earth. (According to stories from the Amazing Lid of Palenque, it seems that perfectly purified souls fast-track through the Soul World to the God World and that impure souls suffer in the underworld (purgatory) for their earthly sins before acquiring the energy to reincarnate on earth for another chance of soul purification.)

The General Theory of Existence

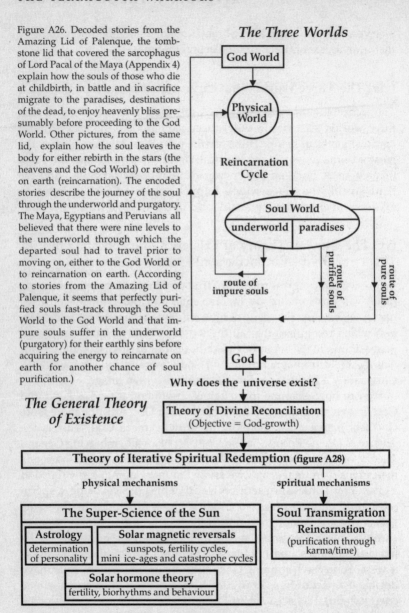

Figure A27. Treasures from the tombs of the Maya, Egyptians and Peruvians suggest that the purpose of the universe is to accommodate God-growth (in accordance with the Theory of Divine Reconciliation, as detailed in the main text). Figure A28 resolves the Theory of Divine Reconciliation and the Three Worlds hypothesis into a working model.

and mass may be converted to energy. The sacrificed energy (E) was then converted into mass (m), the physical universe.

The energy contained in a particular mass is proportional to the atomic weight of the mass (the sum of the constituent parts of the atom) and to the speed of light squared ($E=mc^2$). When a heavy (radioactive) element is smashed to pieces, the energy released is proportional to both its atomic weight and the speed of light (300,000,000 metres per second) squared. The result is a very large bang, a nuclear explosion. We must assume that some kind of *inverse* bang took place when God converted himself into the physical universe and that this event is what orthodox scientists nowadays refer to as 'the big bang' from which our universe was created.

In the beginning, in the spiritual world, there was no such thing as time. The only thing that existed was light. Nothing ever happened. Nothing happened before anything else and nothing happened after anything else, which means that time did not exist. Time began with the creation of the physical universe. Things began to happen after the big bang. Things then happened before other things had happened, and things happened after other things had happened. Time embraced evolution, and mankind biologically advanced. In time, man became more complex and intellectually advanced. The brain developed operating voltages, the opposite charge to that which created them; when +E (positive E) moves across the equation, it must convert to -m (minus m), a simple rule of algebra which explains why biological man has a propensity to be attracted back to God.

These voltages then began to attract further packets of energy – soul energy – from the creator energy. This marks the evolutionary moment at which mankind acquired a soul and became a complete being.

The physical world differs from the spiritual world, just as the physical world differs from the intellectual world. If I have a £1 coin in the physical world and you have a £1 coin in the physical world and we exchange them, then we still each have only £1. However, in the intellectual world, if I have one idea and you, too, have one idea and we exchange them, we both finish up with two ideas, at no cost. Taking this one step further, in accordance with the Scriptures, it seems that (at least in the spiritual world) if I love you my soul voltage increases, grows, at no cost, whereas if I hate you, my soul voltage depletes. If my soul voltage has grown, it is attracted with

The Theory of Iterative Spiritual Redemption

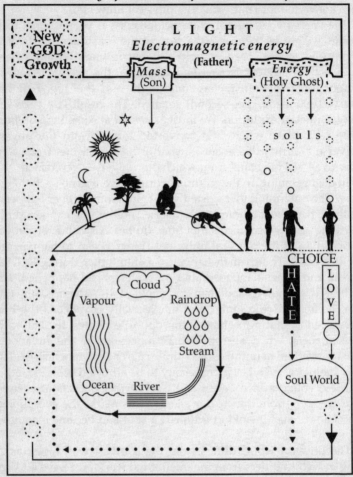

Figure A28. The Scriptures tell us that God is light. Light is electromagnetic energy. Einstein tells us that $E = mc^2$, which means that energy (E) can be converted into physical mass (m) and mass can be converted into energy. The equation tells us that the release of energy, when mass is converted, is proportional to the speed of light squared (c^2). This suggests that in the beginning God sacrificed a part of himself, creating the physical universe (the Son). Physical bodies then evolved to attract discrete packets of electromagnetic energy (souls) away from the source of energy (God). The journey of the soul is analogous to that of a raindrop, which is reborn many times. Purification comes from love and sacrifice. Purified souls return to the creator. As a result, the creator grows. Bad souls return to earth, attempting purification once again.

greater force back to the creator energy (God) on physical death of the body. Conversely, if my voltage has fallen during its lifetime, it instead returns to earth, next time as a lower being, attracted to a lower-voltage body, for another try at purification. In this way God grows, the universe grows and those who have not loved their neighbour suffer again during another incarnation on earth. Figure A28 explains this process diagramatically; the model shows how good souls grow and return to the creator, whereas, conversely, bad souls are again reborn on earth, in an endless cycle of death and rebirth – analogous to raindrops that flow to the rivers and the seas before once again becoming vapour to recondense for another cycle of activity.

(xvi) Heaven and Hell

In 1990 the New Zealand airline pilot Bruce Cathie recalculated Albert Einstein's speed of light to reflect more adequately the movement of light around the spherical earth, rather than in a straight line between two objects. His new figure, calculated in degrees of a circle per second, rather than metres per second, showed that light (God) travelled at 144,000 minutes of arc per second (2,400 degrees per second), meaning that a light beam travels around the physical earth 6.66 times in one second. In the Book of Revelation in the Bible, the number 144,000 represents the number of the purified who will be saved when destruction frequents the earth – the number of souls who will go to heaven – whereas the number 666 is described as 'the number of the beast', commonly understood to refer to the devil, or hell, the opposite to God. Cathie's discovery, therefore, suggests that the number 666 in Revelation may in fact refer to the earth, meaning that the physical earth is the devil, the opposite of God.

The fact that everything in the physical universe is of the opposite polarity charge to that of the creator energy (heaven) also means that everything in the physical universe must likewise be hell, including physical biological bodies. But God, the creative energy, is electro-magnetically attached to each and every one of the biological bodies. A human being is therefore half God (soul) and half devil (body), a person. When we look at life in this way, everything begins to make sense. For every happiness there is unhappiness, for every gain there is loss, for every life there is death, and for every day there is night. Esoteric societies, and the Church, know this already. They know that

The Prisoners of Huaca Cao Viejo, Peru

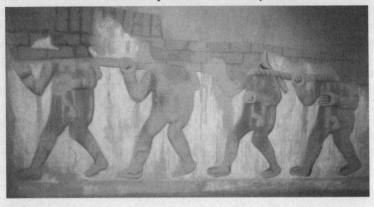

Figure A29. Mochica stucco relief of the 'prisoners' found on the northern wall of the platform on the first level at Huaca Cao Viejo in the Chicama Valley, on the north-west coast of Peru. The characters are bound by the neck with heavy rope and parade with erections. A similar depiction of bound captives can be seen in the tomb of Tutankhamun (see figure A37). The message here reads: *procreation leads to captivity* (procreation leads to reincarnation and eternal imprisonment on earth), reaffirming the message carried by the man with the hat featured beneath Lord Pacal's mouth in the decoded Amazing Lid of Palenque (figure A52): the pure of heart go to heaven while those who procreate find only death and reincarnation on earth.

this place is hell. They, like you, know the sacred secret of the ancients. On the one hand they wish to escape from this endless hell, and yet they know that they cannot escape unless they love God and their neighbour. And therein lies the difficulty: love for God implies love for God's objective, which is growth. God made sex pleasurable to ensure a steady supply of babies that would attract more and more souls from the God World (figure A28), thus enabling perpetual God-growth for eternity. Looked at in this way, mankind is a conduit that facilitates the objective of divine reconciliation, enabling God to grow. This is why the Church opposes birth control and abortion. The objective of individuals in the Church and those in the esoteric societies is therefore to allow God to grow and yet at the same time escape from hell. This is the reason for the secrecy; by keeping this knowledge secret, and loving God and their neighbour, the esoteric orders can purify their own soul and escape, leaving others behind to have more babies, most of which will repeatedly reincarnate on earth.

Physical birth amounts to eternal imprisonment on earth. This is why prisoners appear with erect penises on the walls at Huaca Cao Viejo (figure A29) on the north-west coast of Peru and why prisoners appear in the tomb seals of Tutankhamun (figure A37) bound by ropes that terminate with the divine lotus and why a group of prisoners was buried beside the pyramid of Shi Huangdi. Life on earth amounts to divine imprisonment.

The mechanism of karma (the universal law of cause and effect, action and reaction) provides the final link in the chain of understanding; bad (lower-voltage) souls reincarnate into lower-voltage bodies and suffer during the next incarnation on earth. Suffering in the next life increases the soul voltage during that lifetime, leading to reincarnation again, next time in a higher-voltage body. In this way each earth-life alternates between more suffering or less suffering. This is why the ancients believed in the notion of *inverse transmigration* of souls; the first will become the last and the last the first; the rich will reincarnate as the poor and the poor as the rich; men as women and women as men etc.

The bound prisoners of Huaca Cao Viejo, parading with their erections, and the presence of the bat-god covering the genitals of the man with the hat on the decoded face of Lord Pacal (figure A51) also suggest another step in this process; the man with the hat tells us that purification (a pure heart) comes only to those who do not procreate – the presence of the bat-god across his genitals suggesting that those who procreate find only death. The prisoners of Huaca Cao Viejo also tell us that those who have erections are for ever imprisoned. We need to ask why this should be the case and what physical mechanism might be employed to ensure the propagation of such a scheme.

(xvii) The Ultimate Secret of the Universe

An examination of the chakra centres (figure A30) shows that purification of the spirit is possible only when the physical, emotional and intellectual bodies achieve coordinated equilibrium. This can happen only when the physical, emotional and intellectual bodies are at perfect peace with the universe, God and our neighbour. When we love our neighbour more than ourselves, energy, known as *sushumna* to the mystics, ascends the spine and light radiates from the head; we become one of the 144,000 with light radiating from the forehead. It

Chakras: the Nine Gateways to Heaven

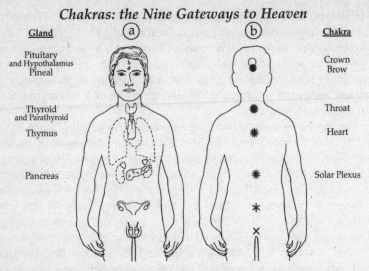

Gland	(a)	(b)	Chakra
Pituitary and Hypothalamus Pineal			Crown Brow
Thyroid and Parathyroid			Throat
Thymus			Heart
Pancreas			Solar Plexus

Figure A30. (a) Chief glands of the endocrine system; (b) chakra (energy) centres; (c) positive (ida), negative (pingala) and light (sushumna) energy flow patterns around chakra centres when the physical, emotional and intellectual bodies achieve coordinated equilibrium; (d) the caduceus representing the cancellation of positive and negative energies, which gives rise to the generation of light, the feathered snake.

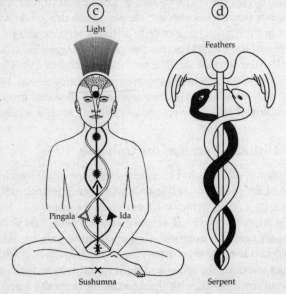

Closing the Gateways to Heaven

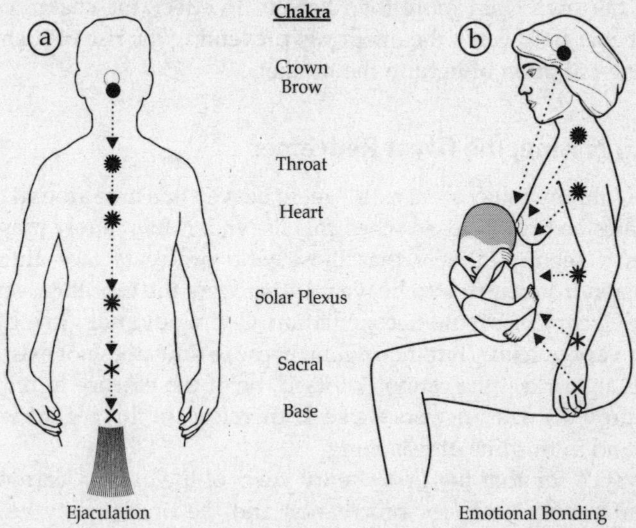

Figure A31. In the male, ejaculation directs energy away from the chakra centres, precluding coordinated equilibrium of energy flows through the body and hence the generation of light. In the female, emotional bonding with the infant directs energies away from chakra centres in the same way.

seems that any unbalance between the three bodies results in disequilibrium.

For males (figure 31a), physical sperm production places great demands on the physical being. Sperm is rich in protein and essential minerals. Ejaculation of sperm results in reverse energy flows down through the body and sushumna flows in the wrong direction. At the same time the great loss of protein means that the body must now produce more, drawing on all its energy reserves and leaving less energy for sushumna production. Ejaculation of sperm hence precludes coordinated equilibrium and purification of the spirit This is why monks, clergy and those belonging to the higher esoteric orders take vows of celibacy, why masturbation is frowned on by the Church and why some religions have adopted circumcision as an impediment to male masturbation.

As far as women are concerned (figure 31b), motherhood, in conjuction with the endocrine system, brings with it a maternal bonding with the offspring greater than with any other. The mother loves her own child more than herself. In effect, the chakra centres direct energy towards the offspring, preventing the rise of sushumna and the radiation of light in the mother.

(xviii) Nature, the Great Redeemer

'Can I,' the anxious parent asks, 'get to heaven this time around or will the gates be firmly closed when this life ends?' In a purely pragmatic sense, it seems unlikely that those who procreate face automatic exclusion from entry into heaven. If that were the case then, mindful of the Theory of Divine Reconciliation, God would not grow by very much very quickly. (But then again, because time does not exist in the spiritual world, time cannot, of itself, be of the essence in regard to God-growth). The answers we seek, therefore, in this regard will not be found in this line of reasoning.

Mystics say that the first twenty years of life are for learning, the second twenty years for procreation and the final twenty years for spiritual redemption.

Appendix 1xiv of *The Tutankhamun Prophecies* explains how the magnetic interaction between the sun and the earth shifts by around thirty degrees each year, resulting in a twelve-year magnetic cycle between the two. That cycle affects the pineal gland and the biorhythmic performance of the body, causing menstruation to commence in females at around twelve years after conception, around the age of eleven years three months on average. The cycle is naturally modified by environmental factors that affect the biorhythmic harmony of the body. After four of these cycles, following conception, forty-seven years three months on average, the body and the sun conspire to ensure decreasing levels of female fertility hormones; the ageing pineal gland produces less melatonin, the pituitary less of the follicle-stimulating and luteinising hormones and the ovaries less oestrogen and progesterone. The perfectly natural menopause is not just nature's way of ensuring that the youngest and fittest of females carry the healthiest of offspring; it is nature's way of closing the gates on sexuality and opening the gates of enlightenment and spiritual awareness, although many fail to follow the plot or see perfection at play. Male testosterone declines at the same time, concentrating the mind on the more important issues of soul purification.

It would seem, then, that even those who procreate *can* be admitted to heaven, although twenty years or so of distraction, rearing offspring, naturally leaves twenty years less time available for the pursuit of spiritual purification. Time *is* of the essence in the physical world.

Mystics also acknowledge that we live in a perfect world where nothing is left to chance. But if God created a perfect world, you may ask, how do we account for natural disasters, and accidents, which take such great loss of life?

God indeed created a perfect physical universe; the sun radiates light and energy that fuels the solar system. The gravitational force of the sun captures and interns the planets.

Over billions of years the once-molten surface of our own planet has cooled sufficiently to support life on its hard outer crust that flexes with the gravitational pull of the sun and the planets. Crustal sections, the great continental plates, drift around the surface, colliding, causing earthquakes that dislodge surface structures.

As the earth turns on its axis it divides night from day, accommodating the rest and regeneration of all living things.

The axial tilt of the earth, together with its orbital movement around the sun, brings the seasons and with them cycles of growth. As it spins, it generates circulating winds and ocean currents that together, with energy from the sun, regulate evaporation, precipitation and glaciation. These geophysical phenomena may not always suit human life, but by accommodating catastrophe cycles that bring periodic destruction and death they do suit the divine objective of perpetual God-growth. If the continental plates did not move gradually and repeatedly, the planet would have been torn apart by torsional stresses caused by the sun and other planets and, in the same way, if the winds did not blow, or the rains fall, then life on earth would cease and all 5.5 billion occupants would perish.

What would you prefer, if you were the great creator? The loss of 5.5 billion people and with it an end to a perfect world and unlimited God-growth or the sacrifice of 50,000 people, through *natural* disasters, every year? If you truly understood the perfection that confronts you, that the soul is imperishable, indestructible, immortal and everlasting, then you would understand that the 50,000 souls will either be reborn on earth or elevated to heaven to live with the creator; you would also be relieved of your intellectual and emotional anxieties.

Perhaps an awareness of reincarnation is not so bad after all; would men pointlessly kill men knowing that killing *releases* the victim from hell, assuring rebirth on earth or escape to heaven? And if killing is not the final solution for man's inhumanity to man, where could enmity seek refuge?

Would the rich be unkind to the poor, men to women, women to men, black to white or white to black if they truly understood that, next time, their roles would be reversed, the first becoming the last and the last becoming the first?

(xix) Why the Ancients Encoded Their Super-Knowledge into Their Treasures

The mechanics of the reincarnation process imply that the super-knowledge, which takes many lifetimes to accumulate, could be acquired more quickly if individuals were able to build on acquired knowledge with each successive incarnation. But a new brain and heart each incarnation precluded such gains. So the purification process takes many more lifetimes than it otherwise might. To overcome this, the ancients encoded their super-knowledge into their treasures. Rediscovery of the same knowledge, in the next incarnation, would enable a higher starting level of purification, giving the soul a better chance of transmigration and transmutation into a star the next time around.

But how could the knowledge be 'written down' so as to guarantee its transmission over vast epochs of time?

Throughout history, nations and languages have been wiped out by conquering armies and political regimes eager to impose their own beliefs on defeated nations. Ideas and cultures are lost through ideological succession. Natural disasters, floods, fire and earthquake likewise erase all evidence of earlier civilisations. Solar-inspired catastrophe cycles that periodically cause the earth to tilt on its axis (figure A21) likewise defeat the transmission of knowledge.

There are two ways to 'write down' knowledge for posterity without the use of words. One way is by using numbers, the cultural common denominator; the number 10 is common to all mankind, because all of mankind has 10 fingers. This is why Lord Pacal chose to use numbers in his encoding of solar magnetic cycles into the pyramid clues at Palenque (Appendix 4). A second way of encoding information

How the Brain Perceives Information

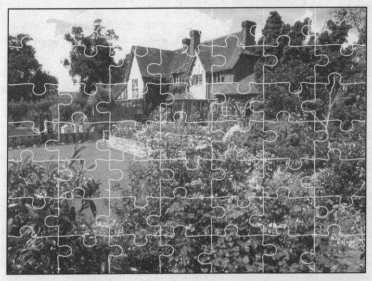

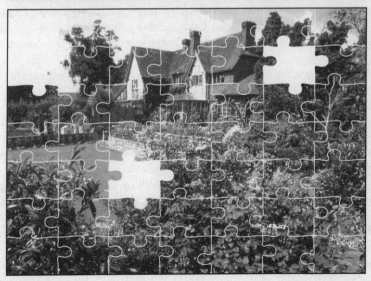

Figure A32. The brain sees nothing unusual in the top picture but immediately spots the defects in the lower picture.

is through the use of pictures; one picture tells a thousand words, and all pictures are common to all people.

Some pictures convey information more efficiently and effectively than others; if we ask ourselves the question 'what's so special about the jigsaw picture (figure 32, top) of an English country garden?', we quickly realise that the human brain finds it difficult to reconcile such a loosely defined interrogation criterion. However, if we ask the same question about the lower picture in figure 32, the answer becomes immediately apparent: pieces of the puzzle are missing. This demonstrates that the human brain finds difficulty in attaching meaning to what it sees; rather it is much easier for it to attach meaning to what it does not see – the exception rather than the rule. This is why we are quick to see the faults in others around us but often fail to see merit where merit is due. It also explains why we are slow to see defects in our own character, because we have no perfect picture of ourselves against which we can be compared. It was for these reasons that the ancients chose to *omit* information from their treasures. *Omission* served as the fundamental mechanism that facilitated the encoding of information. Decoding hence involved a search for, assimilation of and (once located) reorganisation of the missing pieces. The fact that information had been *encoded* itself conveyed a special meaning that differentiated it from other less important information that had not.

It was just after I calculated the duration of the solar neutral sheet magnetic reversal period (figure A20) of 1,366,040 days that I discovered, to my astonishment, that the Maya worshipped a virtually identical number: 1,366,560 (which they referred to as the 'birthdate of Venus' more than a thousand years ago in the jungles of Mexico). It soon became clear that this ancient sun-worshipping civilisation knew more about the magnetic cycles of the sun than we did in 1989.

So I travelled to their ceremonial centre of Palenque, deep in the Mexican jungle, to take a closer look at the treasures they left behind. I was impressed by the lid that covered the sarcophagus of Lord Pacal. But I saw something, it seems, that nobody else had ever noticed: two corners of the lid were missing (see Appendix 4).

APPENDIX 4

Encoding Knowledge

(How the Ancients Encoded Their Super-Knowledge into Their Treasures)

(i) Numerical Encoding in the Temple of Inscriptions, Palenque

In 1952 Mexican archaeologist Alberto Ruz discovered the hidden tomb of Lord Pacal, priest-king leader of the Maya in around AD 750, hidden inside the Pyramid of Inscriptions at Palenque in Mexico.

Ruz had noticed four pairs of circular holes in one of the flooring slabs in the temple (figure A33b) at the top of the pyramid. Having scratched out the mortar filling he was able to lift the slab clear of the floor to expose a single limestone step that was covered with rubble. Brushing away the debris he came to another, and another.

After 26 steps he arrived at a landing, which turned to the right to another flight of rubble-filled steps (figure A33c). Twenty-two steps later, three years after digging began, he was confronted by a solid-limestone wall and a stone box containing eleven jade beads, three red-painted shells, three clay plates and a single pearl in a seashell filled with cinnabar, the powdered form of liquid mercury (figure A33l).

Demolishing the wall, the excavators found themselves in a small square chamber. Through the darkness, their flickering torches picked out the bones of one female and five male skeletons.

To the left, a triangular stone door blocked the entrance to the tomb (figure A33k). Ruz moved the stone. For the first time in 1,250 years the tomb was opened. He was confronted by an enormous, ornately

The Pyramid at Palenque

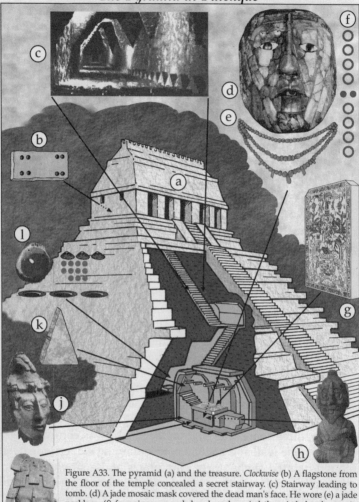

Figure A33. The pyramid (a) and the treasure. *Clockwise* (b) A flagstone from the floor of the temple concealed a secret stairway. (c) Stairway leading to tomb. (d) A jade mosaic mask covered the dead man's face. He wore (e) a jade necklace, (f) four rings on each hand, and carried three jade beads, one in each palm and one in the mouth.(g) A five-tonne carved lid made of limestone covered the sarcophagus. (h) A jade figurine of a white man with a beard accompanied the man in the tomb. Two stone heads, one with a 'low' hairstyle (i) and one with a 'high' hairstyle (j) were positioned on the floor of the crypt. (k) A triangular limestone slab blocked the entrance to the tomb. (l) Three red-painted shells, three clay plates, eleven jade beads and a pearl in a seashell filled with red cinnabar (the powdered form of liquid mercury) were all found in a stone box at the foot of the stairs.

carved slab of limestone measuring 3.65 metres (12 feet) long, 2.13 metres (7 feet) wide, and just under 30 centimetres (1 foot) deep, weighing around five tonnes (figure A33g). Curiously, two of the corners of the lid were missing.

On 15 June, Ruz descended the final four steps inside the tomb and entered the chamber. Two stone heads rested on the floor, one of which carried a 'high' hairstyle and the other a 'low' hairstyle, depicting the man in the tomb (figures 33i and j).

The roof of the crypt was supported by five stone beams, and nine lords of the night, as though in procession, adorned the walls.

With car jacks and poles, they raised the carved lid, exposing the sarcophagus below. This heavy base had one corner missing and was fastened into position with four stone plugs. Then they lifted the lid off the sarcophagus. Before them lay the bones of Lord Pacal, who died in around AD 750 at the height of the Mayan civilisation.

His crumbling face was covered by fragments of a jade mosaic mask (figure A33d). He carried a jade bead in each palm and one in his mouth. He wore four jade rings on his left hand and another four on his right, and around his neck hung a three-tiered jade necklace (figures A33e and f). By his side lay a small green jade figurine of a

A Doorway into the Mind

Figure A34. The doorway into the tomb of Lord Pacal was purposely made triangular to allegorically represent a doorway into the human mind, as illustrated by this ancient Mexican inlaid skull.

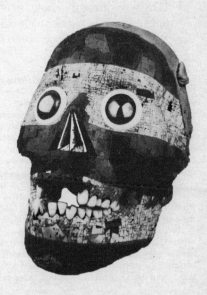

white man with a beard (figure A33h), said to be Quetzalcoatl*
(pronounced 'cat-sell-coe-at-ul'), the feathered snake, the most revered
god in the Mayan pantheon. The feathers represented the soaring
spirit in the sky, while the snake epitomised the physical body on
earth, and the notion of rebirth and reincarnation, every time it shed
its skin.

An inlaid skull (figure A34), today kept in the British Museum,
suggested that the triangular doorway may in fact symbolise much
more than the treasure-trove that confronted Ruz; little did he realise,
this was to be a journey into the mind.

What was the game of the Maya in the pyramid? Was it a game of
numbers? Were the 69 steps on the outside of the pyramid simply an
anagram for the 96 glyphs found on a tablet at the foot of the steps to
the palace (representing the 96 microcycles of the sunspot cycle; figure
A16)? Were the 620 inscriptions in the temple likewise an anagram for
the 260-day Mayan astrological calendar? Were these numbers, taken
together, themselves referring to 360, the base number of the Mayan
calendar system (620 – 260 = 360, the number of degrees in a circle,
representing the sun and sun-worship)?

Were the numbers in the treasures concealing a hidden message?

- Why were there two holes in each corner of the paving slab (2, 2,
  2, 2) as well as two stone heads on the floor of the tomb?
- What was the purpose of the three red-painted shells and three

---

* The name Quetzalcoatl is the Nahuatl (Aztec) translation of the words 'feathered snake'.
The Quiche (Maya) translation of the words 'feathered snake' is 'Ku-kul-kan'. The naming of
the gods of Mexico is a complex subject. Many of essentially the same gods were given different names at different times throughout Mesoamerican history. For example, the god of rain
during the Maya period was known as Chaac, during the Zapotec period Cocijo, and during
the Aztec period Tlaloc. Additionally, many of the gods once thought to have been uniquely
Aztec appear in the recently decoded Amazing Lid of Palenque, meaning, therefore, that the
same gods must have been known during the period of the Maya but that their names are
unknown.

There are other difficulties. Many of the gods change roles at different times. Quetzalcoatl
was the god of the wind (and the west, as well as goodness and wisdom) and perceived as
presiding, like the wind, over all space, the four corners of the sky. When he journeyed into
the southern sky, he was associated with Huitzilopochtli, the god of day, who lived in the
southern quarter of the sky, and hence was associated with daylight (sunlight) and the sun.
When Quetzalcoatl journeyed into the underworld, he was associated with darkness and
hence the god of darkness (and death), Tezcatlipoca Yaotl, of the north. When Quetzalcoatl
occupied the eastern sky, he was associated with Xiuhtechutli, the god of fire. Some commen-
tators insist that Quetzalcoatl was the brother of Huitzilopochtli, Yaotl and Xiuhtechutli, while

clay plates and why did the door to the tomb have three sides? Why did the man in the tomb carry three jade beads, one in each palm and one in his mouth, and why was he wearing a three-tiered necklace?

- Why were there four steps down into the tomb? Why was he wearing four jade rings on his left hand and four on his right, and what was the reason for using four stone plugs to hold down the sarcophagus?
- Why were there five male skeletons, five temple doorways, five ceiling beams and five sides to the sarcophagus?
- And why were there six sides to the tomb lid, and six pillars supporting the roof of the temple?

But here, it seems, the clues come to an end; there were no more sixes in the tomb at Palenque, at least not on first inspection, but counting the beads on the three tiers of the necklace (figure A35a) proved more revealing. There are three groups of thirteen beads in the necklace – (6+7), (6+7), (6+7) – which together give three more missing 6s, as well as three 7s (7, 7, 7). The centre row contains another 7. The centre row likewise contains a string of 15 beads (7+8), which not only gives another missing 7 but throws up an 8. The bottom row contains five oblong beads and four groups of three circular beads which, using the Mayan bar and dot system for counting (where a bar represented 5 and a dot represented 1), amounts to 8, 8, 8, 8.

others believe that they were different emanations of Quetzalcoatl as he occupied the different cardinal points. Because he was the highest of gods, he was seen as the sun itself, or the sun-god. Huitzilopochtli, as the god of day, was also seen as the sun-god. Tonatiuh, another ostensible god of the Aztecs (who also appears on the Amazing Lid of Palenque), was also a sun-god.

To overcome these difficulties, first, Mesoamerican gods mentioned throughout this book have been given names known to have been used during the Aztec period, irrespective of the historical period in which they were thought to subsist. Secondly, to avoid confusion, generic names are used wherever possible; e.g. the 'sun-god' may be used in place of the name of a particular god. Thirdly, to help the reader, pronunciation of the names, where necessary, is given in parentheses following their first appearance in the main text.

It is also worth mentioning that the words *Maya* and *Mayan* are interchangeable, as are the plurals *Maya*, *Mayans* and *Mayas* and that the word *Inca* can be used in two ways: to refer to the race, or to an individual belonging to the race, of South American people of that name, or to the leader of that race, the Inca, king (emperor). Similarly, the word *Incas* may refer to either the race, or to individuals belonging to the race, of South American people of that name, or to more than one king (emperor) of those people.

The Mystery of the Necklace
the 6s, the 7s, the 8s

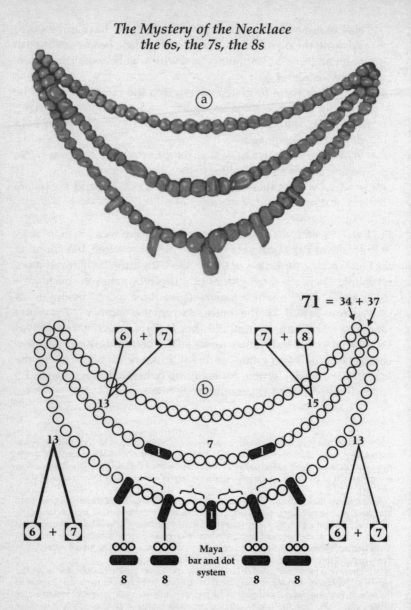

Figure A35. (a) Jade bead necklace from the tomb of Lord Pacal. (b) Numerical analysis of the beads reveals secret astronomical messages.

There were nine levels to the outside of the pyramid and two of the staircases had nine steps, nine on the top and nine on the bottom. Nine lords, in procession, are painted on the wall of the tomb, and the sarcophagus lid containing the carving carries nine 'codes', along each side of its length (9, 9).

There are three *single* oblong beads not yet accounted for in the necklace (1, 1, 1). Only one of the skeletons in the antechamber was female, and let's not forget about the single pearl in the seashell found inside the box at the bottom of the stairs.

The first level of the inside stairway carried twenty-six steps and the second twenty-two, with four more inside the tomb itself (22 + 4 = 26), both representing the 26-day revolutionary period of the sun's equatorial magnetic field.

The middle tier of the necklace carries thirty-seven beads, the revolutionary period of the sun's polar magnetic field in days.

In choosing their anachronistic numbering system to measure periods of time – the Baktun (144,000 days), the Katun (7,200 days), the Tun (360 days), the Uinal (20 days) and the Kin (1 day) – and by providing a host of numerical clues inside the Pyramid of Inscriptions, the Maya encoded the secret super-science of the sun into their architecture, using a handful of numbers. Setting these down, it becomes clear just what they were trying to say; there are more nines in the table matrix than any other number, which is not surprising, since the Maya worshipped the number nine. Taking nine of each of the calendar cycles gives 1,366,560 days (figure A36). They had left modern man a secret message encoded in their jewellery and architecture which, when broken, reveals the duration of magnetic reversals on the sun. These affect the earth, sometimes causing infertility cycles, sometimes catastrophic destruction. They had prophesied their own demise, 1,366,560 days after their calendar began in 3113 BC, and in so doing forewarned us of what might come again, in the year Katun 13 Ahau, AD 2012:

Unattainable is the bread [famine] in the year of Katun 13 Ahau. The sun shall be eclipsed. Double is the charge of the Katun; men without offspring, chiefs without successors [infertility]. For five days the sun shall be eclipsed [pole shift] then it shall be seen again. This is the charge of Katun 13 Ahau (*The Book of Chilam Balam of Chumayel*, Ralph R. Roys, University of Oklahoma Press, 1932, p. 134).

The 666, 99999 and 1,366,560-Day Message of Lord Pacal

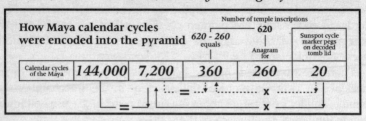

		Number of temple inscriptions		
How Maya calendar cycles were encoded into the pyramid		620 - 260 equals	620 Anagram for	Sunspot cycle marker pegs on decoded tomb lid
Calendar cycles of the Maya	144,000	7,200	360	260	20

Decoding the clues of the pyramid and Temple of Inscriptions				
1 Pearl in seashell	1 Female skeleton in antechamber	1 Single long bead on necklace	1 Single long bead on necklace	1 Single long bead on necklace
2 Holes in paving slab	2 Holes in paving slab	2 Holes in paving slab	2 Holes in paving slab	2 Plaster heads on tomb floor
3 Clay plates in stone chest	3 Red shells in stone chest	3 -sided tomb door	3 Jade beads (1 in each hand, 1 in mouth)	3 -tiered jade necklace
4 Steps down into Tomb	4 Jade rings on left hand	4 Jade rings on right hand	4 Sets of holes in paving slab	4 Cylindrical plugs in sarcophagus
5 Pyramid stairway landings	5 Temple doorways	5 Male skeletons	5 Ceiling beams	5 Sarcophagus sides
6 Temple pillars	6 Sides to tomb lid	missing [6]	missing [6]	missing [6]
missing [7] +	7 Necklace beads	[7] = 13 Necklace beads	[7] = 13 Necklace beads	[7] = 13 Necklace beads
[8] = 15 Necklace beads	8 Dash-dot beads ●●●	8 Dash-dot beads ●●●	8 Dash-dot beads ●●●	8 Dash-dot beads ●●●
9 Bottom steps of pyramid	9 Pyramid levels	9 Top steps of pyramid	9 Lords painted on tomb walls	9 / 9* Codes on left / right sides of lid

| Decoding in relation to calendar cycles used by the Maya | 9 x 144,000 + | 9 x 7,200 + | 9 x 360 + | 9 x 260 + | 9 x 20 |

$$= 1,366,560 \text{ days}$$

Figure A36. Lord Pacal encoded the number of the sun-king Supergods 9, 9, 9, 9, 9 into his treasures in the Temple of Inscriptions, Palenque (figure A33). The number cleverly conceals astronomical information; 9 multiplied by the Mayan calendar cycles of time, in days, amounts to 1,366,560 days, the duration of 20 sunspot cycles, one solar magnetic reversal.

The jade necklace conceals even more information; the first two tiers of the necklace contain 71 beads, which when multiplied by 11 (the number of beads found in the stone chest at the bottom of the stairway) amount to 781. 71 x 11 x 87.4545 = 68,302 days, the exact duration of one 187-year sunspot cycle (Appendix 3x, explains how the solar pole and equator are together every 87.45 days and why this interval is used as the primary interval against which the variables are compared). Twenty of these 187-year cycles amount to the neutral sheet shift figure of 1,366,040 days. (If we recall, it is after twenty of these shifts that the sun's 'neutral warp' shifts its magnetic direction (Appendix 3x).)

Using my knowledge of the sun, I had broken the numbering system of the Mayas and, at the same time, the architectural encoding of the super-science of the sun left 1,250 years ago in the pyramid at Palenque.

The numbers in the matrix of the Pyramid of Inscriptions (figure A36) appear frequently among numbers to be found in the treasures of other Supergod sun-kings: e.g. (figure A37) the door seals on the tomb of Tutankhamun contain the number 9, 9, 9, 9, 9, 9, and Tutankhamun was buried in nine layers of coffin (figure A38). The coffin (figure A39) of the sun-king leader of the Mochica, Viracocha Pachacamac, buried in around AD 300 at Sipan, Peru, was tied down using nine copper straps along each edge, horizontally and vertically (9, 9, 9, 9, 9, 9, 9, 9), while the arrangement of roof timbers that comprise the roof of his tomb (figure A40) also contain the number of the sunspot cycle, 96 (derived by multiplying the total number of roof timbers (16) by the total number of Y-shaped roof-support timbers (6), representing the 96 microcycles of magnetic activity that subsist on the sun during one 187-year sunspot cycle. And, as just mentioned, a stone tablet found at Palenque on the steps of the palace next to the Pyramid of Inscriptions is carved with 96 glyphs (figure A41). Similarly, the stone steps leading to Tutankhamun's tomb (figure A42) encode the same information (derived by multiplying the total number of steps (16) by the number of steps replaced by the burial party (6).

(ii) Pictorial Encoding of the Maya

In *The Mayan Prophecies* I explained how I was able to break the code of the Lid of Palenque by following secret instructions encoded in the

The 99999 Message of Tutankhamun and Viracocha Pachacamac

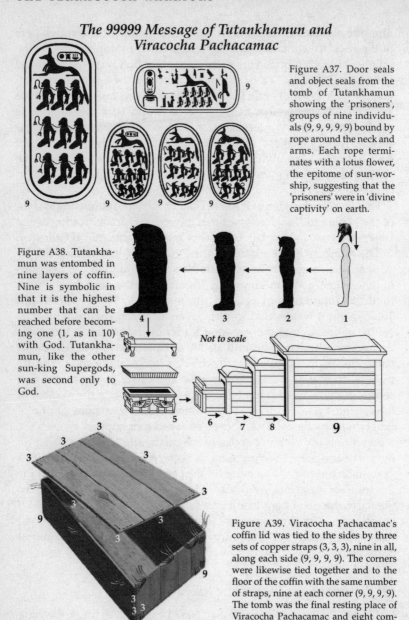

Figure A37. Door seals and object seals from the tomb of Tutankhamun showing the 'prisoners', groups of nine individuals (9, 9, 9, 9, 9) bound by rope around the neck and arms. Each rope terminates with a lotus flower, the epitome of sun-worship, suggesting that the 'prisoners' were in 'divine captivity' on earth.

Figure A38. Tutankhamun was entombed in nine layers of coffin. Nine is symbolic in that it is the highest number that can be reached before becoming one (1, as in 10) with God. Tutankhamun, like the other sun-king Supergods, was second only to God.

Not to scale

Figure A39. Viracocha Pachacamac's coffin lid was tied to the sides by three sets of copper straps (3, 3, 3), nine in all, along each side (9, 9, 9, 9). The corners were likewise tied together and to the floor of the coffin with the same number of straps, nine at each corner (9, 9, 9, 9). The tomb was the final resting place of Viracocha Pachacamac and eight companions, nine in all.

The Tomb of Viracocha Pachacamac, God of the World, of Peru

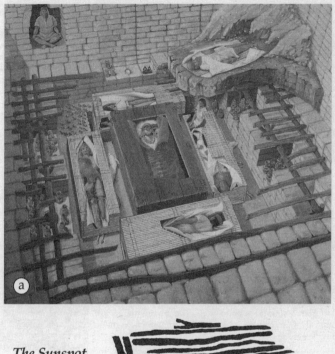

The Sunspot Cycle Message of Viracocha Pachacamac

6 x 16 = 96

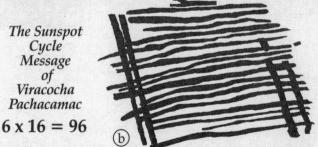

Figure A40. (a) Sixteen wooden beams supported the roof of Viracocha Pachacamac's tomb. (b) Schematic showing beam layout. Five Y-shaped wooden beams supported the roof. 5 x 16 is not astronomically significant. However, we note that one Y-shaped beam was found on top of the roof (*top centre, (b) above*). Why would tomb-builders place one of six supports on top of the roof? The message here is that six is important; 6 x 16 = 96, the number of magnetic cycles in one 187-year sunspot cycle (figure A15c). One more transverse beam was embedded in the bricks, making a total of 97, the number of magnetic cycles that need to be counted when recognising the shifting neutral sheet that produces the 18,139-year solar cycle. The ninety-seventh beam was the odd one out: it did not support the roof.

The Sunspot Cycle Message of Lord Pacal

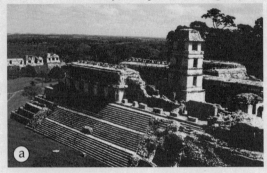

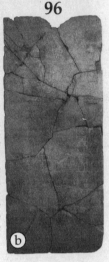

Figure A41. (a) The palace at Palenque. (b) Tablet of 96 glyphs from the steps of the palace – the number of magnetic microcycles in one 187-year sunspot cycle.

96

The Sunspot Cycle Message of Tutankhamun

Figure A42. The bottom 6 steps of the 16-step stairway, which led to the tomb of Tutankhamun, were chiselled away by the burial party to, according to archaeologists, 'permit access of larger pieces of furniture' into the tomb. The steps, originally stone, were reinstated in plaster by the same burial party. But why would a burial party seal a tomb and then repair a broken stairway before filling the stairway with rubble behind themselves? This would simply invite others to use the steps in the future, to gain access to a solid wall. The 6 and the 16 are astronomically significant: 6 x 16 = 96, the number of magnetic cycles in one sunspot cycle (figure A15c).

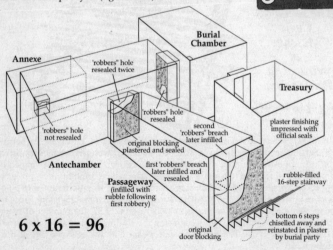

Burial Chamber

Annexe

'robbers' hole resealed twice

'robbers' hole not resealed

'robbers' hole resealed

Treasury

plaster finishing impressed with official seals

original blocking plastered and sealed

second 'robbers' breach later infilled

Antechamber

first 'robbers' breach later infilled and resealed

Passageway (infilled with rubble following first robbery)

rubble-filled 16-step stairway

6 x 16 = 96

original door blocking

bottom 6 steps chiselled away and reinstated in plaster by burial party borders of the lid. The code can only be broken using transparencies of the original carving, then more than a hundred concealed pictures are revealed.

If we are to see the whole picture contained in a puzzle (figure A32), we must first find all the pieces. Our first task with the Lid of Palenque, therefore, is to find the missing corners.

Figure A43a shows a copy of the drawing carved on the lid, and figure A43b shows that part of the lid, box-framed, which is under consideration. Because the corners are missing, half of the pattern drawn in each corner is missing. We need only a mirror to repair each of the missing patterns, or a transparent facsimile of the original design. (Because a transparency is easier to handle this will be used; moreover, because two transparencies are easier to handle than one original and one transparency, two transparencies will be used.)

Figure A44c–f shows how, by overlaying the transparencies, the border patterns may be repaired (completed). In the completed state, one pattern (g) shows the cross of the sun. Sliding the transparencies apart again (h) reveals magnetic loops (representing sunspot loops) at one end, and a twin-star pattern (representing the twin-star Venus) at the other end. With the transparencies locked into this position the border code pattern may now be coloured in to reveal hidden pictures (figures A45a, b and c). These depict pictures: (e), the face of a bird; (f), a human face wearing a blindfold and butterfly patterns across the lips; (g), a tiger face; and (h), a dog-like face wearing a blindfold. (At this stage of the analysis we acknowledge that these border code pictures are inconclusive and unpersuasive.) Other composite codes are obtained from other areas of the border pattern, a few of which are featured in figure A46a–e.

Shifting attention to the opposite end of the lid, we notice that one of the characters carries a defect mark on the nose (figure A47a–d). The defect may be removed using the duplicate transparency (figure A47e).

Referring to the design on the inner lid, we now notice that the central character on the lid also carries a defect mark on his own nose (figure A48). The border code nose defect hence amounts to an *instruction* to remove the defect from the nose of the central character using the same method. When this is done, another composite picture emerges (figure A49a–d) showing a bat flying towards the viewer. The bat-god was the god of death for the Maya.

Border code composite picture (figure A46a) revealed a bat, and the central lid composite picture (figure A49d) likewise featured a bat. It becomes clear that the border code patterns (figure A50) contain a list of contents of other concurrent pictures that can be found in the main part of the inner lid.

The strip of border codes depicted in figure A46b–e contain the following instructions: *to see the man in the tomb* (e), *look for a bird on his head* (d). *The bird is the sun-god Tonatiuh* (c). *To see the man in the tomb with a bird on his head who is the sun-god put the ears* (b) *in the position shown*. When this instruction is carried out, the composite picture of the head and face of Lord Pacal is revealed (figure A51) with a bat, the god of death, covering his mouth. The bat, featured here, takes away Lord Pacal's breath. The high hairstyle, first observed on the stone head carving of Lord Pacal found on the floor of the tomb, here becomes a baby quetzal bird that carries a chain in its beak. On the chain hangs a conch shell, the mark of Quetzalcoatl, the feathered snake. Bringing the information together, this particular scene tells us that when Lord Pacal died he was born again as Quetzalcoatl.

The quetzal bird, from the rainforests of Central America, is treasured for its brightly coloured feathers. These, when used to decorate the serpent, represented the soaring spirit, rebirth, resurrection and everlasting life. The large seashell of the conch snail was used as a 'trumpet' to announce ceremonies and other events and so symbolised control of the wind.

The bat covering Lord Pacal's mouth itself carries the figure of a small man wearing a hat. His arms are held high; giving himself up, in sacrifice. His open shirt reveals a pure heart. On his forehead he carries the number 144,000 (figure A52).

The reference to the number 666, from the Book of Revelation, mentioned earlier, tells of the revelation that appeared to St John. Its meaning is unknown and allegorical and has perplexed many through the ages. It tells of:

a beast which rises from the sea . . . which has seven heads and ten horns and . . . upon his heads the name of blasphemy . . . here is wisdom, let him that hath understanding count the number of the beast: for it is the number of a man; and his number is six hundred three score and six . . .

666 was missing from the clues in the Pyramid of Inscriptions but were found encoded in the beads around Lord Pacal's neck, not as themselves but as factors of higher numbers. There was no place for 666 in the tomb of Lord Pacal.

Revelation continues:

I saw four angels standing on the four corners of the earth [north, south, west and east], holding the four winds of the earth, that the wind should not blow on the earth, nor on the sea, nor on any tree. And I saw another angel ascending from the east having the seal of the living God: And he cried with a loud voice to the four angels, to whom it was given to hurt the earth, and the sea, saying: 'Hurt not the earth, neither the sea, nor the trees, till we have sealed the servants of our god in their foreheads.' And I heard the number of them which were sealed; and there were sealed an hundred and forty-four thousand of all the tribes of the children of Israel . . .

Look again at the decoded picture of Lord Pacal from the Amazing Lid of Palenque (figure A52). He carries the mark of the living God, 144,000, sealed into his forehead. Do not be surprised by the use of modern numerals. Lord Pacal could see the past, the present and the future. This is confirmed by a passage in *The Popol Vuh*, the sacred book of the Maya:

. . . they were endowed with intelligence, they saw and instantly they could see far, they succeeded in seeing, they succeeded in knowing all that there is in the world. When they looked, instantly they saw all around them and they contemplated in turn the arch of the heavens and the round face of the earth. Great was their wisdom, their sight reached to the forests, the rocks, the lakes, the mountains, the valleys. In truth they were admirable men. And they were able to know all (*The Popol Vuh*, University of Oklahoma Press, 1947, pp. 168 and 169).

Jesus (figure A53a) also advocated a pure heart, like the small man covering Lord Pacal's face (figure A53b). Depictions of the same small man wearing a hat were also found in the tomb of Viracocha Pachacamac (figure A53c), associating him with the same number, 144,000. The sun-ray collar worn by Tutankhamun also contains the

Decoding the Amazing Lid of Palenque, Step 1
(Repairing the Missing Corners)

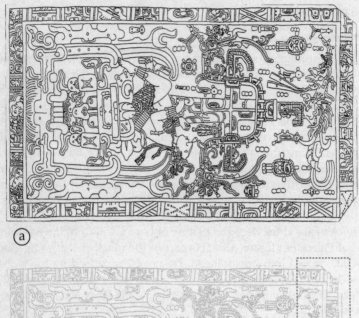

(a)

(b)

Figure A43. Decoding involves several steps. (a) Note that two of the corners (box-framed in (b) are missing. Because of this, the border code patterns, carried by the corners, are *half* missing. The first step is to repair the half-missing border code patterns.

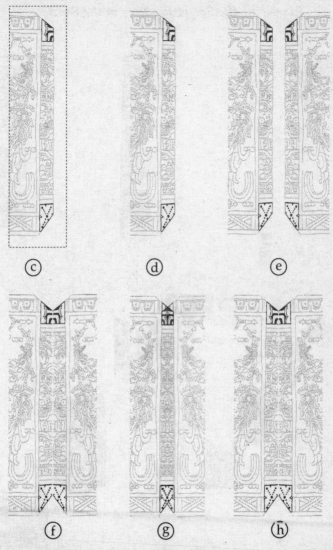

Figure A44. The next step (d) is to highlight the border code patterns affected by the missing corners. These can be repaired (fixed) by making a mirror image of the transparency under investigation (e). Sliding the transparency against the original (f) the top (loop) border code pattern is completed (repaired). Sliding further together (g), the five-dot lower border code pattern is likewise completed (repaired). To continue, the two pieces are arranged as in (f).

Revealing the Secret Pictures in the Border

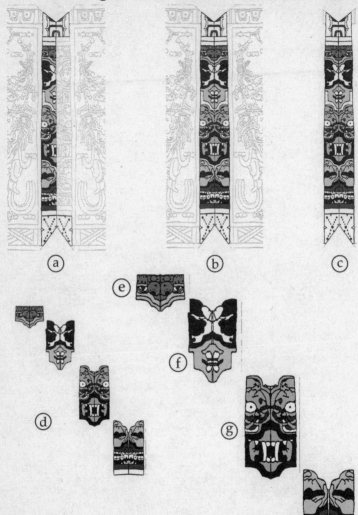

Figure A45. (a–c) Colouring in the border code patterns of figure A44 reveals secret pictures: (e) the head of a bird, (f) a human face wearing a black blindfold sporting tiny wing shapes across the lips; (g) a tiger face; and (h) a dog-like face with teeth and gums exposed wearing a blindfold. At this stage of the decoding process the efficacy of the pictures is inconclusive and unpersuasive.

More Composite Border Code Pictures

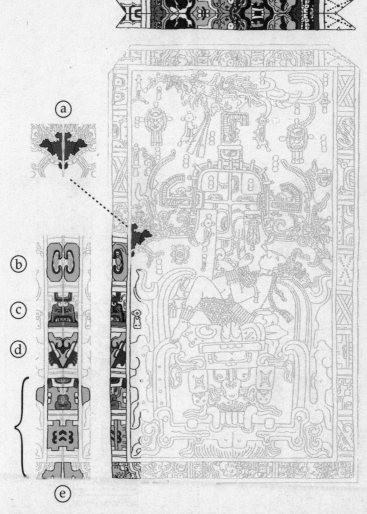

Figure A46. Iconographic composite border code pictures can be found all around the border. A few more are shown above: (a) an open-winged bat, (b) two complementary ear shapes, (c) a picture of Tonatiuh, the sun-god, wearing a magnetic loop on the forehead, (d) an open-winged bird, (e) a small man with bare feet, fingertips touching across the chest, eyes closed and a magnetic loop on the forehead. Once again, at this stage of the decoding the pictures are inconclusive and unpersuasive.

Decoding the Amazing Lid of Palenque, Step 2
(Repairing (Fixing) the Defective Profile-Head)

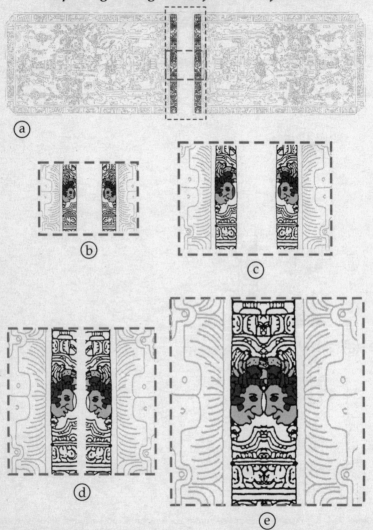

Figure A47. Close examination of the border code pattern (a) (at the opposite end to that already examined) shows a human face, in profile, sporting an unusual banana-shaped defect on the nose. The defect can be removed (repaired) in the same way as before, using a transparency, as in (b–e) above.

Decoding the Amazing Lid of Palenque, Step 3
(Repairing the Defective Head of the Central Character)

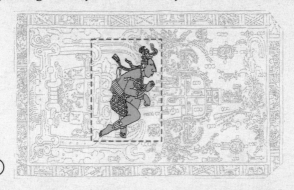

(a)

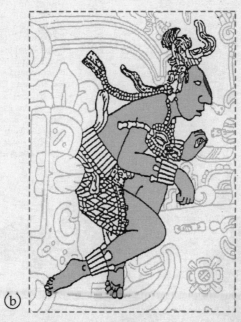

(b)

Figure A48. The repaired border code nose defect draws attention to the nose of the character in the central carving of the lid (a) who carries a similar defect (detailed in b). The border code repair sequence hence amounts to an instruction to apply the same decoding technique to the nose of the central character, in the same way, by making a mirror image of the entire lid and juxtaposing the transparency so that the defect is removed from the nose of the main character.

Decoding the Amazing Lid of Palenque, Step 4
(Revealing the Pictures in the Central Carving)

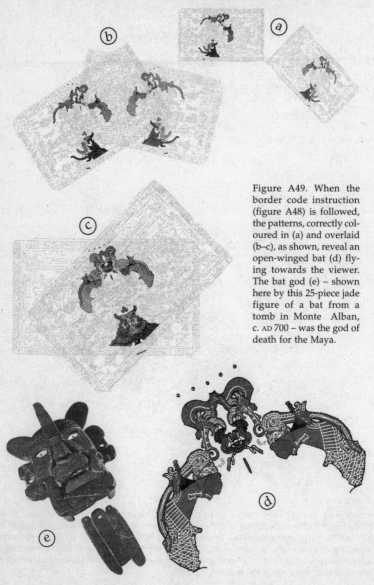

Figure A49. When the border code instruction (figure A48) is followed, the patterns, correctly coloured in (a) and overlaid (b–c), as shown, reveal an open-winged bat (d) flying towards the viewer. The bat god (e) – shown here by this 25-piece jade figure of a bat from a tomb in Monte Alban, c. AD 700 – was the god of death for the Maya.

Decoding the Amazing Lid of Palenque
(Summary Conclusion)

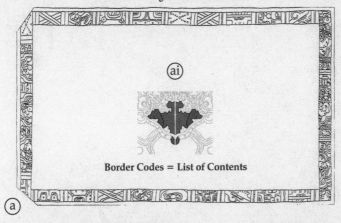

Border Codes = List of Contents

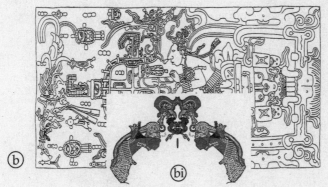

Central Carving = Sacred Book of the Maya
encoded in stone

Figure A50. Figure A46a featured a bat in the border code (*ai, above*). Figure A49d revealed a bat in the central carving (*bi, above*). The bat corresponds to a known archaeological artefact, a 25-piece jade bat, c. AD 700, from Monte Alban, Mexico (figure A49e). The three steps of decoding hence explain that the border codes contain a secret 'list of contents' that refer to corollary secret pictures encoded into the main carving. Other border code pictures refer to other pictures concealed in the central lid. For example: figure A46 (b–e) reads: *To see the dead man from the tomb* (Lord Pacal) *put the ears* (labelled (b) in the border code) *in the correct position* (either side of the head), *then look for a bird* (d) *on his head. The bird is the sun-god* (c). Figure A51 shows the decoded picture that is revealed once these instructions are followed, the face of Lord Pacal, priest-king leader of the Maya, with a bird on his head.

The Amazing Lid of Palenque Story: The Death (and Rebirth) of Lord Pacal, Scene 4

(scenes 1, 2 and 3 not shown here)

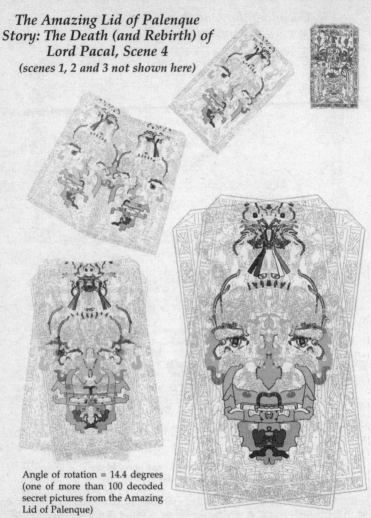

Angle of rotation = 14.4 degrees (one of more than 100 decoded secret pictures from the Amazing Lid of Palenque)

Figure A51. This composite picture, from the decoded Amazing Lid of Palenque, shows the head and face of Lord Pacal, of Mexico, in more detail. His mouth is covered by a bat-mask. A baby quetzal bird sits on his head. The bird carries a chain in its beak from which hangs a conch shell, the mark of Quetzalcoatl. This scene therefore reads: *Lord Pacal died (the bat-god, the god of death, took away his breath); he was reborn as (a baby quetzal bird) Quetzalcoatl.* The number 144,000 is written on his forehead (figure A52). A small man, with outstretched arms and an exposed heart, covers the bat-mask. The same depiction, of the small man, was found prolifically in the tomb of Viracocha Pachacamac, in Peru (figure A53d), identifying Viracocha Pachacamac with Lord Pacal and both with the number 144,000.

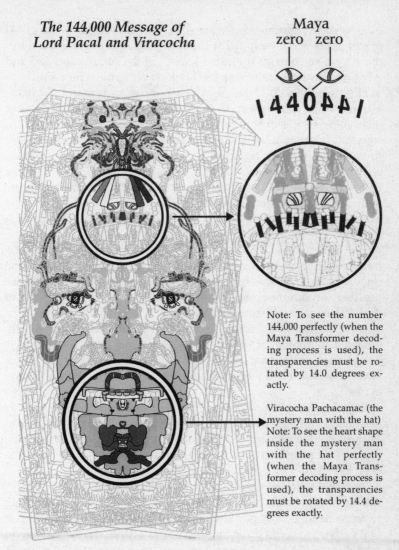

The 144,000 Message of Lord Pacal and Viracocha

Maya zero zero

Note: To see the number 144,000 perfectly (when the Maya Transformer decoding process is used), the transparencies must be rotated by 14.0 degrees exactly.

Viracocha Pachacamac (the mystery man with the hat) Note: To see the heart shape inside the mystery man with the hat perfectly (when the Maya Transformer decoding process is used), the transparencies must be rotated by 14.4 degrees exactly.

Figure A52. In the Bible those with 144,000 written on their foreheads represent the chosen few who will enter the kingdom of heaven. Lord Pacal carries the number 144,000 on his forehead (*above, top, circled*). The perfect heart shape, contained within the composite picture of the man with the hat (*bottom, circled*) can be completed only when the transparencies are inverted, overlaid and juxtaposed by 14.4 degrees. These messages taken together tell us that only the pure of heart will become one of the 144,000, like Lord Pacal and Viracocha.

same encoded information (figure A54). The scarab brooch, one of 143 pieces of jewellery wrapped within the bandages of Tutankhamun's mummy, also contains the super-science of the sun (figures A55 and A56), and Tutankhamun was the 144th object in the wrappings.

How misunderstood the Maya have been for more than 1,250 years. There was so much more to these people of genius who modern archaeologists mistakenly believe worshipped a pantheon of gods in so-called pagan practice and ritual. Their leader, Lord Pacal, was able to use these gods as actors in a grand theatre production, a play, concealed within individual picture frames, which taken together reveal the secrets of life and the universe. The encoded pictures come to life, allowing the gods themselves to tell not only the history of the Maya but also stories of a secret science of a very high order which explains how the sun affects life on earth.

The secret stories of the Amazing Lid of Palenque describe the purpose of life and death, the journey of the soul through the underworld, and how the soul of man can return to the creator purified, or diminish, returning to earth later for another try at purification through suffering.

Other stories (not featured here) interpreted in conjunction with accepted mythological belief, tell us about the 'Paradises' (various destinations of the dead) and the 'five ages of the sun', four of which have ended in destruction. Others tell of solar-inspired infertility cycles.

Stela J (figures 54 and 55) and the information it contains provide new insight into the meaning of the words 'Popol Vuh'. The sixteenth-century written account of the book begins and ends with the same words: 'The [original] Popol Vuh cannot be seen any more . . . it has been hidden from the searcher and the thinker.'

Archaeologists have struggled to understand the words 'Popol Vuh', the literal translation of which becomes 'Book of the Mat'. Attempting to reconcile this oddly perplexing name for a holy book, they suggest that perhaps in olden times the whole family sat on the mat together to read it!

The decoding of Stela J shines new light on this enigma; it seems more plausible to suggest that the Amazing Lid of Palenque is the original Popol Vuh, the Book of the Mat that was hidden from the searcher and the thinker. This is clear for the following reasons. First, two corners of the Amazing Lid of Palenque are missing, suggesting

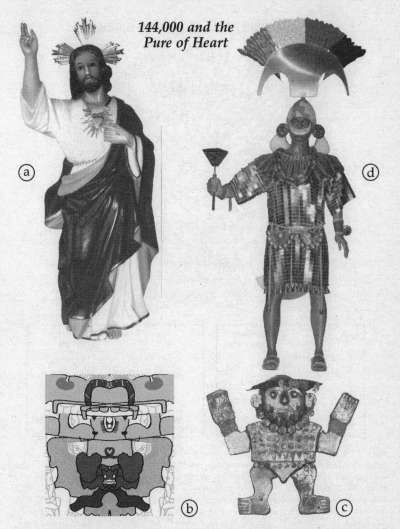

144,000 and the Pure of Heart

(a)

(d)

(b)

(c)

Figure A53. (a) Jesus, pointing to his exposed pure heart that radiates light. (b) The small man, wearing a hat, that covered the decoded face of Lord Pacal (figure A52) proclaimed the same message: the pure of heart, the 144,000, would go to heaven. (In figure A52, Lord Pacal carries the number 144,000 on his forehead.) (c) Gilded copper artefact of a small man wearing a hat, one of many personifications found in the tomb of Viracocha Pachacamac in Peru, c. AD 300; the small man adopts the same stance as the one across Lord Pacal's face and hence conveys the same message: the pure of heart will go to heaven. (d) Reconstruction of the sun-king Viracocha Pachacamac (from the Museum of Archaeology, Lima, Peru) who hence brought the same message to his people.

The 144,000 Message of Tutankhamun

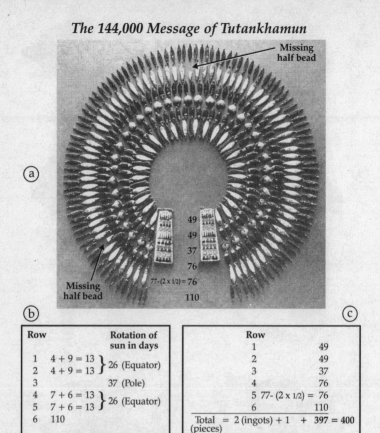

Missing half bead

Missing half bead

	49
	49
	37
	76
77 - (2 x 1/2) =	76
	110

(b)

Row		Rotation of sun in days
1	4 + 9 = 13	} 26 (Equator)
2	4 + 9 = 13	
3		37 (Pole)
4	7 + 6 = 13	} 26 (Equator)
5	7 + 6 = 13	
6	110	

(c)

Row	
1	49
2	49
3	37
4	76
5	77 - (2 x 1/2) = 76
6	110
Total (pieces) = 2 (ingots) + 1 + 397 = 400	

Figure 54. *The Tutankhamun Prophecies* explained how the sun-ray necklace (a) of Tutankhamun contained astronomical and spiritual information. (b) The count of beads on each row of the necklace refers to the rotational rates of the sun's equatorial and polar magnetic fields (26 and 37 days respectively). (c) The total number of beads adds up to 397, which is also astronomically significant (the solar pole rotates 360 degrees in 37 days; 360 + 37 = 397). Multiplying 360 by 400 produces the 144,000 mentioned in the Book of Revelation in the Bible. That this is so is confirmed by table (b): two rows do not add to 13, row 3 and row 6. The Book of Revelation (xiii, 18) goes on to say '. . . here is wisdom, let him that hath understanding count the number of the beast, for it is the number of a man; and his number is six hundred three score and six..' Row 6 multiplied by 110 = 660 which – appearing on row 6 – amounts to 666. That this is so may be confirmed by multiplying row 3 (the only other row which does not add to 13) by 37, which equals 111. Hence the necklace carries both 144,000 and 666, as mentioned in Revelation. The same numbers can be found by decoding the clues in the Temple of Inscriptions at Palenque. Moreover, Tutankhamun carried 143 pieces of jewellery wrapped within the bandages of his mummy; he was object number 144.

The Secrets of Tutankhamun's Scarab Brooch

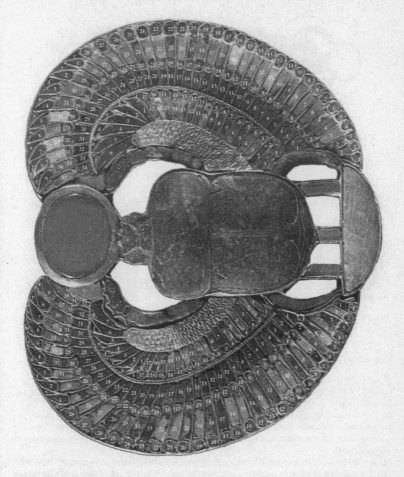

Figure A55. The brooch (pectoral) found wrapped within the weave of Tutankhamun's mummy contains several levels of encoded information (see figures A56 (I) and (II)). (i) The sun, the scarab and the crescent together form the name Neb-Khepru-Re, Tutankhamun. (ii) It explains how solar radiation from the sun impinges on the earth, affecting life on our planet (figure A3). (iii) The quantities of inlaid stones, in the two wings, amount to 397, explaining that the solar pole (figure A6a) revolves through 360 degrees in 37 days, the revolutionary period of the sun's polar magnetic field. (iv) Analysis of the encoded numbers reveals the number 781 (figure A16b), the duration of the sunspot cycle in 87.4545-day periods (781 x 87.4545 = 68,302 = one 187-year period). A solar neutral sheet magnetic reversal occurs after 20 of these cycles.

The Secrets of the Scarab Brooch (I)

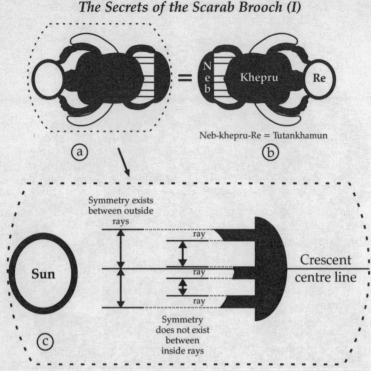

Neb-khepru-Re = Tutankhamun

Figure A56 (I).

Figure A56 (I) and A56 (II). The scarab brooch contains several layers of information:
(a) and (b) Disc, scarab and crescent together form the hieroglyphic name Neb-Khepru-Re, Tutankhamun.
(c) The distance between rays and the centre line of the crescent is symmetrical. However, the distance between the inside rays is asymmetrical. This tells the observer that the outside wings of the scarab are symmetrical, but the number of stones inside each wing is asymmetrical.
(d) 186 feather stones are inlaid in each wing, which shows symmetry; together these total 366, the number of days in a leap year. However, each group of 186 stones is comprised of different numbers of stones on respective feather rows; 31 stones are distributed asymmetrically in gaps between feathers (*see boxed figures, e*). The total number of stones is therefore 366 + 31 = 397.
(e) The solar disc and crescent appear to contain another level of information; the solar disc, consisting of 360 (degrees), and the crescent (representing the polar cap of the sun, which takes 37 days to rotate once) together add up to 397. This allows a further step in the interpretation of the symbolic significance of the brooch.
(f) shows a schematic of the sun and its magnetic field showering particles, the solar wind, towards the earth. This bombardment results in compression of the earth's magnetic field on the sunward side, a bow shock.

The Secrets of the Scarab Brooch (II)

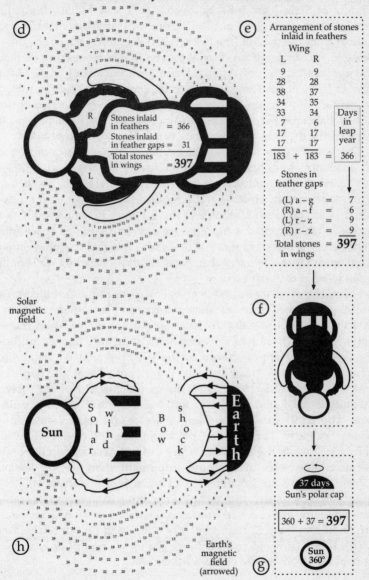

(d)

Stones inlaid in feathers = 366
Stones inlaid in feather gaps = 31
Total stones in wings = **397**

(e) Arrangement of stones inlaid in feathers

	Wing	
	L	R
	9	9
	28	28
	38	37
	34	35
	33	34
	7	6
	17	17
	17	17
	183 + 183 =	366 Days in leap year

Stones in feather gaps

(L) a – g	=	7
(R) a – f	=	6
(L) r – z	=	9
(R) r – z	=	9
Total stones in wings	=	**397**

(f)

(g)

37 days
Sun's polar cap

360 + 37 = **397**

Sun 360°

(h)

Solar magnetic field

Sun

Solar wind

Bow shock

Earth

Earth's magnetic field (arrowed)

Figure A56 (II).

that information has been encoded into it, and we note that all four corners of Stela J are missing. Secondly, it was hidden from the searcher (archaeologists) in the Pyramid of Inscriptions and it was hidden from the thinker (the information it contains is not obvious). Being an *encoded* book, it is logical to refer to it as resembling *the book that was encoded*. The only known *obviously* encoded book of the Maya is Stela J of Copan. The encoding technique used in that resembled the pattern of a woven, or plaited, mat. The decoded version of the Lid of Palenque, what I call the Amazing Lid of Palenque, must therefore be the long-lost holy book of the Maya, *The Popol Vuh*.

The Popol Vuh, the lid, was hidden from archaeologists because the encoded stories are primarily spiritual (as well as super-scientific) – not aimed at, or intended for, grave-robbers or archaeologists. It was encoded to protect, preserve and safeguard the information for those who placed the spiritual ethos first and foremost in their lives. It also succeeded in compressing more information into a smaller space and, importantly, it demonstrates that those who encoded the information were much more intelligent than we are today – meaning we should listen to what they have to say.

Sceptics, primarily orthodox archaeologists, argue that the Maya could never have encoded such information into their artefacts, that they did not possess the technology, that they had no transparencies, that they had no computers, that they had no understanding of the super-science of the sun. But this is, firstly, the wrong way to look at the enquiry. It was Lord Pacal, the miracle-maker, who encoded the treasures of the Maya, not the Maya themselves (just as it was Jesus, and not the entire Israeli population, who 2000 years ago, walked on water and turned water into wine). Secondly, I believe that the Maya themselves did have the ability to encode the treasures. They did not need our technology because they were much more intelligent than we are today. Moreover, there are documented cases in recent human medical history that demonstrate that the human brain can process information perfectly, both back to front and upside down. A quarter-page article in *The Times* (7 December 1995) reported on one such case: 'Girl's Bump Cures Mirror-Writing'. The article described how ten-year-old Vicky Wilmore of Manchester was

. . . a happy child of normal ability until she complained of a headache one morning a year ago. From that moment, she started writing everything back to front and upside down.

Apart from that, she was perfect. Her schoolteachers found that they could read her handwriting perfectly providing they used a mirror and turned her work-paper upside down. One year later Vicky suffered a bang on the head and her neural processing returned to normal. The article concluded: 'Doctors are baffled.'

Other examples of transparency-free pictorial decoding proliferate today. Over the past few years the advent of computers has allowed the encoding of information by digitally scrambling images to deliberately conceal information. The so-called Magic-Eye 3-D pictures, often featured in the popular press, provide hours of fun to enthusiasts. At first glance the image appears to be a jumble of nonsense. But the information can be decoded by staring at the image, slightly cross-eyed. Eventually the left and right hemispheres of the brain process the information separately, and the underlying encoded image snaps into consciousness.

Bishop Diego de Landa (second Bishop of Merida, in the Yucatán Peninsula of Mexico, following the Conquest) reported, in his book *Relacion de las Cosas de Yucatán* (1565, published by the Abbé Brasseur de Bourbourg in 1864) that

> . . . squint-eye was considered a mark of beauty, and mothers strove to disfigure their children in this way by suspending pellets of wax between their eyes in order to make them squint, thus securing the desired effect.

And so, in this simple way, the secrets of Lord Pacal were handed down through Mayan cultural practice, generation after generation; a physiological *instruction* telling us how to decode the Transformers left behind in antiquity.

Maya Transformers: designs that 'transform' into many more pictures when the secret code is broken

There are thousands of Mayan carvings, only a few of which contain these hidden stories. The Amazing Lid of Palenque is the 'Rosetta stone' of Mexican archaeology. It contains the decoding instructions which can be applied to other artefacts. Some other carvings contain simple ordinary pictures, which are mere allegories: e.g. many show 'blood-letting practices', proof, modern archaeologists would have us believe, that these people were no more than barbarians who pierced their penises and tongues with spikes and thorns, fought bloody battles and went to war. But how else could the message about declining fertility – the loss of, and need for, menstruation (blood) – be conveyed to future peoples like ourselves?

In *The Supergods*, I dispelled the 'pagan' myth, this travesty of one of the world's most gifted people. Using the decoding instructions from the Amazing Lid of Palenque, I showed that the paintings of the Maya (the Mural of Bonampak, featured later in the chapter), just like their jewellery (the jade necklace – figure 33e – and the mosaic mask – figure A33d) and architecture (the Pyramid of Inscriptions – figure A33), also contain hidden knowledge of their traditions and history.

(iii) The Mythological Sun

The Legend of the Feathered Snake

In *The Tutankhamun Prophecies* I explained the true meaning of the feathered snake. It was in my earlier work *The Supergods*, while writing about Augustus le Plongeon, the son of a naval commodore and Maya explorer at the end of the nineteenth century, that the pieces of the puzzle came together. He believed that the Maya practised mesmerism, induced clairvoyance and used 'magic mirrors' to predict the future. He was sure they had sailed westwards from Central America to develop civilisations in the Pacific and then onwards across the Indian Ocean and Persian Gulf to Egypt. To substantiate this, he compared many examples of Mayan and Egyptian architecture, writings and beliefs, which extended to sun-worship.

Le Plongeon's interpretation of one of the treasured Mayan bark books, the Troano Codex, suggested that several pages were devoted to a cataclysm, the sinking of the lost continent of Mu, in the Pacific.

In the 1930s the American businessman and self-styled explorer James Churchward supported le Plongeon's ideas and at the same time valued his own persuasive evidence to substantiate the earlier existence of Mu; these were sketches of ancient stone tablets (figure A57a) he had stumbled on in a monastery in Brahmaputra, Tibet, while serving as an undercover agent for the British Army. The tablets were named after the legendary Mayan adepts, the Naacal, the 'exalted ones', who travelled the world teaching their science, engineering and language.

Churchward also believed that the Muvians exploited technologies surpassing our own, including anti-gravity, which enabled the Muvians to move large objects and construct colossal buildings. He says their civilisation was in no way primitive and that their under-standing of the cosmic forces of 'energy' was remarkable. He believed the higher knowledge that allowed the building of pyramids in both Egypt and Mexico had come from Atlantis and before that from Mu, some 25,000 years ago.

He was sure the Naacal tablets contained the exposition of a profound knowledge that is only just dawning on the scientific world of today. He believed the tablets described how the cataclysmic sinking of the lost continent of Mu was caused by an increase in solar radiation that led to overheating of the landmass, causing the expansion of underground gases that bubbled to the surface. The land resettled, submerged beneath the Pacific, taking with it the sixty-four million inhabitants.

But what has this to do with the feathered snake? Churchward had meticulously sketched the accounts of the deluge from the Naacal tablets: one (figure A57a) showed the disc of the sun carrying a tiny feathered snake-like mark in the region of the equator (figure A57a, sketch 1B). If the tablet were from Mu, it must have been 25,000 years old.

Often the smallest of clues turns an investigation, and so it was with Churchward's sketch. The Muvians, it seems, understood the super-science of the sun and knew, just like the Maya, of the existence of the sun's neutral warp (figure A17–19). They knew that when the 11.5-year sunspot cycle is superimposed on the sun's neutral warp the combined shape takes the form of a feathered snake (figure A57b) that lives in the equatorial region of the sun. So important was this to them that they carved it into one of their precious tablets, a feathered snake across the face of the sun.

It soon became clear that the legend of the feathered snake described the story of how the sun affects life on earth. The feathered snake *was* the sun.

The Egyptians revered the feathered snake in their monuments and paintings (figure A57c). Tutankhamun carried the mark of the feathered snake school of initiates on his forehead and his beard (figure A58). In Mexico, Lord Pacal was known as the feathered snake. In Peru, Viracocha Pachacamac encoded the same message into the hieroglyphic carving (figure A59) of Viracocha on the Gateway of the Sun, which stands in the temple of the Kalasasaya and, as I explained in *The Lost Tomb of Viracocha*, he left the same enigmatic message carved in the sand pictures (figure A60b and c) at Nazca.

The Feathered Snake and the Mosaic Mask of Palenque

Alberto Ruz removed the sarcophagus lid of Palenque from the sarcophagus to discover the occupant wearing a mosaic jade mask (figure A33d) which was restored and polished and placed in the museums of Mexico for everyone to admire.

Using the same technique as before, I made two transparent colour copies of the mask, placed one on top of the other, and several composite pictures emerged (previously published in *The Tutankhamun Prophecies*). Plate 3a shows just one of those pictures – the head of a snake with wings on its forehead – Lord Pacal as the feathered snake.

The stories encoded in the mask explain that the man in the tomb brought life, and brought death, and that he ruled the four corners of the heavens. He was the feathered snake who took to the throne at the age of nine to become priest-king of the Maya. The decoded stories explain that as the good god (999) he fought the bad god (666) and won. And they suggest that he has lived many times before, as other spiritual leaders, throughout history.

The orientations of the pictures encoded into the mask (not shown here) likewise provide clues; a picture of the god of the south, upside down, becomes the god of the north. Similarly, a picture of the god of the east, upside down, becomes the god of the west. This tells us that when the earth tilts upside down, following a solar magnetic reversal, south becomes north and north becomes south, east becomes west and west becomes east and that Quetzalcoatl was the good god, the opposite of bad.

The Sun as the Feathered Snake

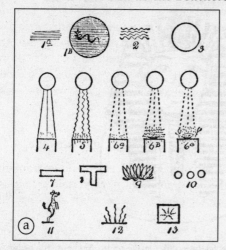

Figure A57. (a) Sketches, by James Churchward, of the Naacal tablets showing the sinking of Mu; increased levels of solar radiation led to the overheating of the landmass, causing the release of subterranean gases and the sinking of the land itself. One of the sketches (labelled as 1B) shows a feathered snake-like mark across the face of the sun. (b) The sunspot cycle and solar neutral sheet (figure A17) represented as a feathered snake.

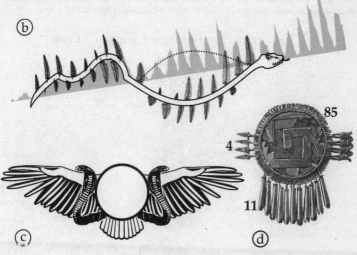

(c) The sun, as the feathered snake, was worshipped and depicted in carvings and paintings throughout Egypt. (d) The magnetic field of the sun shifts every 1,366,040 days: 1,366,040 ÷ 365.25 = 3,740 years exactly. This gold and turquoise sun-shield from Monte Alban, Mexico, encodes this period: 4 (arrows) x 11 (pendants) x 85 (gold loops) = 3,740. The four arrows (that fly through the air – wings) symbolise the four previous ages of the sun, which all ended in destruction. The 85 loops around the perimeter represent magnetic field loops of sunspots that occur on the sun's surface.

Tutankhamun, the Feathered Snake of Egypt

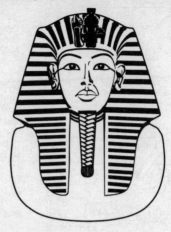

Figure A58. Tutankhamun carried feathers and a snake on his forehead. His beard was fashioned as the body of a snake which ended with the tail feathers of a bird.

Viracocha, the Feathered Snake of Peru

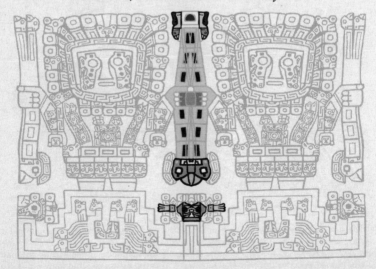

Figure A59. The Viracocha Transformer from the Gateway of the Sun, Tiahuanaco, showing Viracocha Pachacamac as the feathered snake. Plate 3a shows Lord Pacal as the feathered snake encoded into the Mosaic Mask of Palenque.

266

The Feathered Snake Drawings of Nazca

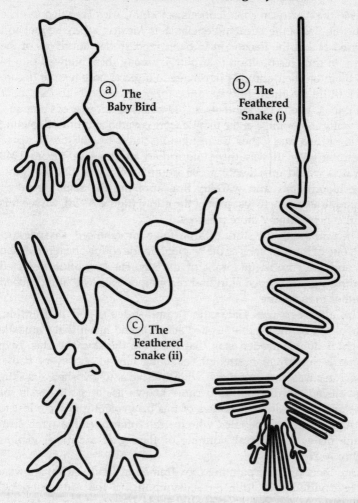

Not to scale. Orientation and position shown for illustration purposes only.

Figure A60. (a) Nazca line drawing of the baby bird with five fingers (claws) on the left foot and four fingers (claws) on the right foot. The bird has one finger missing, like the Viracocha bas-relief carving. The feathered snake as depicted on two separate desert line drawings in the Nazca desert: (b) bird with a snake-like neck; (c) bird with a snake-like neck. Parts of this drawing have been damaged (erased) over time.

267

The Legend of the Stag

In 1946 the American conscientious objector Carlos Frey fled to exile in the jungles of the Yucatán Peninsula, in Mexico, where he met and married one of the Lacondon Indians, modern-day survivors of the Maya. In time his position of privilege among them allowed him to join them on their annual pilgrimage to a secret holy temple (figure A61) built by their Mayan ancestors, in around AD 750, near Bonampak, about 160 kilometres (100 miles) south-east of Palenque. The walls and ceilings of the temple were covered in murals depicting battle scenes and other paintings obscured by the build-up of limestone scale. It was these more than anything that from 1946 onwards would mistakenly persuade archaeologists that the Maya were bloodthirsty and warlike. But, applying the same decoding technique as before to just part of the mural (figure A62a), we see this again conceals many more pictures.

The mural tells the story of Xipe Totec (pronounced 'shy-pee-toe-tec'), one of the four sons of the original divine couple; he represented fire and the eastern quadrant of the sky. He was often depicted wearing a green striped skirt and carrying two sticks that he rubbed together to make fire.

His alter ego was Camaxtle ('cam-ash-lee'), god of hunting, symbolised by the double-headed stag. Legend has it that Camaxtle caught a double-headed stag that fell from the sky. The stag gave Camaxtle superhuman strength, enabling him to win every battle. Xipe Totec was also associated with the snake, which sheds its skin, symbolising rebirth, and so became known as the god of skin, or foreskin. The positive attributes of this benevolent god were lost to the Aztecs and later peoples, who instead interpreted his symbolism as the malevolent literal skinning or flaying of sacrificial victims (figure A62b).

One section of the painting (box-framed in figure A61b) shows a circle divided into four parts, symbolising the cross-sectional schematic of the sun's magnetic fields (figure A62a, arrowed). Archaeologists maintain that the scene simply shows a group of dancers dressed up as lobsters, crabs and sea-monsters. But closer examination, using the Maya Transformer decoding process, reveals a picture of a man carrying two sticks (figure A63). His chest is formed from the complementary heads of two stags. Above his head a poppy-headed chalice contains the seeds of renewal. A foreskin-covered penis hangs down between his legs. This is the story of Xipe Totec, god of rebirth, skin, foreskin and his other emanation, Camaxtle, the double-headed stag. This initial scene is located using the solar-cross mark as the first centre of transparency rotation.

Other decoded scenes appear when different areas of the picture are coloured in and other centres of rotation are used. Figure A64 tells the story of Chimalma. Mainstream scholars, for the most part, agree that Camaxtle married a girl called Chimalma, who reportedly swallowed a jade bead that impregnated her without even touching the insides of her body. Following this immaculate conception she gave birth to twins.

Another account, by historian Ignacia Bernal, suggests that Chimalma was also the second wife of the warrior Mixcoatl, who conquered the valley of Mexico after chancing on her during one of his military sojourns into Morelos. He took her, lay with her and she later conceived, giving birth to Ce Acatl Topiltzin Quetzalcoatl, a legendary leader (ostensibly), who was believed to have become the king of the ancient Toltec city of Tula that flourished from around AD 750 to 1068, 74 kilometres (46 miles) north-west of today's Mexico City. Figure A64 shows pregnant Chimalma modestly covering her naked chest when chanced on by the warrior Mixcoatl, who fired arrows above her head. The large (arrow-shaped) head of Mixcoatl can be seen in the foreground of the picture bowing in front of Chimalma. These remarkable pictures, from Lord Pacal's Maya Transformer collection, seem to confirm that a living woman, Chimalma, did indeed conceive through an immaculate conception, that she did give birth to Lord Pacal (the twins, the planet Venus, eponym of Quetzalcoatl), who was born through an immaculate conception and went on to rule at Tula, before his death in AD 750 at Palenque; another incarnation of the great Quetzalcoatl, the feathered snake Supergod of the Maya.

The next scene, figure A65, shows the birth of Camaxtle, the double-headed stag. The baby – whose head carries two sets of horns – emerges from his mother's womb. The mother is restrained by two midwives, and her head is licked by two stags' heads, one fleshed, the other skeletal, symbolising the *rebirth* of Camaxtle, born again from bones. Note that the scene shows the birth of Camaxtle among animals (in a stable?). Eventually (figure A66), we are told that Xipe Totec

The Temple in the Jungle

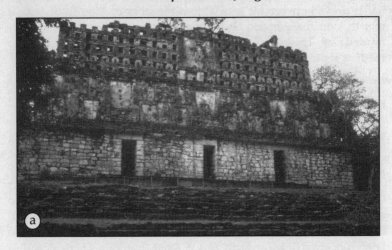

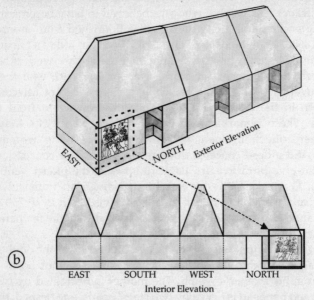

Figure A61. (a) The mysterious temple in the jungle discovered by Carlos Frey in 1946. (b) Every wall and ceiling in the temple is covered with (according to archaeologists) strange and baffling murals. (The area box-framed is discussed in this section.)

The Mural of Bonampak

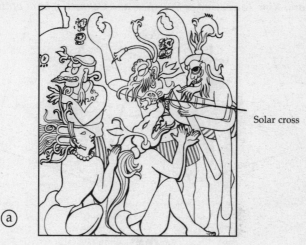

Solar cross

(a)

Xipe Totec/Camaxtle (Lord of the Stags)

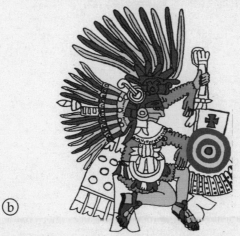

(b)

Figure A62. (a) Mural from the first room of the temple at Bonampak. A circle with a cross, representing the sun (*arrowed*) is featured in the design. (b) A depiction of Xipe Totec, from the Borbonic Codex 14, wearing the skin of a flayed victim whose hands hang like gloves from his wrists. He was the god of spring, rebirth and fertility. One of his emanations was Camaxtle (lord of the stags), the god of hunting. Here, Xipe Totec carries a shield showing the solar cross and radiating-sun symbols. He wears a striped skirt, and a banner, showing the five ages of the sun, hangs from his back.

The Transformer of Bonampak
Story: Xipe Totec, God of Sacrifice, and Camaxtle, Lord of the Stags

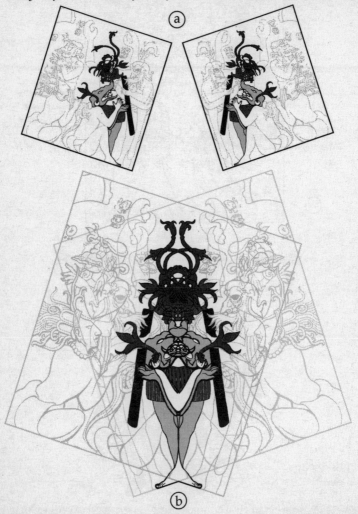

Figure A63. When the solar cross mark is used as a centre of rotation, with the acetates positioned as shown, a picture of Xipe Totec/Camaxtle can be seen. Xipe Totec, as the god of fire, carries two sticks, which he rubbed together to make fire. On his head, as the god of fertility, he carries a poppy-headed chalice filled with seed, and his foreskin hangs down beneath his striped skirt. His chest, as Camaxtle, the god of hunting (lord of the stags), is made from two complementary stags' heads.

The Transformer of Bonampak
Story: The Immaculate Conception of Chimalma

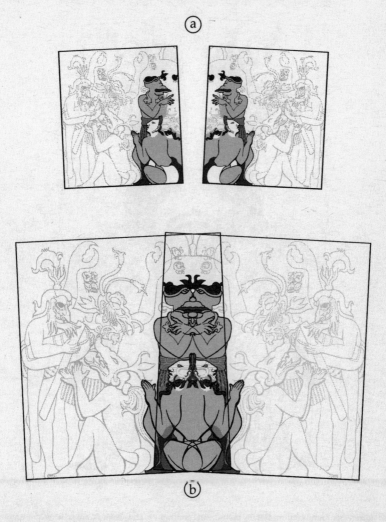

Figure A64. Repositioning the transparencies, a composite picture appears telling the story of Chimalma, the mother of Quetzalcoatl (the twins), who became pregnant after she swallowed a jade bead. Here she carries the twins in her womb. She stands with her arms folded across her chest to protect herself from the lecherous warrior Mixcoatl, who bows in the foreground of the picture.

The Transformer of Bonampak
Story: The Birth of Camaxtle, Lord of the Stags

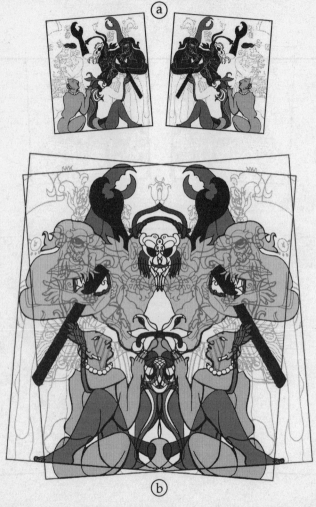

Figure A65. Here, two midwives restrain the mother of Xipe Totec/Camaxtle as she gives birth to her son, Xipe Totec, in his emanation as Camaxtle. The head of Camaxtle, the double-headed stag, is represented by the emerging head with two sets of complementary antlers, or horns, in the lower centre of the scene. A large stag's head, which carries another skeletal stag's head, fills the composite picture above. The stag licks the head of the female in labour, suckling and comforting the mother during the painful process of birth.

The Transformer of Bonampak
Story: The Man with a Beard who Died on a Cross

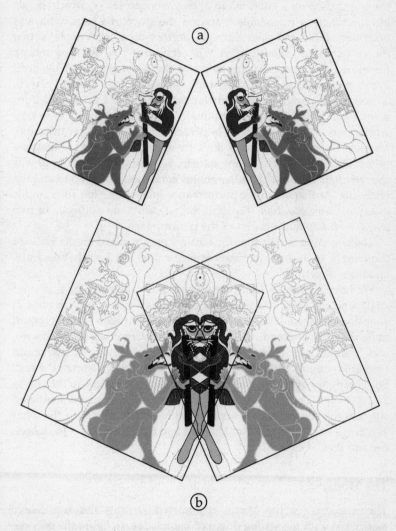

Figure A66. Here, Xipe Totec, the god of sacrifice, appears as the white man with a beard. His arms are folded across his chest, and he carries two wooden sticks in his hands. The two seated stags pull back the skirt of Xipe Totec to reveal his crossed legs. This tells us that Xipe Totec, the white man with a beard, died on a wooden cross.

becomes a white man with a beard. This man carries two wooden sticks and stands cross-legged, informing us that the white man with the beard died on a cross made of two wooden sticks, which, if this interpretation is reasonable, parallels the story of Christ, who was born in a stable and died through sacrifice on a cross made of two pieces of wood. The story in this section of the decoded mural, therefore, strongly links the belief of the Maya (inspired by Lord Pacal) to that of the Christian faith, implying that the Maya were aware of the paradigm of Christianity, and of the Christ-child born through an immaculate conception, in a stable, who grew up to be a white man with a beard who was sacrificed and died on the cross. Moreover, the significance of the two stags' heads, one skeletal, the other fleshed out, symbolising rebirth, suggests that Lord Pacal was the *rebirth* of Christ. This is the genius concealed in the myth and the encoding. At the end of the performance (plate 3b), Xipe Totec, in his guise as Camaxtle, half stag, half man, bows to an audience of two stags, who applaud the end of the performance.

The decoding shows that the battle scenes painted on the walls of the temple should not be taken at face value, but for what they are: creations of genius.

We have seen how Lord Pacal was known as both the feathered snake and the stag. The dragon of China (as we have seen in plate 2) was also a feathered snake and a stag. And the dragon was the chosen insignia of Shi Huangdi, the first emperor of China who, legend says, was 'the Son of Heaven', just like Lord Pacal, Jesus, Tutankhamun ('tut-ankh-amun' = 'the son of god') and Viracocha, 'foam of the sea'. Shi Huangdi never died but became a dragon that flew to the sun to live for ever. The dragon *is* the feathered snake, and the feathered snake *is* the sun, which means that Shi Huangdi must, like the other sun kings – Lord Pacal, Tutankhamun and the Viracochas – have been the sun itself, God.

The Monkey

The monkey, for the Maya, epitomised writing and was hence associated with the setting down of knowledge. In Egypt the baboon, Hapi, features widely in the tomb paintings of Tutankhamun. In Peru, a picture of a monkey (figure A67), drawn by Viracocha Pachacamac, features in the lines of Nazca. The monkey is hence associated with higher knowledge and hence the Supergods. The Viracocha monkey (figure A67) has one finger missing from the right hand. The carving of Viracocha Pachacamac (figure A59) from the temple of the Kalasasaya, at Tiahuanaco, also shows him with one finger missing, this time from each hand (indeed, this ostensible defect led to the decoding of that Transformer). The baby bird line drawing of Nazca (figure A60a) is also depicted with one finger (claw) missing from the right hand, suggesting that the baby bird is associated not only with the feathered snake but also with Viracocha Pachacamac, who drew the pictures at Nazca, and also with Lord Pacal who carries the baby bird on his forehead (figures A50 and A51). The monkey, therefore, can be identified with the feathered snake, the Supergods and, hence, with the number of the Supergods, 999.

(iv) The Supergods as Venus

In *The Supergods* I explained that, in the past, superior beings visited earth teaching mankind the higher orders of science and spirituality. They were not from this planet, although where they were 'from' is unclear. What is clear is their relationship to the living God who created the earth and the heavens; they were one and the same.

Krishna of India who incarnated on earth 5,000 years ago, Buddha, 500–420 BC in India, and Christ, from 2,000 years ago, all brought the same messages as Lord Pacal: that purification comes through sacrifice, self-control and duty to others. Since then, new knowledge from the decoded treasures of Tutankhamun (see *The Tutankhamun Prophecies*) and Viracocha and Viracocha Pachacamac (see *The Lost Tomb of Viracocha*) encourage us to include these sun-kings among the list of Supergods, given that they, too, shared much in common. Each of the teachers taught in 'parables', allegorical stories that invoked 'pictures' in the mind, enabling the ancient esoteric teachings to be handed down through generations, on the one hand, and yet hidden from the disbeliever on the other. Each performed miracles and was born through an immaculate conception. Each was associated as the twin-star Venus; in the Bible Jesus says '. . . I, Jesus . . . am the bright and morning star' (Revelation xxii, 16) (see also figure A70); Lord Pacal, in a scene from the Amazing Lid of Palenque (figure A71) is reborn as the twins; Tutankhamun, in a wall painting in his tomb (figure A72), is shown greeting Nut, goddess of the night sky before

The Monkey

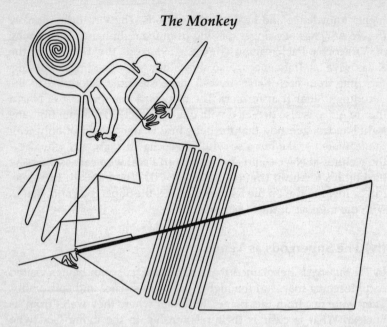

Figure 67. The monkey line drawing from the desert sands of Nazca, Peru. The monkey has four fingers on the right hand and five on the left; one finger is missing from the hands, just like the Viracocha bas-relief carving from the Gateway of the Sun at Tiahuanaco (figure A59). The monkey embraces the largest of three identical shapes (triangles).

Viracocha of Tiahuanaco

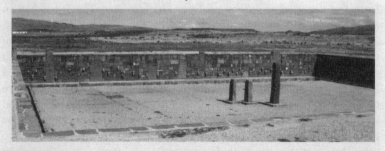

Figure A68. Statue of Viracocha (large) and the children of Viracocha (small) at the Temple of the Stone Heads, Tiahuanaco. The hands (not shown here) of the large statue (on close inspection) make the same gesture as those of the monkey (figure A67). This correspondence suggests that the asymmetrical hands of the monkey belong to the statue of Viracocha and that Viracocha drew the picture of the monkey in the sand at Nazca.

The Supergods

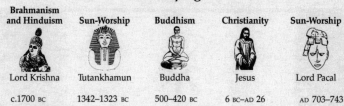

Brahmanism and Hinduism	Sun-Worship	Buddhism	Christianity	Sun-Worship
Lord Krishna	Tutankhamun	Buddha	Jesus	Lord Pacal
c.1700 BC	1342–1323 BC	500–420 BC	6 BC–AD 26	AD 703–743

Figure A69. Several religious leaders shared much in common (see *The Supergods*). Each was the embodiment of the one living God who created the universe; each was born through an immaculate conception; each performed miracles; and each believed in reincarnation and everlasting life. Each was identified with the twin-star Venus, the brightest and purest source of light in the heavens. In Revelation (xxii, 16), Jesus says: '. . . I, Jesus...am the root of David, and the bright and morning star' (figure A70). One of the stories from the Amazing Lid of Palenque (figure A71) shows the rebirth of Lord Pacal as the twins, Venus. When Tutankhamun died, he became twins (figure A72) and joined Osiris in the heavens. Evidence from the tombs of Viracocha and Viracocha Pachacamac, in Peru, says that those legendary white gods were earlier incarnations of Lord Pacal more than 1,500 years ago (see *The Lost Tomb of Viracocha*). When Viracocha Pachacamac died, he, too, journeyed to Venus in the heavens (figure A73). The sun-kings shared even more in common: each encoded their knowledge of the super-science of the sun, together with the higher orders of spirituality, into their treasures.

becoming twins and greeting Osiris in the heavens; the statues of Viracocha and the children of Viracocha from Tiahuanaco (figure A73) tell us that Viracocha became the twins, while the layout of the three statues, laid out to reflect the position of stars in Orion's belt, tell us that he became the twins in the heavens, Venus.

Our investigations show that there is little doubt that the decoded treasures of the Maya tell the same story as St John's Revelation, as do those from Tutankhamun, Viracocha and Viracocha Pachacamac, through the use of pictures and numbers. The numbers are unique and specific: 26 (the rotational duration of the solar equator on the surface of the sun); 37 (the rotational duration of the solar pole on the surface of the sun); 96 (the number of magnetic microcycles in one 187-year sunspot cycle), 97 (the number of magnetic microcycles that need to be recognised when considering the 18,139-year great solar cycle); 20 (the number of 187-year sunspot cycles that comprise one directional shift of the sun's warped magnetic sheet); 1,366,560 (the number of 20 sunspot cycles; 1,366,040 days, or 1,366,560 days measured as 2,340 intervals of the planet Venus); 666 (the mark of the devil, hell and the beast); and 999 (the mark of God, heaven, the sun and the Supergods).

Jesus as the Twin-Star Venus

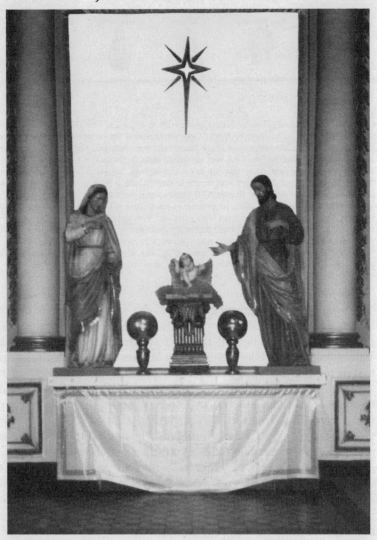

Figure A70. Shrine, from the cathedral at Guadalajara, Mexico, showing the newborn baby Jesus beneath a twin star, together with Mary and Joseph. Silver spheres, mounted on urns on either side of Jesus, represent the various manifestations of the planet Venus as the morning star and the evening star. Joseph and Mary hence introduce Jesus as the twin-star Venus.

Lord Pacal as the Twin-Star Venus
The Amazing Lid of Palenque
Story: The Death (and Rebirth) of Lord Pacal, Scene 6 (Scenes 1–5 not shown here)

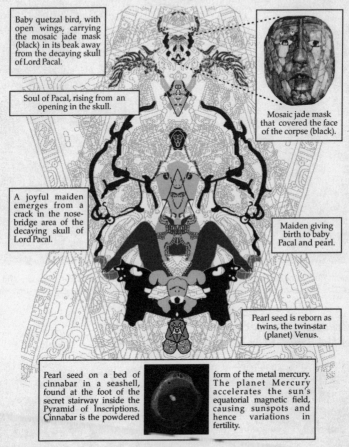

Baby quetzal bird, with open wings, carrying the mosaic jade mask (black) in its beak away from the decaying skull of Lord Pacal.

Soul of Pacal, rising from an opening in the skull.

Mosaic jade mask that covered the face of the corpse (black).

A joyful maiden emerges from a crack in the nose-bridge area of the decaying skull of Lord Pacal.

Maiden giving birth to baby Pacal and pearl.

Pearl seed is reborn as twins, the twin-star (planet) Venus.

Pearl seed on a bed of cinnabar in a seashell, found at the foot of the secret stairway inside the Pyramid of Inscriptions. Cinnabar is the powdered form of the metal mercury. The planet Mercury accelerates the sun's equatorial magnetic field, causing sunspots and hence variations in fertility.

Figure A71. Here an open-winged quetzal bird (*top, centre*) carries away the green mosaic mask, the physical identity of Lord Pacal when he was alive, in its beak. At the same time it carries away Lord Pacal's soul in its tail feathers through the hole in the skull at the top of the head. The rest of the scene explains the rebirth of Lord Pacal: a maiden appears across the face of Pacal with her legs wide open. A baby emerges from her womb and delivers a pearl from its mouth. The pearl becomes two 'solar babies', the twins, Venus, the morning and the evening star. This tells us that Lord Pacal was reborn as Venus, brightest of the night-time heavenly bodies.

Tutankhamun as the Twin-Star Venus

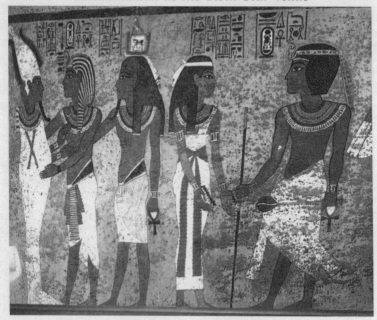

Figure A72. Tutankhamun (*right*) meeting his escort Nut, goddess of the night sky and the stars. Tutankhamun, after death (*centre*) with his twin, greeting Osiris, god of resurrection.

Viracocha Pachacamac as the Twin-Star Venus

Orion's Belt

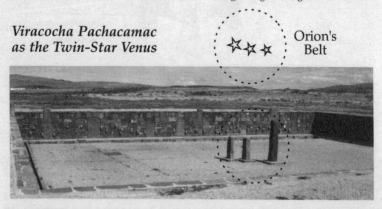

Figure A73. Statue of Viracocha Pachacamac (largest of the three) and the ostensible children of Viracocha (the twins) at the Temple of the Stone Heads, Tiahuanaco, laid out to reflect the stars in Orion's belt. Viracocha Pachacamac was reborn as two children in the heavens, the twins, the planet Venus.

APPENDIX FIVE

Mexico, Peru and China

Decoding the Squared Circle, Viracocha, the Gateway of
the Sun and the White Man with a Beard of China

The Sun-Shield of Monte Alban

Figure A57d showed how the mosaic sun-shield from Monte Alban,
Mexico, contained the super-science of the sun: the four arrows, eighty-
five loops and eleven pendants, when multiplied (4 x 85 x 11) amount
to 3,740 – which corresponds with the solar neutral sheet reversal
period of 3,740 years.

The artefact resembles the disc of the sun with golden loops around
the perimeter. Clearly, whoever encoded the numerical information
into the sun-shield intended to communicate the association between
the sun and the solar neutral sheet reversal period. The sun-shield, of
the Zapotec period, c. AD 700, was made at around the time that a
white man with a beard (Quetzalcoatl) was thought to have lived in
Mexico.

Plate 16c shows a terracotta figure of a white man with a beard
(c. AD 400–600) that was found in a tomb near Ankang, China. He,
curiously, sports a serrated dorsal fin, similar to a step-like mark
found on the mosaic shield (figure A76), suggesting that a story of a
white man with a beard, who shared something in common with the
sun-shield, circulated in China, at least in around AD 400–600.

Stories from the Mural of Bonampak (figures A62–A66) explain
that Lord Pacal (c. AD 700–750), the product of an immaculate conception, was born in a stable, performed miracles and died in sacrifice on
a wooden cross.

Decoding the Squared Circle

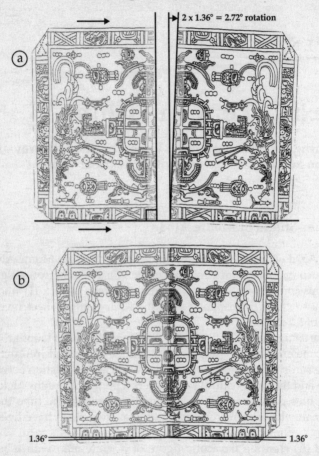

Figure A74. The bronze canopy of the funerary chariot (figure 68) takes the shape of a 'squared circle', an esoteric reference to the sun. That this is so is confirmed by the Amazing Lid of Palenque Sub-Transformer. The squared-circle composite is produced by slicing the lid design through the central cross portion of the picture (a). The half-loop marks on two complementary acetates may now be buttressed together to provide the final composite arrangement (b), as long as each acetate is rotated by 1.36 degrees, as shown. The **1.36**-degree rotation refers to the **1,36**6,040-day solar magnetic reversal period. The half-loop marks hence refer to solar magnetic activity, and the 20 marker pegs (which can be seen only when the half-loop marks are brought together to become complete loops (cycles)) refer to the 20 magnetic cycles of one solar magnetic reversal period. Supporting proof is given by figure A75; in this position the Sub-Transformer reveals a composite picture of the sun between the morning star and the evening star (the twins).

Decoded stories from the Amazing Lid of Palenque (figure A52) show Lord Pacal's mouth covered with a picture of the man with a hat. Facsimiles of the man with the hat (one of which is shown in figure A53c) were also found in the tombs of Viracocha (c. AD 500) and Viracocha Pachacamac (c. AD 300) in Peru. These two so-called mythical figures were known as the fair-skinned blue-eyed gods that travelled the length of Peru, from Lake Titicaca in the south to Sipan in the north, where, legend has it, they disappeared – into the foam of the sea.

'Foam of the sea' appears to decribe the *perfect person*; he who is in harmony with the elements of the earth, water, air and fire (sun). This simultaneous contact only happens when standing in the foam of the sea, hence the metaphor.

The Book of Revelation says:

> And I saw another mighty angel come down from heaven, clothed with a cloud: and a rainbow was upon his head and his face was, as it were the sun . . . and he set his right foot upon the sea and his left foot on the earth . . . [in the foam of the sea] (Revelation x, 1–2).

Figure A53d, remarkably, shows a reconstruction (from the Museum of Archaeology in Lima, Peru) of Viracocha ('foam of the sea') Pachacamac ('god of the world') wearing a rainbow on his head and a golden sun disc across his face.

Examining the sun-shield more closely, using the Maya Transformer decoding process, several pictures emerge. Figure A76d shows the 'Gateway of the Sun' that stands in the temple of the Kalasasaya in Tiahuanaco, Bolivia, the birthplace of Viracocha. At one time the gateway stood on the water's edge of Lake Titicaca (the lake has since receded several miles from the gateway). The decoded picture shows the monolith reflected in the waters of the lake. The scene is embraced by a large triangle, in the centre, similar to the shape of the doorway that leads to the tomb of Lord Pacal at Palenque. The triangle is one of two that form a star of David, the emblem of Israel.

Figure A77a shows another decoded picture, the head of Lord Pacal with his distinctive hairstyle, leaning forwards (in a pose very similar to the scene of Camaxtle in plate 3b) regurgitating a pearl, the symbol of rebirth and Venus. Pacal's face is contained within a vesica pisces, a geometric fish-like shape (the symbol of Christianity) formed by the intersection of two overlapping circles.

Another scene (figure A77b) shows the face of Viracocha, from the bas-relief carving on the Gateway of the Sun.

In the Book of John, in the Bible, Jesus says '. . . let not your heart be troubled . . . I will go away but will come again unto you' (St John xiv, 27–28).

The newly discovered evidence, in this and my previous books, suggests that Jesus, the son of God the creator, *has* already returned to earth on many occasions. It suggests that the Christ-spirit has taken on many incarnations at different times during the history of the planet. It suggests that he has walked the lands of India (as Krishna and Buddha), Peru (as Viracocha and Viracocha Pachacamac), Mexico (as Lord Pacal and other Quetzalcoatls), Egypt (as Tutankhamun) and China (as the Sons of Heaven), each time leaving his mark and his message behind. Accounts in Revelation, decoded miracles from the Maya Transformers, and archaeological evidence bear testimony to such a hypothesis.

The Amazing Lid of Palenque Sub-Transformer
Story: The Sun and Venus

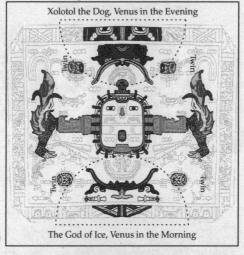

Xolotol the Dog, Venus in the Evening

Twin

Twin

Twin

Twin

(a)

The God of Ice, Venus in the Morning

Figure A75. (a) Decoded story from the Amazing Lid of Palenque Sub-Transformer (figure A74) showing (*top*) Xolotol, the blind dog (Venus in the evening), who cried so much that his eyes fell out, and (*bottom*) the god of ice (Venus in the morning) with a morning ice dagger on each cheek. The sun (the squared circle) sits between the morning

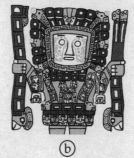

(b)

star and the evening star. (b) Line drawing of the bas-relief carving of Viracocha from the Gateway of the Sun (c and d) that once stood on the shore of Lake Titicaca (before the lake receded). The crack in the lintel was thought to have been caused by a lightning strike. Notice the highly advanced carving of the architrave around the doorway.

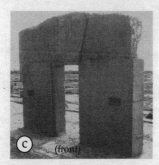

(c) (front)

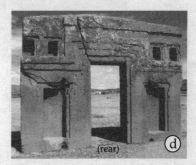

(rear) (d)

The White Man with the Beard of China,
The Sun-Shield of Monte Alban, Mexico,
and Viracocha of Peru

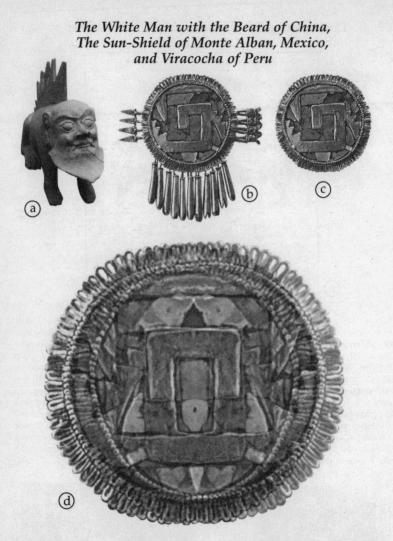

Figure A76. (a) Terracotta figure of a white man with a beard from the Han tomb near Ankang (plate 16c). The serrated edge down the spine resembles a similar pattern featured on the mosaic sun-shield (b) from Monte Alban, Mexico (see also figure A57d for numerical analysis). Closer inspection of the sun-shield reveals a hitherto unknown Maya Transformer, which when decoded reveals pictures of (d), the Gateway of the Sun from Tiahuanaco and its reflection in the waters of Lake Titicaca showing detail of the architrave and the crack on the lintel (ostensibly caused by lightning). Other orientations of the transparencies reveal pictures of Lord Pacal and Viracocha (figure A77a and b).

The Sun-Shield of Monte Alban Transformer
Story: Lord Pacal and Viracocha

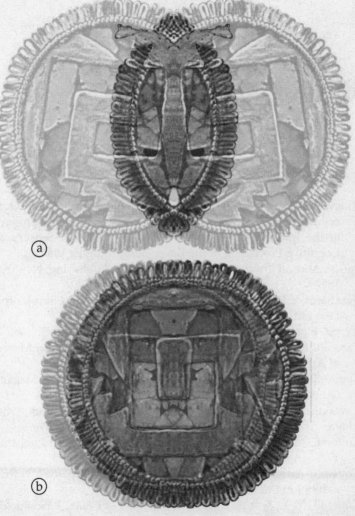

Figure A77. (a) Composite picture of Lord Pacal (the white man with a beard) regurgitating a pearl, inside a vesica pisces (the fish-shaped symbol of Christianity, created by two overlapping circles). (b) Composite picture of Viracocha. These decoded pictures show further correspondence between the serrated dorsal fin carried by the white man with the beard from Ankang and the same serrated pattern found on the sun-shield.

Bibliography

Aidey, Dr W. Ross, 'Cell Membranes, Electromagnetic Fields and Inter-cellular Communication', Basar, E. (Ed.), from a paper presented at the International Conference on Dynamics of Sensory and Cognitive Processing in the Brain, Berlin, August 1987

Bailey, Alice, *A Treatise on White Magic*, Lucis Publishing, New York, 1892

Burkhardt, V. R., *Chinese Creeds and Customs*, The South China Morning Post Ltd, 1953

Capon, E., and MacQuitty, W., *Princes of Jade*, Sphere, 1973

Caroselli, Susan L., *The Quest for Eternity*, Los Angeles County Museum of Art, 1988

Cathie, Bruce L., *The Harmonic Conquest of Space*, NEXUS Magazine (Australia), 1995

Cavendish, R., *An Illustrated Guide to Mythology*, W. H. Smith, 1984

Clayre, Alasdair, *The Heart of the Dragon*, Harvill Press, 1976

Cotterell, Arthur, *A Dictionary of World Mythology*, Guild Publishing, 1979

Cotterell, Arthur, *The First Emperor's Warriors*, Emperor's Warriors Exhibition Ltd. (London), 1987

Cotterell, Y. Y. & A., *The Early Civilization of China*, Weidenfeld & Nicolson, 1975

Cotterell, M. M., *Astrogenetics*, Brooks Hill Robinson & Co., 1988

Cotterell, M. M., *The Amazing Lid of Palenque*, Vol. 1, Brooks Hill Perry & Co., 1994

Cotterell, M. M., *The Amazing Lid of Palenque*, Vol. 2, Brooks Hill Perry & Co., 1994

Cotterell, M. M., *The Mayan Prophecies*, Element, 1995 (co-authored)

Cotterell, M. M., *The Mosaic Mask of Palenque*, Brooks Hill Perry & Co., 1995

Cotterell, M. M., *The Mural of Bonampak*, Brooks Hill Perry & Co., 1995

Cotterell, M. M., *The Supergods*, Thorsons, 1997

Cotterell, M. M., *The Lost Tomb of Viracocha*, Headline, 2001

Cotterell, M. M., *The Tutankhamun Prophecies*, Headline, 1999

Eberhard, Wolfram, *A History of China*, Routledge & Kegan Paul, 1960

Eysenck, H. J., and Nias, D. K. B., *Astrology: Science or Superstition?*, Maurice Temple Smith, 1982

Goepper, Roger, *The Oriental World*, Paul Hamlyn, 1967

Fagan, Brian, *New Treasures of the Past – Fresh Finds that Deepen our Understanding of the Archaeology of Man*, Guild Publishing, 1998

Goetz, D., and Morley, S. G., (after Recinos), *The Popol Vuh*, University of Oklahoma Press, 1947

Grosier, J. B., *The World of Ancient China*, John Gifford, 1972

His Majesty's Special Command (translation), *Holy Bible*, Eyre & Spottiswoode, 1899

Huxley, Francis, *The Dragon*, Thames and Hudson, 1979

Jordan, M., *Encyclopaedia of Gods*, Kyle Cathie, 1992

Knowles, Christopher, *Explorer China*, AA, 1999

Lafferty, Peter and Rowe, J. (Eds), *The Hutchinson Dictionary of Science*, Helicon, 1996

Legge, James, *Chinese Classics*, Vols I-V, University of Hong Kong Press, 1960

le Plongeon, Augustus, *Sacred Mysteries among the Mayas and the Quiches 11,500 Years Ago*, Macoy, 1909

Luxiang, Wang, *China's Cultural Heritage – Rediscovering a Past of 7,000 Years*, Morning Glory Publishers (Beijing), 1995

Mackenzie, Donald A., *Myths and Legends of China and Japan*, Studio Editions, 1994

Millidge, J. (Ed.) *Chinese Gods and Myths*, Grange, 1998

Moon, Peter, *The Black Sun*, Sky (New York), 1997

Moore, Hunt, Nicolson and Cattermole, *The Atlas of the Solar System*, Mitchell Beazley, 1995

Morley, S. G., *An Introduction to the Study of Maya Hieroglyphs*, Dover, 1915

Needham, Joseph, *Science and Civilisation in China*, Vol.1, Cambridge University Press, 1954).

Oldenburg, Prof., *Sacred Books of the East*, Vol. X, translated by Max Müller, Clarendon Press, 1881

Ozaniec, Naomi, *The Elements of Chakras*, Element, 1990

Paludin, Ann, *Chonicle of the Chinese Emperors – The Reign by Reign Record of the Rulers of Imperial China*, Thames and Hudson, 1999

Pearson, R., *Climate and Evolution*, Academic Press, 1978

Peterson, Roland, *Everyone is Right – A New Look at Comparative Religion and Its Relation to Science*, De Vorss & Co (California), 1986

Pierpaoli, Walter and Regelson, William, with Colman, Carol, *The Melatonin Miracle*, Simon & Schuster, 1995

Posnansky, Arthur, *Tihuanacu, the Cradle of American Man*, J. J. Augustin, New York, 1945

Powell, Neil, *The Book of Change – How to Understand the I Ching*, Orbis, 1979

Reiche, Maria, *Nazca, Peru, Mystery of the Desert*, Hans Shultz-Severin, 1968

Reinhard, Johan, *The Nazca Lines: A New Perspective on their Origin and Meaning*, Editorial Los Pinos, 1985

Price, Glickstein, Horton and Bailey, *Principles of Psychology*, Holt Rinehart and Winston, 1982

Rawson, Jessica (Ed.), *Mysteries of Ancient China*, British Museum Press, 1996

Rawson, Philip, *Tao*, Thames and Hudson, 1973

Shri Purohit Swami, *The Geeta*, Faber & Faber, 1935

Sullivan, Michael, *The Arts of China*, Cardinal, 1973

Sykes, Egerton, *Dictionary of Non-Classical Mythology*, J. M. Dent, 1952

Temple, Robert, *The Genius of China, 3,000 Years of Science, Discovery and Invention*, Simon & Schuster, 1986

Tianchou, Fu, *The Underground Terracotta Army of Emperor Qin Shi Huang*, New World Press (Beijing), 1996

Thomson, W. A. R., *Black's Medical Dictionary*, A. & C. Black, 1984

Thorp, Robert L., *Son of Heaven, Imperial Arts of China*, Son of Heaven Press (Seattle), 1988

Von Hagen, W., *The Ancient Sun Kingdoms of the Americas*, Thames and Hudson, 1962

Walters, Derek, *Chinese Mythology – An Encyclopaedia of Myth and Legend*, Diamond Books (London), 1995

Walters, Derek, *Ming Shu – The Art and Practice of Chinese Astrology*, Pagoda, 1987

Warner, R. (Ed.), *Encyclopaedia of World Mythology*, BPC, 1970

Watson, William, *The Genius of China*, Times Newspapers, 1973

Welker, H. A., Semm, P., Willig, R. P., Wiltschko, W., Vollrath, L., 'Effects of an artificial magnetic field on seratonin-N-acetyltransferase activity and melatonin content of the rat pineal gland', *Exptl. Brain Res. 50:426–531*,1983

Whitaker, Clio (Ed.), *An Introduction to Oriental Mythology*, Quantum, 1997

White, J., *Pole Shift*, ARE Press (USA), 1993

Willis, Roy (consultant), *Dictionary of World Myth*, Duncan Baird, 1995

Xiaocong, Wu (Chief Ed.), *Valiant Imperial Warriors 2,000 Years Ago*, Xi'an Branch of China National Publications, 1998

Yuchen (Ed.), *Great Sites of Beijing*, Beijing Arts and Crafts, 1999

Yutang, Lin, *Imperial Peking, Seven Centuries of China*, Elek (London), 1961

Yutang, Lin, *Chinese–English Dictionary of Modern Usage*, University of Hong Kong Press, 1972

Tianxing, W., and Yongan, Shi (Eds), *Imperial Tombs of the Ming and Qing Dynasties*, China Esperanto (Beijing), 1981

Zhongyi, Yuan, *Terra Cotta Warriors*, People's China Publishing House, 1996

Index

Note: Page references in *italics* refer to illustrations